HUMAN RESOURCE MANAGEMENT FOR THE HOSPITALITY AND TOURISM INDUSTRIES

Dennis Nickson

Deputy Head of Department, Department of Human Resource Management, Strathclyde Business School, University of Strathclyde, Glasgow, Scotland

ELSEVIER

AMSTERDAM • BOSTON • HEIDELBERG • LONDON • NEW YORK • OXFORD
PARIS • SAN DIEGO • SAN FRANCISCO • SINGAPORE • SYDNEY • TOKYO
Butterworth-Heinemann is an imprint of Elsevier

Butterworth-Heinemann is an imprint of Elsevier
Linacre House, Jordan Hill, Oxford OX2 8DP
30 Corporate Drive, Suite 400, Burlington, MA 01803, USA

British Library Cataloguing in Publication Data
A catalogue record for this book is available from the British Library

Library of Congress Cataloging in Publication Data
A catalog record for this book is available from the Library of Congress

ISBN–10: 0-7506-6572-6
ISBN–13: 978-0-7506-6572-8

For information on all Butterworth-Heinemann publications visit our
web site at http://books.elsevier.com

Typeset by Charon Tec Ltd (A Macmillan Company), Chennai, India
www.charontec.com
Printed and bound in Great Britain by MPG Books Ltd. Bodmin, Cornwall

HUMAN RESOURCE MANAGEMENT FOR THE HOSPITALITY AND TOURISM INDUSTRIES

Contents

List of figures

List of tables

List of abbreviations

ACAS	Advisory Conciliation and Arbitration Service
AIDS	Acquired Immune Deficiency Syndrome
BA	British Airways
BHA	British Hospitality Association
CIPD	Chartered Institute of Personnel and Development
CEHR	Commission for Equality and Human Rights
CRE	Commission for Racial Equality
DDA	Disability Discrimination Act
DRC	Disability Rights Commission
DTI	Department of Trade and Industry
EOC	Equal Opportunities Commission
EAP	Employee Assistance Programme
ET	Employment Tribunal
EU	European Union
EWC	European Works Councils
HCN	Host-Country Nationals
HIV	Human Immunodeficiency Virus
HRD	Human Resource Development
HRM	Human Resource Management
HSE	Health and Safety Executive
ICE	Information and Consultation of Employees Regulations 2004 (ICE Regulations)
IDS	Income Data Services
IIP	Investors in People
IRS	Industrial Relations Services
IHRM	International Human Resource Management
JCC	Joint Consultative Committees
LPC	Low Pay Commission
LRD	Labour Research Department
MNC	Multinational Company

NMW	National Minimum Wage
N/SVQ	National/Scottish Vocational Qualification
PCN	Parent-Country National
QC	Quality Circles
RFO	Race for Opportunity
RRA	Race Relations Act
SSC	Sector Skills Council
SDA	Sex Discrimination Act
SME	Small and Medium-sized Enterprise
TCN	Third-Country National
TGWU	Transport and General Workers Union
TQM	Total Quality Management
WERS	Workplace Employment Relations Survey
WTR	Working Time Regulations

Preface

This book stems from a longstanding interest in how tourism and hospitality organizations and managers seek to manage their employees. As a highly labour-intensive industry, tourism and hospitality organizations are often heard to talk of how their people are 'their greatest asset'. However, even a cursory understanding of the nature of work, employment and people management in tourism and hospitality points to the many paradoxes and contradictions that are apparent in studying human resource management (HRM) in the sector. This book aims to explore some of these paradoxes and contradictions in seeking to submit the cliché of 'our people are our greatest asset' to critical scrutiny. That said, the book is in many respects a standard HRM text for the tourism and hospitality sector, recognizably following the traditional concerns of organizations as to how they best attract, maintain and develop an effective workforce.

In talking about tourism and hospitality the book is also aware of the many debates about how the sector is best conceptualized. There are many common attributes that are associated with both hospitality and tourism activities, which could encourage them to be seen synonymously. Equally though some would argue for distinctiveness between the two. Like most colleagues writing in this area the book acknowledges these debates, whilst also at times rather fudging the distinction between tourism and hospitality. In fudging what some might consider a largely semantic debate it is important not to lose sight of the one thing that is clearly paramount in all organizations in tourism and hospitality: the need to deliver service to customers and the need to manage people in such a way that they offer a quality service. The manner though in which organizations in different countries, cultures and market niches address this issue may vary enormously and this difference sustains many of the concerns outlined in this book. Indeed, an appreciation of culture – and the importance of organizational culture in particular – is a strong, and hopefully novel, feature for a book of this nature.

In attempting to understand the importance of context to explain HRM practices this book also aims to be international in its focus and its use of sources and examples. Thus, whilst the primary focus of the book is the UK, there are numerous examples from a variety of other countries across the world. The same point is also true in terms of examples of organizational practice. A number of examples are drawn from what is usually described as the commercial hospitality sector, which is well served by research. Many of those activities which are more oriented towards travel and tourism are also represented, though material of this nature is not quite so voluminous. A further aspect of context is the need to understand the dynamic and changing environment in which tourism and hospitality organizations operate. Political, economic, social and technological changes significantly affect tourism and hospitality organizations and the experience of work for those people who work in the sector; and the book is cognizant of this point throughout. This dynamism is also apparent with regard to emergent debates about new concepts which allow for an appreciation of the changing nature of the employment experience of the tourism and hospitality workforce. For example, work I have done with colleagues on aesthetic labour – how employees embody the tourism and hospitality product by 'looking good' or 'sounding right' – points to the manner in which organizations increasingly take an interest in their employees' appearance as a source of competitive advantage. This book is designed to provoke thought and debate about aesthetic labour and a myriad of other issues and encourage the readership to challenge its conclusions and stimulate further reading and research.

As has already been stated this book is the culmination of a longstanding interest in the area of tourism and hospitality employment, both as teacher and researcher. In that sense it is also an opportunity to draw on many of the ideas and writings of innumerable students and colleagues who have influenced my thinking. In particular, I would very much like to acknowledge a huge debt to the work of Tom Baum, Yvonne Guerrier, Rosemary Lucas and Roy Wood. Over the years they have given freely of their time, advice and ideas, and shaped many of the ideas expressed in this book. I hope this book can take its place alongside the work of my illustrious colleagues in encouraging students and practitioners to think about how to improve the working lives of the many who rely on tourism and hospitality for their employment.

Chapter 1

Human resource management and the tourism and hospitality industry: An introduction

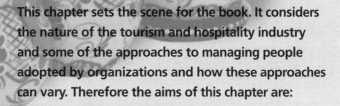

Chapter objectives

This chapter sets the scene for the book. It considers the nature of the tourism and hospitality industry and some of the approaches to managing people adopted by organizations and how these approaches can vary. Therefore the aims of this chapter are:

- To recognize the importance of tourism and hospitality as an employment sector.
- To outline the diverse range of sub-sectors and occupations within the broad heading of tourism and hospitality.
- To consider the nature of the workforce.
- To review the range of models/theories concerned with human resource management (HRM) and how these might be applied to the tourism and hospitality sector.

1

Introduction

The importance of tourism and hospitality employment in both developed and developing countries is attested to by the World Travel and Tourism Council (WTTC), who suggest that travel- and tourism-related activities account for over 230 million jobs, or 8.7 per cent of jobs worldwide (WTTC, 2006). However, whilst the quantity of jobs is unquestionable, the *quality* of many of these jobs is of great concern to academics and policy-makers alike. Despite the rhetoric of policy-makers and business leaders that people are the industry's most important asset, many remain unconvinced that such a view is borne out by empirical evidence. For example, Douglas Coupland, the notable cultural commentator, has for many captured the *zeitgeist* when he talks pejoratively of 'McJob' which he describes as, 'A low-pay, low-prestige, low-dignity, low-benefit, no-future job in the service sector. Frequently considered a satisfying career choice by people who have never held one' (Coupland, 1993: 5; and see also Lindsay and McQuaid, 2004). MacDonald and Sirianni (1996) recognize the challenges of living and working in a service society which, according to them, is characterized by two kinds of service jobs: large numbers of low-skill, low-pay jobs and a smaller number of high-skill, high-income jobs, with few jobs being in the middle of these two extremes. Such a situation leads labour analysts to ask what kinds of jobs are being produced and who is filling them. This point is also true for the tourism and hospitality industry and it is important at the outset of this book to add a caveat about the generalizability (or otherwise) of the conditions of tourism and hospitality employment worldwide. Hence Baum (1995: 151) reflecting the diversity of employment within the sector notes that:

> In some geographical and sub-sector areas, tourism and hospitality provides an attractive, high-status working environment with competitive pay and conditions, which is in high demand in the labour force and benefits from low staff turnover ... The other side of the coin is one of poor conditions, low pay, high staff turnover, problems in recruiting skills in a number of key areas, a high level of labour drawn from socially disadvantaged groups, poor status and the virtual absence of professionalism.

Organizations and managers in the tourism and hospitality industry face real challenges in recruiting, developing and maintaining a committed, competent, well-managed and well-motivated workforce which is focused on offering a high-quality 'product' to the increasingly demanding and discerning customer. This book seeks to address some of the key human resource (HR) issues that have to be tackled in order that organizations can maintain such an environment. To do so it will critically review some of the problems which lead many to characterize tourism and hospitality employment as generally unrewarding and unappealing, whilst also considering examples of good practice, important policy responses and models of HRM which may offer cause for greater optimism in the way people are managed within the tourism and hospitality industry.

What are the tourism and hospitality industries?

Many academics, industrialists and policy-makers have attempted to define the nature of the tourism industry – and the place of the hospitality sub-sector within this broader conceptualization – yet there is still no one commonly accepted definition. Hence, there are inherent problems seeking to define what is a large and diverse sector, which means many of the activities may overlap, and could be described as encompassing tourism and hospitality. For example, Lucas (2004) in her recent work on employment relations in the hospitality and tourism industries chose to talk in broad terms about the Hotel, Catering and Tourism Sector (HCTS). This characterization of the HCTS recognizes that, in reality, many jobs in hospitality and tourism, 'share common attributes and are associated with both hospitality and tourism activities' (p. 4). Clearly, then, we should recognize the potential for a lack of precision in describing the tourism and hospitality industries.

In an attempt to avoid too much imprecision and, at the same time, capture the diversity of the sector this book uses the framework offered by People 1st, which is the Sector Skills Council (SSC) for the hospitality, leisure, travel and tourism sector, to exemplify the broad range of activities that may be seen in the HCTS. The reason for using People 1st is that SSCs are the government-licensed bodies in the UK responsible for improving skills within the industry. SSCs are employer led and amongst other things aim to be the voice of industry on skills matters and encourage best practice approaches to employment (and see Chapter 7 for the role of People 1st in improving skills and training in hospitality, leisure, travel and tourism). Therefore, People 1st suggest that the sector as a whole is made up of 14 sub-sectors (People 1st, 2006):

- hotels;
- restaurants;

- pubs, bars and night-clubs;
- contract food service providers;
- membership clubs;
- events;
- gambling;
- travel services;
- tourist services;
- visitor attractions;
- youth hostels;
- holiday parks;
- self-catering accommodation;
- hospitality services.

Moreover within this broad classification of travel, tourism and hospitality there is massive diversity in the types of jobs generated, in relation to their technical and skills' demands, educational requirements, terms and conditions and the type of person that is likely to be attracted to employment in them. To illustrate this point we can consider Baum's (1997: 97–98) description of the range of people a person buying a package holiday is likely to interact with:

- the retail travel agent;
- insurance companies;
- ground transport to and from the airport;
- at least two sets of airport handling agents (outbound and return);
- airport services (shops, food and beverage outlets, bureaux de change) (outbound and return);
- the airline on all legs of the journey;
- immigration and customs services;
- local ground transportation;
- the hotel or apartment;
- tour services at the destination;
- companies and individuals selling a diversity of goods and services at the destination (retail, food and beverage, entertainment, cultural and heritage, financial, etc.);
- emergency services at the destination (medical, police, legal);
- service providers on return (photography processing, medical).

Baum characterizes all of these possible intermediaries, and the interactions they will have with the holiday maker, as crucial in 'making or breaking the tourist experience'. Thus while the physical product is important, for most tourists the quality of their experience is likely to be also reliant to a large degree on the interactions they will have with the variety of front-line staff in the travel, tourism and hospitality industry. These so-called 'moments of truth' (Carlzon, 1987) are therefore crucial for organizational effectiveness, success, competitiveness and profitability. Indeed, within an industry that is characterized by diversity and heterogeneity in terms of the purpose, size, ownership and demands of the enterprise, the only real point of homogeneity is delivering service to customers and the need to manage people in such a way that they offer a quality service. The corollary of this point would be the belief that such front-line staff would therefore be sufficiently well paid, trained and motivated to offer outstanding service. The reality however is that often such staff have the lowest status in the organization, are the least trained, and are the poorest paid employees of the company.

In recognizing the diversity both of the range of sub-sectors and types of jobs they are likely to generate, this book cannot consider all of these aspects in detail. Indeed, more is known about employment in certain sub-sectors than others. For example, the commercial hospitality industry encompassing hotels, restaurants and pubs, bars and nightclubs is the largest sub-sector with around 70 per cent of employees in the UK (People 1st, 2006). Unsurprisingly, then, the commercial hospitality industry is well served with extensive research on the nature of employment and HRM strategies (D'Annunzio-Green et al., 2002; Lucas, 2004). On the other hand, little has been written on the events industry or the nature of HRM in youth hostels, for example. As a consequence many of the examples drawn on in this book are from the commercial hospitality industry, although, where possible, illustrations of organizational practice from travel and tourism organizations are also used. Ultimately, the main aim of the book is to attempt to understand the potentially diverse employment experience of those working in what we will broadly think of as the tourism and hospitality industries. Thus, how does the experience of an airline flight attendant differ from that of a pot washer in the kitchen in a small restaurant to a receptionist in the front desk of an international hotel or to a tour rep working on an 18–30-type holiday?

A further issue to consider is the manner in which the sector is heterogeneous in terms of the predominance of small- and medium-sized enterprises (SMEs). People 1st (2006) note that within the UK hospitality, leisure, travel and tourism sector 76 per cent of establishments employ fewer than ten people and 50 per cent fewer than five. Heterogeneity is also seen in relation to the way that organizations adopt differing routes to competitive advantage, depending on which type of market they operate in. For example, full service carriers in the airline industry are likely to have very different approaches to HRM compared to low-cost airlines (Eaton, 2001; Spiess and Waring, 2005). The same is true for the hospitality sector, which may range from first class and luxury hotels providing extravagant, full 24-hour service to the more homely comforts of a bed and breakfast establishment; from fast food restaurants to Michelin starred restaurants. In turn, the jobs provided by these various organizations demand a variety of skills and attributes from those employees interacting with customers, which again will impact on HR strategies such as recruitment and selection and training.

Who makes up the tourism and hospitality workforce? A brief snapshot

The International Labour Organization (ILO, 2001) in their wide-ranging report on the global tourism and hospitality industry provides evidence that suggests that the industry globally is largely reliant on what Wood (1997) has described as so-called 'marginal workers', such as women, young workers, casual employees, students, relatively high numbers of part-timers and migrant workers. For example, within the UK women make up around 58 per cent of the broader hospitality, leisure, travel and tourism workforce (People 1st, 2006). More specifically, the hospitality sub-sector is indicative of the broader sector in having a higher proportion of part-time employees (52 per cent) than most other industries with the all industry figure being 25 per cent (HtF, 2003). Young people are also prominent within the hospitality, leisure, travel and tourism sector. For example, 37 per cent of the total UK workforce is under 24 years and 58 per cent under 34 years (People 1st, 2006). Related to this last point a significant part of the tourism and hospitality workforce consists of student, seasonal and migrant workers. Students are an increasingly important segment of the labour market for hospitality and tourism organizations (ILO, 2001). They are prepared to work for low wages and be flexible in their working patterns (Canny, 2002), creating what Curtis and Lucas (2001) describe as a 'coincidence of needs' between employers and students. Thus, nearly three quarters of all students who are working are employed in the retail and hospitality industries and the vast majority of students who are working do so in front-line jobs such as sales assistants, waiters/waitresses and check out operators (Curtis and Lucas, 2001; Canny, 2002). The number of ethnic minority workers in the broader hospitality, leisure, travel and tourism sector is 11 per cent, slightly higher than the all industry figure of 9.6 per cent (People 1st, 2006). With regard to qualifications only 12 per cent of employees in hospitality, leisure, travel and tourism have a degree or equivalent compared to an all industry figure of 29 per cent, with 15 per cent of the workforce having no qualification compared to 11 per cent of the total workforce (People 1st, 2006).

Review and reflect

If you are currently working in the tourism and hospitality industry whilst completing your studies list what you consider good and bad aspects of your job and your reasons for this.

Having briefly considered the nature of the hospitality and tourism industry and the characteristics of its workforce attention now turns to understanding HRM and the increasingly important role it is felt to play in organizational success.

What is HRM?

Definitions of HRM

There have been many attempts to define what exactly HRM might be and indeed Heery and Noon (2001) recognize that it is a subject of considerable academic analysis and that, ultimately, 'there is no common agreement on what HRM means' (p. 161). Resultantly, they offer 10 definitions, which they feel capture the complexity and dynamism of HRM as a subject of academic study:

- *A label* HRM is seen as simply being another name for personnel management and there is nothing distinct or special about HRM.
- *A convenient shorthand term* that allows for the grouping together of a whole series of sub-disciplines that are broadly concerned with people management: such as employee relations, industrial/labour relations, personnel management and organizational behaviour.

- *A map* to help guide students and practitioners to understand the concept and ideas associated with the management of people.
- *A set of professional practices* suggests that there are a range of personnel practices that can be integrated to ensure a professional approach to managing people. In this view a potentially key role is likely to be played by the Chartered Institute of Personnel and Development (CIPD), which is the professional association for those entering the HR and personnel profession.
- *A method of ensuring internal fit* again sees the need to co-ordinate approaches to people management, but here the co-ordination needs to be with other areas of the organization.
- *A method of ensuring external fit* where HRM activities have to be fully integrated with the demands of the external environment.
- *A competitive advantage* where HRM is the means by which an organization can gain competitive advantage, a view best captured by the cliché of 'our people are our greatest asset'.
- *A market-driven approach* in that decisions will often be market driven and the needs of the business determine the manner in which employees are treated; some may be treated well, others less so well.
- *A manipulative device* sees it as inherently exploitative and manipulative.
- *A hologram* captures much of the above discussion in recognizing the fluid identity of HRM and the fact that it has multiple meanings.

Clearly what the above discussion points to is that HRM means many things to many people, depending on whether you are a manager, an employee or an academic and there is no one definition that will adequately capture the potential complexity of the topic.

Review and reflect

Which definition do you find most persuasive and why?

That said, for the purposes of this book we will recognize HRM as being broadly about how organizations seek to manage their employees in the pursuit of organizational success. Reflecting this point the book utilizes the concise definition offered by Storey (1995: 5). Thus, HRM 'is a distinctive approach to employment management which seeks to achieve competitive advantage through the strategic deployment of a highly committed and capable workforce, using an integrated array of cultural, structural and personnel techniques'. The challenge of HRM then would seem to be how to recruit, deploy, develop, reward and motivate staff, leading to them being a source of competitive advantage. As the above discussion suggests, however, there is more than one route to seeking competitive advantage and this point is further considered in examining the notion of 'hard' and 'soft' HRM.

Hard vs. soft?

As well as providing the concise definition utilized above, Storey (1987) also provided one of the earliest and most enduring attempts to recognize different approaches to HRM. These different approaches are captured by the idea of hard and soft HRM, each of which are now briefly described. The *hard* version is seen to be an instrumental and economically rational approach to human resource management. In this view people management strategies are driven by strategic considerations to gain competitive advantage, maximizing control while achieving the lowest possible labour cost. This approach is quantitative and calculative and labour is a commodity/resource, the same as any other. The focus is on human *resource management*. On the other hand the *soft* version is seen to be much more about adopting a humanistic and developmental approach to human resource management. As a result an organization's people management approach is likely to be more consensual and based on a high level of managerial commitment to employees, which is intended to lead to mutual high commitment from employees, high trust, high productivity and so on. Employees are seen as being proactive, capable of being developed and worthy of trust and collaboration. This approach focuses on *human resource* management.

Review and reflect

Reflecting on your answers from the first review and reflect question to what extent do the good and bad aspects you listed equate to hard or soft aspects of HRM?

What hard and soft approaches to HRM point to is that employers will vary their people management strategies. Clearly as well there are likely to be a number of external influences as HRM in practice 1.1 suggests. These external influences will

HRM in practice 1.1   Hard and soft approaches to HRM in the airline industry

The tourism and hospitality industry is particularly sensitive to economic cycles and political trouble and can be badly affected in times of uncertainty. For example, the global nature of the industry means that it is vulnerable to external events that cause fluctuations in tourist visits and spend. The global 2001–2004 economic downturn, 9/11, the Iraq war and the outbreak of SARS in the Far East all led to a drop in revenue in the industry. These factors reduced the number of travellers internationally and left uncertainty and fragility in the tourism market. Many of these aspects are particularly pronounced in the airline industry and trade unions have often railed against the manner in which employees are used as 'shock absorbers' to protect the industry from the cyclical nature of the market. These hard approaches to HRM have seen major redundancy programmes in a number of airlines in recent years, especially after 9/11. On the other hand, a number of companies have sought a more soft approach to HRM which aimed at increasing the customer responsiveness of their front-line staff. British Airways, for example, had a series of initiatives in the 1980s and 1990s such as 'Putting People First' and 'Winning for Customers'. Amongst other things these initiatives sought to introduce team working, extensive training programmes, enhance quality procedures and multi-skill staff. As companies alternate between hard and soft approaches to HRM employees may become confused as to what the company message is. Ultimately, employees may well be a company's 'greatest asset', but in times of uncertainty and downturn are equally expendable as recent history suggests.

Derived from Grugulis and Wilkinson (2002); ITF (2004).

reflect a variety of political, social, economic and technological aspects which will have an effect on HRM policies and practices. Hard and soft HRM point to the manner then in which organizations can vary their approaches to HRM and as a result the impact on employees may vary. A similar attempt to recognize that there may be different approaches to HRM is also seen in the debate over whether organizations should aim to achieve 'best fit' or 'best practice'.

Best fit vs. best practice?

Boxall and Purcell (2000) suggest that attempts to understand the way in which organizations approach the management of their HR can be seen with regard to whether they aim for 'best fit' or 'best practice'. On the one hand, the best fit school argues for an approach to HRM, which is fully integrated with the specific organizational and environmental context in which they operate. On the other hand, best practice advocates argue for a universalistic approach to HRM where all firms who adopt a range of agreed HR policies and practices are more likely to create a high-performance/commitment workplace, as organizations aim to compete on the basis of high quality and productivity.

Best fit

One of the earliest and most influential attempts to develop a model that recognized the need for a fit between the competitive strategy and HRM was that offered by Schuler and Jackson (1987). Schuler and Jackson developed a series of typologies of 'needed role behaviours' that enabled the link between competitive strategy and HRM practices to be made. The type of needed role behaviours within Schuler and Jackson's model was contingent on the overall strategies that an organization could adopt to seek competitive advantage and the HRM approached adopted to sustain this.

First, there is an *innovation* strategy, where organizations seek to develop products or services that are different from competitors, such that the focus here is on companies offering something new and different. Organizations adopting this approach seek to develop an environment where innovation is allowed to flourish. Resultantly, the employee needed role behaviour in such a scenario is characterized by things like a willingness to tolerate ambiguity and unpredictability, the need to be creative and risk taking. Given these characteristics the type of HRM strategy flowing from this approach is based on having a large number of highly skilled individuals who are likely to enjoy high levels of autonomy. Second, is the *quality enhancement* strategy wherein firms seek to gain competitive advantage by enhancing the product and/or service quality. The approach once again points to certain HRM practices to support a total-quality approach. These practices include the encouragement of feedback systems, teamwork, decision-making and responsibility being an integral part of an employee's job description and flexible job classifications. The intent of these practices is to create needed employee behaviour such as co-operative, interdependent behaviour and commitment to the goals of the organization. Lastly, the *cost reduction strategy* sees firms attempting to gain competitive advantage by aiming to be the lowest-cost producer within a particular market segment. The characteristics of firms seeking to pursue this strategy are tight controls, minimization of overheads and pursuit of economies of scale, in the pursuit of increased productivity. In following such a strategy organizations may use higher number of part-timers, seek to simplify and measure work via narrowly defined jobs that encourage specialization and efficiency, and offer short-term results oriented appraisal. Needed employee behaviours include, repetitive and predictable behaviour, low-risk taking activity and a high degree of comfort with stability.

This support for the importance of HRM practices 'fitting' the organizations own strategically defined market segment to create a fit between the functional areas of marketing, operations and HRM is also seen in the work of Lashley and Taylor (1998). Lashley and Taylor describe four basic archetypes within which tourism and hospitality organizations can be potentially located. These archetypes are the service factory, the service shop, mass service and professional services. These characterizations are based on the degree of customization and labour intensity involved in the service offer, in terms of the degree of customer contact required between employees and customers.

The service factory is relatively low labour intensity and low customization (i.e. high standardization). The service factory is most obviously exemplified by fast food operators, especially McDonald's. The service shop involves more customization, but relatively low labour intensity. The defining difference to the service factory lies in the degree of standardization within the process. Lashley and Taylor draw upon the example of TGI Fridays to argue that although there are high levels of standardization in the tangible aspects of the organization, such as the menus, layouts, décor and staff uniform, there is also some scope to customize the customers' eating and drinking experience. This customization is by virtue of their more extensive menu, and more importantly, greater spontaneity and authenticity in the intangible aspects of the service provided by front-line staff. The next classification is mass service where service processes involve a relatively high degree of labour intensity, though a limited amount of customization. Lashley and Taylor assert that the Marriott hotel brand typifies a mass service organization, as their four star offering is similar to others in relation to the tangibles reflecting the highly competitive nature of the mid to upper segment of the hotel market. As a result of this convergence of the tangibles the key lies in the intangibles and the scope available to organizations to differentiate themselves on the basis of service quality. Within this process of differentiation a key role is played by the staff via the relatively high level of contact with customers. The final grouping is professional services where there is a high level of service to individual customers and a high degree of labour intensity, as exemplified by hospitality management consultants.

The key point which emerges from the work of Lashley and Taylor is the likely relationship between the service operation type adopted by the organization and the style of HRM which best fits it. For example, it is apparent that in the four star hotel sector a broadly soft approach to HRM, as exemplified by high discretion in relation to the intangibles, moral involvement and a moderate trust culture, is suggested as being important to sustain a high quality, total quality management (TQM) based approach to the service offering. At the other end of the spectrum, McDonald's are suggested as exemplifying a command and control style which is characterized by things such as low discretion for employees, limited responsibility and autonomy, and scripted service encounters. Importantly, Lashley and Taylor (1998: 161) see the command and control approach as being right for what McDonald's are aiming to offer their customers:

> … the historic success of the McDonald's organization in delivering their market offer … is partly due to the ability to develop and maintain a close fit between the key characteristics of the strategic drivers and actual service delivery through utilization of an appropriate HRM style.

The key point remains that organizations in developing a certain product market strategy then ensure that their HR policies and practices are congruent and cost effective with this strategy.

Best practice

Whilst arguments for best fit advocate a close fit between competitive strategies and HRM, those in favour of best practice approaches to HRM suggest that there is a universal 'one best way' to manage people. By adopting a best practice approach it is argued that organizations will see enhanced commitment from employees leading to improved organizational performance, higher levels of service quality and ultimately increases in productivity and profitability. Usually couched in terms of 'bundles', the HRM practices that are offered in support of a high commitment and performance model are generally fairly consistent. For example, Redman and Matthews (1998) outline a range of HR practices which are suggested as being important to organizational strategies aimed at securing high-quality service:

- *Recruitment and selection*: Recruiting and selecting staff with the correct attitudinal and behavioural characteristics. A range of assessments in the selection process should be utilized to evaluate the work values, personality, interpersonal skills and problem-solving abilities of potential employees to assess their 'service orientation'.
- *Retention*: The need to avoid the development of a 'turnover culture', which may of course be particularly prevalent in tourism and hospitality. For example, the use of 'retention bonuses' to influence employees to stay.
- *Teamwork*: The use of semi-autonomous, cross-process and multi-functional teams.
- *Training and development*: The need to equip operative level staff with team working and interpersonal skills to develop their 'service orientation' and managers with a new leadership style which encourages a move to a more facilitative and coaching style of managing.
- *Appraisal*: Moving away from traditional top down approaches to appraisal and supporting things such as customer evaluation, peer review, team-based performance and the appraisal of managers by subordinates. Generally, all of these performance appraisal systems should focus on the quality goals of the organization and the behaviours of employees needed to sustain these.
- *Rewarding quality*: A need for a much more creative system of rewards and in particular the need for payment systems that reward employees for attaining quality goals.
- *Job security*: Promises of job security are seen as an essential component of any overall quality approach.
- *Employee involvement and employee relations*: By seeking greater involvement from employees the emphasis is on offering autonomy, creativity, co-operation and self-control in work processes. The use of educative and participative mechanisms, such as team briefings and quality circles are allied to changes in the organization of work which support an 'empowered' environment.

In simple terms best practice is likely to entail attempts to enhance the skills base of employees through HR activities such as selective staffing, comprehensive training and broad developmental efforts like job rotation. Additionally, it also encourages empowerment, participative problem-solving, teamwork as well as performance-based incentives.

Review and reflect

Think of an organization that you are familiar with, for example where you are currently working or one where you have spent time on placement, to what extent do their HR practices evidence either a best fit or best practice approach? Why would you characterize it as best fit or best practice?

Models or reality?

Of course ideal types and academic models may not always reflect the complex reality of what really goes on in tourism and hospitality organizations. Schuler and Jackson, for instance, freely admit the description of their three competitive strategies as pure types often does not reflect the reality of, for example, organizations pursuing two or more competitive strategies simultaneously. The same point can also be made with regard to hard and soft HRM; it is not uncommon for organizations to vary their approaches to employees depending on any given practice. For example, with regard to labour flexibility the use of numerical flexibility may well reflect fairly hard approaches to HRM, whilst functional flexibility and multi-skilling exemplifies a much softer approach (see Chapter 4). A further issue is the predominance of SMEs in tourism and hospitality. It is often suggested that their small scale means that they are unlikely to have the necessary means to employ the kind of HRM expertize to develop sophisticated soft approaches, for example. Nevertheless, they are still likely to require HR policies that require at least some thought with regard to their business circumstances.

Whilst some understanding of debate about soft and hard and best fit and best practice are important to place HR practices within a broader theoretical context, in reality, regardless of these various ideal types all organizations have to manage employees on a day-to-day basis. We can illustrate this in Figure 1.1, which outlines the notion of an HRM cycle.

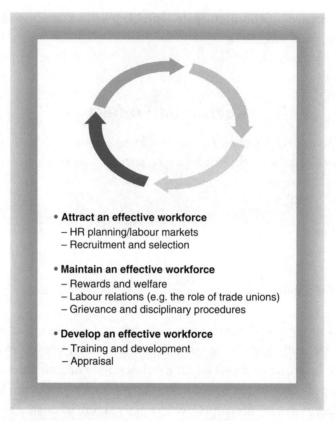

- **Attract an effective workforce**
  - HR planning/labour markets
  - Recruitment and selection

- **Maintain an effective workforce**
  - Rewards and welfare
  - Labour relations (e.g. the role of trade unions)
  - Grievance and disciplinary procedures

- **Develop an effective workforce**
  - Training and development
  - Appraisal

Figure 1.1   The HRM cycle

Figure 1.1 is useful in allowing us to appreciate that these broad aspects of attracting, maintaining and developing a workforce are constant and that organizations and managers, both specialist HR and line managers, are wrestling with HR issues on a day-to-day basis. However, whilst a number of the functional aspects of HRM are unlikely to differ, the manner in which organizations actually develop their overall strategy will. In these circumstances models that allow for recognition of differing strategic intent in HRM are still useful in allowing us to appreciate why and how companies differ in their approaches to HRM in tourism and hospitality. It would be naïve to imagine we could talk in very broad terms about HRM in tourism in hospitality. The reality is far too complex and as we have already noted the employment experience for employees can vary enormously depending on the type of organization they work in and the job or role they have within their organizations. With this recognition we should consider the key question: so what does HRM in hospitality and tourism look like? Reflecting some of our earlier discussion of hard and soft and best fit and practice we can also crudely distinguish between those who argue for a pessimistic view of HRM in the sector and those who suggest that increasingly organizations are seeking a much more progressive approach to managing their employees.

The bad news … pessimistic views of HRM in tourism and hospitality

Generally tourism and hospitality has often struggled with negative perceptions about employment practices and conditions and this perception has often been matched by the reality. Keep and Mayhew (1999) for example in their review of the skills issue in the tourism and hospitality industry suggest the industry has a number of personnel problems, including:

- generally low wages, unless skill shortages act to counter this (e.g. chefs);
- unsocial hours and shift patterns that are not family friendly;
- overrepresentation of women and ethnic minorities in low-level operative positions, with better paid, higher status and more skilled jobs filled by men, pointing to undeveloped equal opportunities policies in the sector;
- poor or non-existent career structures and use of casualized seasonal employment;
- over reliance on informal recruitment methods;
- lack of evidence of good practice personnel/HRM practices;
- little or no trade union presence;
- high levels of labour turnover;
- difficulties in recruitment and retention of employees.

Recognizing this reality of poor employment practices, Riley et al. (2000) argue that economics is the key determining factor for HRM policies and practices in tourism and hospitality. Of course this point is likely to be true of any industry, but as Riley et al. point out it carries a particular resonance in tourism and hospitality, due to the nature of the sector. That is not to say that organizations and managers in the industry are not well aware of new managerial thinking on HRM. However, they also find themselves wrestling with 'traditional problems', which are underpinned by 'fundamental labour economic imperatives' (p. 120). Importantly, these problems limit managerial actions and this leads Riley et al. to argue the behaviour of managers is determined 'by the structures and forms under which they live' (p. 119). This economic imperative creates a short-term perspective on managerial decision-making and strategy in relation to HRM, and also means that management are more likely to deploy a weak internal labour market. An obvious impact of this is that HRM concerns of tourism and hospitality organizations are constantly directed to short-term responses to issues such as recruitment, selection and basic training, rather than more long-term areas which could conceivably offer more development and career progression for existing employees.

Another reason for continuing pessimism is the general attitude of employers and particularly the extent to which they are willing to recognize the extent of the HRM problem in the sector. The DfEE (2000) registers with some incredulity the awareness of low pay, for example, existing alongside the naïve view of employers of tourism and hospitality as a 'good' employing sector. Thus, although in a number of locations labour shortages were clearly reflective of an unwillingness of employers to offer competitive pay and terms of conditions of employment, the DfEE (2000: 35) notes how, 'We were struck by the extent to which employers described pay and working conditions as "reasonable" or even "good" while at the same time report-ing extensive recruitment problems, skills gaps and labour turnover.' This disjunc-ture between the views of employers and employees is also noted by the ILO in a recent report on the international tourism industry. They recognize how:

> Employers' representatives generally consider that the turnover in the indus-try should be attributed to the essentially transient nature of part of the workforce, namely students, young mothers and young people as a whole, as well as the general difficulty in retaining staff. Employees, on the other hand, frequently cite low pay as a reason for changing employment, though a lack of career structure and benefits would appear to be of even greater importance (ILO, 2001: 6).

This inability by industry to recognize the most glaring of issues is long standing and can also be seen in relation to things like a degree of hostility and opposition from the employers associations in the industry, such as the British Hospitality Association (BHA), to governmental initiatives such as the minimum wage and working time directive. The BHA still remains unsure of the benefits of such initiatives, despite support from others who argue these initiatives are likely to have a potentially positive impact on the industry (e.g. see Lucas, 2004).

Given the above discussion it is unsurprising to see a long history of support for the proposition that tourism and hospitality remains a poor employing sector. From Orwell's *Down and Out in Paris and London* in the 1930s to recent work by the likes of Price (1994), Kelliher and Perrett (2001), Kelliher and Johnson (1997) and McGunnigle and Jameson (2000), the dominant paradigm has tended to stress the negative aspects of working in the sector. For example, McGunnigle and Jameson surveyed a selected number of hotels from the top 50 hotel groups ranked by ownership of bedroom stock, which were considered to be most likely to exhibit good practice HRM. Despite this they concluded, 'This study suggests that there is little adoption of HRM philosophy in corporately owned hotels in the UK sample ... [and hospitality] ... has a long way to go before it can claim that it is encouraging a "culture of commitment"' (ibid. p. 416). Similarly, Kelliher and Perrett (2001), drawing explicitly on Schuler and Jackson's typology, develop a case study analysis of a 'designer restaurant'. Such a restaurant might be though of as potentially developing a more sophisticated approach to HRM as they sought to differentiate themselves from chain establishments such as Hard Rock Café and TGI Friday's. However, although the restaurant had moved to a more sophisticated approach to HRM in areas like planning, training and development and appraisal, and ostensibly sought an 'innovation' strategy, 'there was little real evidence that human resources were seen as a source of competitive advantage' (p. 434). Instead, the HRM approaches adopted by the restaurant were much more reflective of immediate environmental constraints, such as the difficulties in recruiting and retaining staff.

In sum, any number of reasons may account for poor personnel practice in the tourism and hospitality industry. Economic determinism, the predominance of SMEs, a low-skills base, employer antipathy to a more progressive approach to HRM, labour market characteristics, organizations ensuring best fit HRM practices to support a high volume, low-cost strategy; all are plausible reasons for a view of HRM which is not necessarily premised on high-skills, high-wages and a high-quality route to competitive advantage. That said, it would be equally wrong to paint a wholly pessimistic picture. It was recognized earlier in the chapter that there are also examples of good practice HRM, particularly in certain sub-sectors of the industry and in market segments where organizations are likely to seek differentiation on the basis of offering high-quality services.

The good news … best practice in tourism and hospitality

Some of the most important work to emerge in recent years on the question of the extent of good practice in the HCTS is the work of Hoque (2000). Based on his work on the hotel sector, he argues that arguments which portray the industry as backward and unstrategic are now outdated, at least where larger hotel establishments are concerned. Indeed, he suggests that 'it is perhaps time researchers stopped highlighting the example of "bad management" and branding the industry as under-developed or backward, and started identifying approaches to hotel management capable of generating high performance' (2000: 154). The research conducted by Hoque consists of a questionnaire-based survey of 232 hotels and a number of follow-up interviews conducted in targeted hotels, based on the results of the survey.

Based on this research he discusses three key issues. First, the extent to which hotels have experimented with new approaches to HRM. Secondly, the factors that influence HRM decision-making and whether these factors are any different in the hotel industry compared to elsewhere. Finally, he reviewed the relationship between HRM and performance in the hotel industry. Hoque is able to claim that, compared to a sample of over 300 greenfield-site manufacturing establishments, the hotels in his sample where utilizing a number of practices that were very similar to best practice. Indeed, in illustrating the manner in which academic models can, in reality, overlap it is also worth noting that there is significant overlap between Schuler and Jackson's quality enhancement and innovation approaches with much of the 'best practice' approaches. This point about such overlap is further illustrated in HRM in practice 1.2.

Hoque's work remains useful in offering a description of organizational practices that support a professional, high-quality approach to service. That said, there are a number of criticisms that can be levelled at the research (Nickson and Wood, 2000). As Hoque himself recognizes his sample of hotels is large by industry standards, averaging 125 employees per unit compared to an industry 'standard' of 81 per cent of establishments employing fewer than 25 people, and thus as Hoque (2000: 51) himself recognizes 'patently unrepresentative of the industry as a whole'. Furthermore his reliance on city-centre hotels with a high proportion of corporate clients is equally unrepresentative. Lastly, the reliance on managerial voices in his research, to the exclusion of those on the receiving end of many of the initiatives

HRM in practice 1.2   The HRM quality enhancer hotel

The hotel in Hoque's (2000) research, which is termed the HRM quality enhancer hotel, employed 140 staff and was part of a large international chain. In relation to their approach to HRM a number of practices were prominent in the hotel. Recruitment and selection emphasized the need for employees to have an aptitude for customer care, although this tended to be 'spotted' at interview rather than through psychometric or behavioural tests. The hotel used extensive induction programmes to lessen the potential of employee turnover. The use of cross-functional teams aimed to generate co-operation and team building and staff were encouraged to view the hotel as a unit rather than a collection of discrete functions. Allied to this extensive multi-skilling and cross-functional flexibility was encouraged, this 'cross-exposure' allowed staff to see a number of the other parts of the hotel. There was extensive decentralization, which sought to encourage responsible autonomy, for example through a well-understood empowerment scheme operating in the hotel. Consultation via a representative consultative committee allowed employees to voice their views on the running of the hotel. Further to this consultation the hotel also operated an annual attitude survey. Employees were appraised on a yearly basis. The appraisal system was used for succession planning and the hotel was also working towards linking appraisal with a merit-based remuneration system. Employees were also encouraged by a strong internal labour market which promoted from within, whenever possible. Finally, throughout the hotel there was an overriding emphasis on quality and the need to offer 'outstanding customer service'.

described (i.e. employees), may be considered an important omission. To be fair, Hoque's exclusive reliance on managerial voices is not unique and is shared by much of the literature on HRM. The key point emerging from the work of the likes of Redman and Matthews and Hoque is what good practice HRM is likely to look like in the tourism and hospitality industry.

Where this book stands

Whilst, Boxall and Purcell (2003: 61) suggest that 'there is quite a lot of agreement on what constitutes "bad" or "stupid" practice' in relation to HRM, this does not stop organizations often developing rather bad or stupid HR practices. As we have already noted tourism and hospitality is likely to offer huge diversity with regard to HRM policies and practices and it would be nice to think that these are rarely bad or stupid. Experience equally tells us though that this is not always the case. In recognizing this point, this book aims to develop a realistic account of how employers in tourism and hospitality develop and implement their HRM policies and practices and what this will mean for employees. It will certainly celebrate good practice, but equally will not be afraid to point to bad practice. This sentiment points to the fact whilst best practice is something to which organizations should aspire to, the reality is that there may be a number of constraints in achieving best practice, a point which Boxall and Purcell (2000: 199) recognize:

> While all employers will benefit from avoiding the real 'howlers' of HRM practices that are well known for their dysfunctional or perverse consequences – they are often constrained by industry and organizational economics from implementing a deluxe version of best practice.

In sum, whilst all tourism and hospitality employers are, for a variety of reasons, unlikely to aspire to the deluxe version of best practice they should at least aim to avoid the real howlers as suggested by Boxall and Purcell. The remainder of the book considers how they might do this in considering policies and practices in a variety of organizational and occupational settings.

Conclusion

This chapter recognized the importance of tourism and hospitality as an employment sector. The sector provides a large and diverse number of jobs and will be important for future job creation throughout the developed and developing world. Whilst the number of jobs produced by the tourism and hospitality industry is impressive there are some concerns about the type of employment experience within the sector. The nature of the labour market and the reliance on 'marginal' workers has led to a number of pessimistic views of HRM practice. More upbeat accounts point to the manner in which concerns with providing good-quality service are improving HR practices. Underlying this debate are a number of models of HRM which provide a framework in which to locate the strategies adopted by tourism and hospitality organizations. Ultimately though we have to be cautious to not over generalize the nature of HRM in tourism and hospitality and there is a need to examine differing practices and try to understand why these differences might exist.

References and further reading

Baum, T. (1995) *Managing Human Resources in the European Hospitality and Tourism Industry – A Strategic Approach*, Chapman and Hall.

Baum, T. (1997) 'Making or breaking the tourist experience: the role of human resource management', in C. Ryan (ed.) *The Tourist Experience: A New Introduction*, Cassell, 92–111.

Boxall, P. and Purcell, J. (2000) 'Strategic human resource management: where have we come from and where should we be going?', *International Journal of Management Reviews*, 2(2), 183–203.

Boxall, P. and Purcell, J. (2003) *Strategy and Human Resource Management*, Palgrave.

Canny, A. (2002) 'Flexible labour? The growth of student employment in the UK', *Journal of Education and Work*, 15(3), 277–301.

Carlzon, J. (1987) *Moments of Truth*, Ballinger.

Cheng, A. and Brown, A. (1998) 'HRM strategies and labour turnover in the hotel industry: a comparative study of Australia and Singapore', *International Journal of Human Resource Management*, 9(1), 136–154.

Coupland, D. (1993) *Generation X: Tales for an Accelerated Culture*, Abacus.

Curtis, S. and Lucas, R. (2001) 'A coincidence of needs? Employers and full-time students', *Employee Relations*, 23(1), 38–54.

D'Annunzio-Green, N., Maxwell, G. and Watson, S. (2002) *Human Resource Management: International Perspectives in Hospitality and Tourism*, Continuum.

Department for Education and Employment (2000) *Employers Skill Survey: Case Study Hospitality Sector*, DfEE.

Eaton, J. (2001) *Globalization and Human Resource Management in the Airline Industry*, Ashgate.

Grugulis, I. and Wilkinson, A. (2002) 'Managing culture at British Airways: hype, hope and reality', *Long Range Planning* 35(2), 179–194.

Heery, E. and Noon, M. (2001) *A Dictionary of Human Resource Management*, Oxford University Press.

Hoque, K. (2000) *Human Resource Management in the Hotel Industry*, Routledge.

Hospitality Training Foundation (2003) *Labour Market Review 2003*, HtF.

International Labour Organization (2001) *Human Resource Development, Employment and Globalization in the Hotel Catering and Tourism Sector*, ILO.

International Transport Workers Federation (ITF) (2004) 'The cuts don't work', available at http://www.itfglobal.org/transport-international/ti10cuts.cfm (accessed 2 July 2006).

Jollife, L. and Farnsworth, R. (2003) 'Seasonality in tourism employment: human resources challenges', *International Journal of Contemporary Hospitality Management*, 15(6), 312–316.

Keep, E. and Mayhew, K. (1999) *The Leisure Sector (Skills Task Force Research Paper 6)*, DfEE.

Kelliher, C. and Johnson, K. (1997) 'Personnel management in hotels – an update: a move to human resource management?', *Progress in Tourism and Hospitality Research*, 3, 321–331.

Kelliher, C. and Perrett, G. (2001) 'Business strategy and approaches to HRM – a case study of new developments in the United Kingdom restaurant industry', *Personnel Review*, 30(4), 421–437.

Lashley, C. and Taylor, S. (1998) 'Hospitality retail operations types and styles in the management of human resources', *Journal of Retailing and Consumer Services*, 5(3), 153–165.

Lindsay, C. and McQuaid, R. W. (2004) 'Avoiding the "McJobs": unemployed job seekers and attitudes to service work', *Work, Employment and Society*, 18(2), 297–319.

Lucas, R. (2004) *Employment Relations in the Hospitality and Tourism Industries*, Routledge.

MacDonald, C. and Sirianni, C. (1996) *Working in the Service Society*, Temple University Press.

Marchington, M. and Grugulis, I. (2000) '"Best practice" human resource management: perfect opportunity or dangerous illusion?', *International Journal of Human Resource Management*, 11(6), 1104–1124.

McGunnigle, P. and Jameson, S. (2000) 'HRM in UK hotels: a focus on commitment', *Employee Relations*, 22(4), 403–422.

Nickson, D. and Wood, R. C. (2000) 'HRM in the hotel industry: a comment and response', *Human Resource Management Journal*, 10(4), 88–90.

Nickson, D., Baum, T., Losekoot, E. et al. (2002) *Skills, Organizational Performance and Economic Activity in the Hospitality Industry: A Literature Review*, Universities of Oxford and Warwick: SKOPE.

People 1st (2006) *Skills Needs Assessment*, People 1st.

Price, L. (1994) 'Poor personnel practice in the hotel and catering industry – does it matter?', *Human Resource Management Journal*, 4(4), 44–62.

Redman, T. and Matthews, B. (1998) 'Service quality and human resource management: a review and research agenda', *Personnel Review*, 27(1), 57–77.

Riley, M., Gore, J. and Kelliher, C. (2000) 'Economic determinism and human resource management practice in the hospitality and tourism industry', *Tourism and Hospitality Research*, 2(2), 118–128.

Schuler, R. and Jackson, S. (1987) 'Linking competitive strategy with human resource management', *The Academy of Management Executive*, 1(3), 207–219.

Spiess, L. and Waring, P. (2005) 'Emotional and aesthetic labour: cost minimization and the labour process in the Asia Pacific airline industry', *Employee Relations*, 27(2), 193–207.

Storey, J. (1987) 'Developments in the management of human resources: an interim report', *Warwick Papers in Industrial Relations*, 17, IRRU.

Storey, J. (1995) 'Human resource management: still marching on, or marching out?', in J. Storey (ed.) *Human Resource Management: A Critical Text*, Routledge, 3–32.

Vaughan, E. (1994) 'The trail between sense and sentiment: a reflection on the language of HRM', *Journal of General Management*, 19(3), 20–32.

Wood, R. C. (1997) *Working in Hotels and Catering*, International Thomson Press, 2nd edition.

World Travel and Tourism Council (WTTC) (2006) *Travel and Tourism Climbing New Heights: The 2006 Travel and Tourism Economic Research*, at http://www.wttc.org/2006TSA/pdf/Executive%20Summary%202006.pdf (accessed 1 July 2006).

Websites

The Chartered Institute of Personnel and Development (CIPD) is the main professional body for HRM practitioners in the UK. There website can be found at http://www.cipd.co.uk/default.cipd and includes a number of downloadable items for non-members.

http://www.hrmguide.co.uk/is a very good general guide to HRM issues in the UK. Within the site there is also links to HRM issues and practices in a range of other countries including Australia and the US.

The International Labour Organization produced a very comprehensive report in 2001 on HR issues in global tourism and hospitality and this can be found at: http://www.ilo.org/public/english/dialogue/sector/techmeet/tmhct01/tmhct-r.pdf

The Work Foundation (formerly the Industrial Society) has some interesting material on their site at http://www.theworkfoundation.com/index.aspx

Caterer and Hotelkeeper is the trade magazine for the hospitality industry and has a search engine at http://www.caterersearch.com/Home/Default.aspx. The archive has numerous stories on aspects of HRM in the sector.

Chapter 2

International human resource management

Chapter objectives

As tourism and hospitality organizations increasingly internationalize they face a number of challenges in managing their human resources. This chapter considers these challenges and specifically the aims of the chapter are:

- To consider the nature of international human resource management (IHRM).
- To outline and discuss different strategic dispositions to internationalization.
- To appreciate the importance of a multinational company's (MNC's) country-of-origin and the effects of host countries on HRM policy and practice.
- To assess challenges facing MNCs operating in the tourism and hospitality industry in attempting to transfer HRM practices across national boundaries.

Introduction

The continuing growth of world markets, increased availability of management and technological know-how in different countries, advances in telecommunications, and greater regional political and economic integration are just some of the factors that are increasingly leading to the globalization of many tourism and hospitality MNCs. Resultantly, the contemporary tourism and hospitality industry is increasingly global and this is important in a number of ways. As more and more tourism and hospitality MNCs are now selling their products outside their home countries they face a number of issues in terms of how they approach a range of HRM issues. For example, to what extent will they try to transfer policies and practices that are successful in the home country to host countries? In thinking about the mix between parent country and local managers, how will they staff their units overseas? The globalization of business is making it increasingly important to understand how multinational enterprises can operate more effectively in seeking to answer these types of questions. As they cross national boundaries tourism and hospitality MNCs face many challenges related to issues like: language, culture, economic and political systems, legislative frameworks, management styles and conventions. To assess some of these issues the chapter will consider the emergence of IHRM; and relatedly the issue of comparative HRM. In many respects the former aspect is largely concerned with how MNCs manage their geographically dispersed workforce. The latter aspect is more about why and in what ways HR practices and policies may differ in a variety of different countries. Of course, these two aspects are very much intertwined. For example, MNCs may attempt to transfer certain HRM practices and this process may be successfully achieved in certain countries and be much more problematic in others, the chapter will seek to assess why this might be the case.

The emergence of IHRM

We should begin by firstly defining what IHRM is. Torrington (1994: 6) suggests that, 'In many ways IHRM is simply HRM on a larger scale; the strategic considerations are more complex and the operational units more varied, needing co-ordination across more barriers'. A slightly different view is offered by Schuler et al. (1993: 720), who define IHRM as, 'human resource management issues, functions, and policies and practices that result from the strategic activities of multinational enterprises and that impact on the international concerns and goals of those enterprises'. In a similar vein Boxall (1995: 5) also locates the locus of IHRM primarily within the choices faced by MNCs, and sees it as being, 'concerned with the HR problems of multinational firms in foreign subsidiaries (such as expatriate management) or, more broadly, with the unfolding HR issues that are associated with the various stages of the internationalization process'. Thus, on the basis of these definitions it can be seen that, compared to domestic HRM, IHRM is likely to involve the MNC in more diverse activities, greater involvement in employees private lives (e.g. the impact of the expatriation cycle), greater risk exposure, more external influences and generally greater complexity than would be found managing domestically. Most obviously these issues can be seen in terms of how MNCs seek to co-ordinate and integrate a range of units throughout the world, leading Schuler et al. (1993: 719) to ask a crucial question: 'Can MNCs link their globally dispersed units through HR policies and practices, and if so, how?' In many respects any attempt to answer this question can be found in the seminal work of Howard Perlmutter.

Perlmutter: the 'father' of IHRM

Harzing (2004) is representative of much of the IHRM literature which suggests that the typology outlined by Perlmutter (1969) is crucial in attempts to characterize the approach adopted by MNCs not only to HRM, but also finance and accounting, marketing and production. Indeed, Mayrhofer and Brewster (1996) recognize how Perlmutter's typology has become a virtual synonym of analytical approaches to understanding IHRM, such that they talk of his role as the originator and 'father' of the discipline.

Perlmutter's (1969) work attempts to delineate differing orientations, or strategic dispositions, adopted by multinational organizations with his starting point being that claims to multinationality should be based on more than simply generating sales overseas. Consequently Perlmutter outlines an ethnocentric approach which is home-country oriented, a polycentric approach which is host-country oriented and a geocentric approach which is world-oriented (a further orientation of regiocentric, i.e. regionally oriented, was added in 1979 by Perlmutter and Heenan). In general, the ethnocentric strategy suggests that companies should maximize their parent company control to integrate subsidiaries, at the cost of local responsiveness. Resultantly the ethnocentrically oriented MNC believes in the superiority of the way of doing things in the home country and this informs their strategies for staffing and managing overseas units. Therefore this approach implies centralized systems with authority high at headquarters with much communication in the form of orders, commands and advice. Managers of the home country of the parent company are, therefore, recruited, trained and developed for key positions anywhere in the world to ensure that the home country approach is easily transferred and that host-country nationals (HCNs) fully understand the headquarters culture. The polycentric approach allows for more local responsiveness and is premised on the view that the MNC should respond to prevailing local conditions where practicable. Hence, in this orientation local people know best and organizations thus seek to pursue an approach of localizing operations as quickly as possible. Local staff are employed in core positions in the host country and enjoy high levels of autonomy and local opportunities for further promotion. The final orientation of geocentrism is, as Caligiuri and Stroh (1995: 497) note, 'When MNCs desire an integration of all of their foreign subsidiaries and the melding of a worldwide corporate culture'. Consequently organizations seek 'the best man (*sic*), regardless of nationality, to solve the problems anywhere in the world' (Perlmutter, 1969: 13). The geocentric approach envisages competitive advantage emanating from the organization's ability to draw on a rich array of national and cultural perspectives, allowing for a global strategy which is also respectful of local circumstances – the notion of 'think global act local'.

Which of these approaches an international organization could be characterized by is dependent on attitudes inferred from 'the assumptions upon which key product, functional and geographical decisions were made' (ibid.: 11). Importantly though, Perlmutter feels that, 'There is some degree of ethnocentricity, polycentricity or geocentricity in all firms' (ibid.: 11), and it is thus unlikely that any of these orientations are ever found in pure form. Nonetheless Perlmutter argues strongly that one predominant disposition can usually be discerned, with Pauuwe and Dewe (1995: 84) suggesting that any dominant attitude or state of mind of the corporation is likely to be 'determined by the phase of internationalization in which the company finds itself and by its history'. The implicit sense of an evolutionary approach to internationalization is a clear and important theme of Perlmutter's work and equally clear is his recognition of the difficulties and complexity of attaining the most advanced form of the 'ideal' geocentric approach, such that 'The route to pervasive geocentric thinking is long and torturous' (1969: 16). This view that the most developed form for the MNC is the geocentric 'ideal' is something now routinely supported in much of the international business and management literature, as exemplified by Caligiuri and Stroh (1995: 495) who suggest that the geocentric strategy is:

> ... the 'ideal', as it attempts to balance both global integration and local responsiveness. In a hierarchy, the geocentric strategy would be the best because it incorporates both of the theoretical ideals. Polycentric and regiocentric strategies would be second because they satisfy the local responsiveness ideal (usually at the cost of global integration). Ethnocentric strategies, focusing on headquarters control are neither globally integrated nor locally responsive.

A shift to a global orientation is likely to be dependent on the organization having the wherewithal to create and appoint a pool of genuinely 'global' managers, assuming this is in fact possible. This approach requires a sophisticated HR planning system and training infrastructure to enable an organization to enact such a strategy. Some of the issues engendered by this discussion are identified in Table 2.1, which suggests some of the implications for organizations which wish to pursue a geocentric HRM strategy.

The impact of centricity in the tourism and hospitality industry

Roper et al. (1997, 1998) examine the factors that influence and determine success for international hotel groups in the global market place. They argue that centricity – defined by them as an approach to international management – is one of the key factors that influence all business decisions and their subsequent successful implementation. Consequently they examine the possible causal relationship between centricity and organizational success and particularly whether organizations should be seeking to move to the geocentric 'ideal'. Interestingly they disaggregate centricity at a number of levels both in terms of orientation and functional areas of management. First, they suggest that centricity can be viewed from three interrelated perspectives: management's mind set and the attitudes and beliefs of key senior managers in the organization; corporate strategic predisposition and the

Table 2.1 A geocentric human resource profile

Organization	Key decision makers from diverse backgrounds operating on a global basis.
Company culture	Integrated and draws on experiences, attitudes and beliefs held by people from different countries.
Recruitment	Based on ability rather than nationality. Recruits drawn from a range of different countries to core positions.
Training and development	Managers from all countries treated as equal. People developed through a range of overseas assignments and drawn together in cross-cultural teams to learn from each other.
Terms and conditions	General principles adopted which draw on practice from around the globe yet also allow for a response to local circumstances.
Employee relations	General principles adopted which draw on best practice from different countries. European Works Council, international committees/task groups, etc. may be established.

Source: Roper et al. (1997: 381) Reprinted by permission of the author.

way this will shape the company's mission, governance structure, strategy, organization structure and organizational culture; and finally, subsidiary level predilection. Of these, Roper et al. suggest that the first two have the most influence, particularly in the way that management attitudes and beliefs will inform and dictate strategic and operating decisions.

Nickson (1999) reports research from three pseudonymous tourism and hospitality companies, Americo, Frenco and Swedco. Using Perlmutter's framework the three companies evidenced differing orientations, as outlined in HRM in practice 2.1.

Review and reflect

What are some of the likely advantages and disadvantages of companies pursuing an ethnocentric, polycentric or geocentric approach to internationalization?

HRM in practice 2.1   Orientations in the global hotel industry

Americo was an American company who had internationalized relatively recently. The company was now undergoing a fairly rapid process of internationalization and seeking a more global orientation. Americo seemed to have a control-oriented ethnocentric approach to internationalization, with use of American expatriates or long-standing 'Americanized' Americo people in key positions, such as general manager. Control was further enhanced by the use of 'task forces' to transfer the corporate message. There was some evidence of the beginnings of attempts to aspire to a more global outlook, for example, by the use of well-known consultants and academics who were working with the company to encourage a less Amerocentric view.

Frenco was a major travel and tourism multinational who were seeking a more global orientation. The Frenco corporate culture was used as a unifying mechanism across the company, as the organization attempted to sustain a broadly geocentric approach. Nonetheless, there was some evidence of post- or neo-colonialism in use of French expatriates in certain parts of the world. Attempts to sustain a 'global' approach were facilitated by the movement of a cadre of 'global' managers across brands/countries. Many of these managers also attended Frenco's corporate university which attempted with some success to encourage a more global outlook.

Swedco was a relatively small MNC with a small presence outside of Scandinavia. Generally Swedco were seeking a control-oriented ethnocentric approach facilitated by Swedish or Danish expatriate managers in pivotal positions in overseas units. The company seemed largely successful in their attempts to transfer the 'Swedco Way', the company's core corporate culture, though there was some scepticism in the only unit in the UK with a non-Scandinavian/Swedish manager.

International staffing

A further key issue in IHRM is the way in which MNCs seek to staff their overseas unit. Contingent upon the predominant headquarters orientation – as based on Perlmutter's typology – MNCs are likely to use a mix of parent-country nationals (PCNs), third-country nationals (TCNs) and host-country nationals (HCNs). For example, MNCs may utilize PCNs in the early days of an overseas unit's existence, but over time it is likelier that TCNs and particularly HCNs will play an ever greater role. Consequently organizations are likely to see a range of advantages and disadvantages of the utilization of PCNs, HCNs or TCNs and these are considered in Table 2.2.

International organizations would usually have three broad motives for sending managers abroad. The first one of those is to fill positions, when HCNs are unavailable or difficult to train. Although in a more control-oriented ethnocentric approach, PCNs or suitably socialized TCNs may be sent to maintain control due to them knowing the organizational 'rules' and culture better, thus allowing them to make the 'right' kind of decisions. Second, organizations may seek to develop managers with long-term potential by giving them valuable international experience, which is likely to enhance their standing in the organization. Such transfers may occur even when suitably qualified HCNs exist. Lastly, there may be attempts to develop a more geocentric approach, whereby control is achieved by acculturation, socialization and interaction among managers of different nationalities, with the intent of creating a 'global' corporate culture, which de-emphasizes national cultures, and a cadre of managers able to disseminate such an approach. The idea would be that managers would become less ethnocentric if they were to come into contact with a variety of cultures and different cultural perspectives.

The role of international managers in tourism and hospitality

Gliatis and Guerrier (1994) report on research conducted with a small sample of expatriate managers. The research was based on interviews conducted in four large international hotel companies with seven personnel specialists and eight hotel managers (all from different countries and interestingly all male), on assignments outside their home country. The research was carried out in the UK and in Greece and sought to answer several key questions (Gliatis and Guerrier, 1994: 230):

- Why and how do hotel chains use international assignments for managers?
- When would they seek to fill a post with an expatriate manager and when with a local manager?
- How is the use of expatriates changing?
- What problems do they perceive in their use of international transfers?
- What type of person is attracted to an international career?

Table 2.2 Advantages and disadvantages of using PCNs, TCNs and HCNs

	Advantage	Disadvantage
PCNs	Familiarity with the home offices goals, objectives, policies and practices	Difficulties in adapting to the foreign language and the socio-economic, political, cultural and legal environment
	Technical and managerial competence	Excessive cost of selecting, training and maintaining expatriate managers and their families abroad
	Effective liaison and communication with home-office personnel	The host countries' insistence on localising operations and promoting local nationals
	Easier exercise of control over the subsidiary operation	Family adjustment problems
HCNs	Familiarity with the socio-economic, political and legal environment and with business practices in the host country	Difficulties in exercising effective control over the subsidiaries operation
	Lower costs incurred in hiring HCNs	Communication difficulties in dealing with home-office personnel
	Provides opportunities for advancement of local nationals and, therefore, increases motivation and commitment	Lack of opportunities for home country's nationals to gain international and cross-cultural experience
	Responsive to demands for localization of subsidiary operation	
TCNs	Perhaps the best compromise between securing needed technical and managerial expertise and adapting to a foreign socio-economic and cultural environment	Host countries' sensitivity with respect to nationals of specific countries
	TCNs are usually career international business managers	Local nationals are impeded in their efforts to upgrade their own ranks and assume responsible positions in the multinational subsidiaries
	TCNs may be better informed about the host environment than PCNs	

Source: Harzing (2004a: 254) Reprinted by permission of Sage Publications Ltd from Wil-Harzing A. and Van Ruysseveldt, J. *International Human Resource Management*, Copyright (Sage, 2004).

- What do managers who follow international career paths perceive they gain from this type of career path?
- What do they perceive as their main problems?

The main focus of this research was why expatriate managers fail, although Gliatis and Guerrier do tangentially address wider questions on organizational strategy towards crossing national boundaries. They suggest that companies would ordinarily see the rationale for expatriation as comprising three main reasons. The first of these is to solve specific staffing problems in a particular location, for example, a lack of suitably qualified personnel. The second is as part of a management development process, thus managers would benefit from the exposure to a range of countries, cultures and international issues. The final reason would be as a process of organizational development, whereby transfers are seen as encouraging global co-ordination, integration and commitment to the company. A further element to this may also be more control-oriented, in the sense that organizations will seek to integrate via the use of (usually home country) expatriate managers to spread the co-ordinating 'glue' of corporate culture to ensure that organizational practices and policies are 'correctly' followed. As a result of the research Gliatis and Guerrier also added a fourth reason as suggested by the personnel specialists, namely the use of expatriation as a tool for motivating and retaining managers within a company. Gliatis and Guerrier found evidence of all of these strategies in their research and also found that expatriation tended to be more appropriate for operational roles, such as general manager, resident manager, food and beverage manager and rooms division manager, whilst locals would ordinarily fill the positions of personnel managers, financial managers and chief engineers due to their local expertise.

D'Annunzio-Green (1997) reporting on research within five international tourism and hospitality organizations – representing the airline, fast food and hotel sector – suggests that her case study organizations were largely pursuing a geocentric or polycentric approach. Her work is useful both in its reporting of the research but also in terms of its contextual discussion of how organizations approach international management development (IMD). An organization which aspires to a more global outlook faces a number of issues in terms of approaches adopted to things such as: international career pathing, organizations developing international managers, adaptability of employees to new cultures and language and the effect of training and adaptation. MNCs intending to pursue a geocentric approach must address a number of questions, these being:

- Is there a constant supply of mobile staff?
- Can they be released on time from existing positions?
- Is there a database advanced enough to manage a geocentric approach to training and development?
- Is the company willing to invest the time and money required to ensure such a system will operate effectively?

As D'Annunzio-Green (1997: 200) suggests, 'For organizations wishing to develop a truly international manager, there needs to be a major transformation in managerial careers and development opportunities to enable the acquisition of the skills, knowledge and experience needed to work in a global market place'.

Based on findings from a self-completed postal questionnaire sent to the senior human resources specialist within the organizations, D'Annunzio-Green found that three of the organizations in her research were pursuing a geocentric approach, with the other two being characterized respectively as polycentric/geocentric and geocentric to regiocentric. The questionnaire was followed up with in-depth interviews with the HR director in three of the organizations and this allows D'Annunzio-Green to add more detail as to why the organizations are characterized in such a way. For example, in a British-owned airline company, which is conceptualized as shifting from an ethnocentric to a geocentric approach, a key role is increasingly played by HCNs and TCNs and all of the 30–40 graduates taken on to the company's management training scheme had to undertake a number of international postings during their training period. Allied to this approach the company also had a sophisticated database to track career moves and mechanisms to ensure all vacancies worldwide were notified to company personnel.

Similarly, an American-owned hotel MNC communicated all international postings via a computerized personnel database. This company, also considered geocentric and committed in the words of the company themselves to '"developing truly international managers"' (ibid.: 204), selected international managers on the basis of good performance appraisals, a minimum of 5 years with the company and language proficiency in at least two languages. Additionally the selection criteria was also based on adaptability, international background and a high level of mobility. The common strand of a sophisticated computerized global transfer system was also found in the final organization, a Japanese-owned hotel MNC. Again this company was considered geocentric and as part of their IMD had a 10-year training and development plan which culminates in a general manager's position. During this time the candidates, who theoretically could come from any country, would undertake a part-time MBA and placements in at least three countries to encourage mobility, cultural empathy and global business awareness.

Review and reflect

What are some of the key skills needed to be a successful expatriate manager in the international tourism and hospitality industry?

In sum, Gliatis and Guerrier's and D'Annunzio-Green's work is useful in pointing to the likelihood of organizations within the tourism and hospitality sector adopting different approaches to internationalization and their utilization of international managers. In particular, the attempt by D'Annunzio-Green to add greater detail as to what may denote a geocentric approach is useful in suggesting a range of organizational practices and policies which appear crucial in facilitating such an approach.

Much of what we have been discussing to date has largely been about the manner in which MNC companies seek to develop their overall orientation and the implications of such an approach with regard to international staffing. Beyond this focus, there is also a need to consider the broader aspect of comparative HRM, which is more concerned as to why certain HRM practices may differ from country to country. To begin to discuss this we should recognize the importance of the country-of-origin of MNCs.

Country-of-origin

Ferner (1997) provides a review of the country-of-origin literature and some of the substantive issues engendered by this work. From the relatively small body of research examining the country-of-origin effect, Ferner believes that two important generalizations can be extrapolated.

The first generalization is that the literature provides support for the notion that the nationality of ownership is a significant determinant of MNC behaviour and thus any examination of MNCs strategies should take cognizance of the national economic and business cultures out of which they emerged. An example of this would be the proposition that American and Japanese MNCs have in the past tended to be more ethnocentric and reliant on expatriate managers to ensure organizational practices and polices are 'correctly' followed. Therefore this 'imperial' approach was concerned with close control over foreign subsidiaries and led to greater formalization and centralization and a reliance on formal systems, policies and standards to manage human resources globally.

A further interesting aspect identified by Ferner (1997) is whether it is sensible to characterize, as an example, differences between Japanese and British MNCs as being due to some inherent quality of 'Japaneseness' or 'Britishness', or whether such differences stem from other factors, such as stage of internationalization, corporate structure and proportion of units represented overseas. Furthermore the implications of national specificity would seem to preclude any real possibility of either a literal or even figurative 'stateless' organization, reflecting Van Maanen and Laurent's (1993: 283) view that 'All MNCs bear something of a cultural stamp that originates in the society where the organization was first designed' (see also Hu, 1992). Therefore, as Ferner (1997) cogently agues even if the home country does not provide the bulk of sales, operations and employment, in reality it is likely to play a highly significant role in relation to locus of ownership and control, staffing of board and senior positions, strategic decisions emanating from the home country and also in the location of innovative activities such as research and development. Given Ferner's support for the notion of an MNC's entrenched rootedness to a national economic and business culture it is unsurprising to find him asking the question of 'what features do they "absorb" from the national background?' (ibid.: 24).

In answer to that question the second generalization is that the extent of the possible national influence on MNC behaviour is contingent upon the issues under consideration. Consequently nationality manifests itself more in relation to some issues than others. For example, industrial relations practices are more likely to resemble the practices of the local environment. These considerations are also closely related to the convergence/divergence debate, and the extent to which the forces of convergence may be subverting national differences. At its broadest macrosocial level, convergence theory is a recognition of the influence of over-arching trajectories and logic of capitalist development. This socio-structural argument suggests that societies and organizations will increasingly come to resemble each other as they accept the inevitability of universalistic tendencies in relation to technology, economic development, industrial policies, management style and HR practices. Consequently, over time a universal type of business organization will emerge and management practices and organizational performance would be shaped by the 'logic of industrialization' and technological change, rather than cultural or environmental variables. Within this process a key role will be played by MNCs who act as carriers of 'best practice' across national boundaries.

Clearly a key role in this process is ascribed to MNCs and this raises the interesting spectre of MNCs acting as forces for convergence around the practices of the most 'successful' national business regimes. In essence this means that nationally specific versions of capitalism emerge to be disseminated by the hegemonic country's multinationals (Smith and Meiksins, 1995). There is still much support for the notion that the US continues to be the predominant source of what are considered 'good practice' approaches to both general business management and, more particularly, HRM. Brewster (1995: 207), for example, argues that 'the analyses and prescriptions laid out in the standard management textbooks are, fundamentally, drawn from one particular culture: that of the USA'. Guest (1990: 377) also makes a clear connection between HRM and the 'American Dream':

The growth of HRM in the UK clearly owes something to the political, economic and business climate of the 1980s and the tendency during the decade to look to the United States as a model of good practice in all these fields. American multinationals have been to the forefront of HRM innovation in the UK and the leading advocates are all American.

Branine (1994) makes the cogent point that it is much more likely that non-American managers would adopt American management styles or techniques, whilst at the same time suggesting it is difficult to envisage American managers adopting policies that were originally from, for example, Mexico, Fiji or Peru. The important point then is the applicability and transferability of the putatively American approach to management and whether there may be an enduring American influence on any convergent tendencies if HRM is to be the new model for managing organizations throughout the world (and see HRM in practice 2.2).

Review and reflect

Does the American dominance of the globalization process mean that we are all increasingly 'Americanized'?

HRM in practice 2.2   American dominance of global economy and the international hotel industry

Many writers argue that there are three key dimensions underpinning the process of globalization, these being economic, political and cultural. It is also often argued that globalization is, in reality, better conceptualized as Americanization. With regard to economics a key aspect is the rise of the multinational firm. By the early twentieth century US firms were becoming more important players in the international economy, beginning to eclipse their established European competitors. During the Second World War and into the post-war period, US firms were in a position to exploit, by trade and with foreign direct investment (FDI), firstly the inadequacies and then the decline in European manufacturing capacity, aided of course by Marshall Aid and US Government desires to create bulwarks against communism in Europe and Asia – *Pax Americana*. During this time American management methods were vigorously exported through FDI, and education and training institutions in Europe. With regard to politics, and particularly global governance, many argue that it is the US particularly and to a lesser extent the industrialized countries of the European Union which drive the operations and policies of institutions such as the World Bank, International Monetary Fund and the World Trade Organization. Finally, there appears to be a growing passion around the world for all things American and few things reflect American culture better than the likes of Coca-Cola, Disney and McDonald's, who seem to embody Americana. A number of these aspects are seen in the history of hotel internationalization, which was initially attributed to Conrad Hilton. He sought to place his 'little Americas' across the globe, leading many to talk of Hilton in venerable terms as the 'founder' of internationalization in the hotel industry. As well as explicitly offering a challenge to communism, many of the operating standards and procedures established by Hilton and other pioneering American hotel chains are still apparent today. This dominance can be seen with regard to aspects of the 'hardware', that is the physical product; but importantly also the 'software', that is the management of people. This software increasingly aims to support high quality approaches to service via aspects such as empowerment.

Source: Nickson and Warhurst (2001).

Country-of-operation

However strong the country-of-origin effect it is likely that units of MNCs in overseas locations will be influenced, to a greater or lesser extent, by what Ferner (1994: 92) has termed 'the host-country effect'. This effect is likely to be manifested in one of two ways, namely, the 'culturalist' perspective and the 'institutionalist' perspective (Olie, 1995).

The importance of culture in IHRM

The 'softer' culturalist perspective draws attention to cultural distinctiveness in terms of the differing values, ideas and beliefs shared by people within any given society. These aspects will then be taken into the organizational setting and uniquely influence individuals workplace behaviour. Tayeb (1994) suggests that the culturalist perspective is important primarily due to three reasons. First, it recognizes the differences of cultural norms, values and attitudes from one society to another, such that peoples' thinking is likely to be shaped by what is considered appropriate behaviour within that society. Second, different cultural groups will behave differently under similar circumstances because of the differences in their underlying values and attitudes. Lastly, culture will play a major part in shaping social institutions, work organizations, managerial behaviour and personnel policies.

It is important to recognize that culture remains an essentially vague and contested concept with literally hundreds of definitions. Equally though many have attempted to research the impact between culture and workplace behaviour, with one of the most famous writers in this area being Geert Hofstede. Hofstede (1980, 2001) studied 117 000 IBM staff across more than 50 countries and identified the following four basic dimensions which describe the differences of national culture:

- *Power distance*: This is the extent to which inequalities among people are seen as normal. This dimension stretches from equal relations being seen as normal to wide inequalities being viewed as normal. Where high power distance exists there may well be a very clear hierarchy and managers would be expected to manage and direct subordinates. Cultures with low power distance are likely to be more consensual, with employees expecting to be consulted in decision-making.

- *Uncertainty avoidance*: This refers to a preference for structured situations vs. unstructured situations. This dimension runs from being comfortable with flexibility and ambiguity to a need for extremely rigid and certain situations. Cultures with high uncertainty avoidance would prefer clear rules, whilst low uncertainty avoidance cultures would be more comfortable working with few rules.
- *Individualism*: This examines whether individuals are used to acting as individuals or as part of cohesive groups. This dimension ranges from collectivism to individualism. In individualistic cultures there is likely to be a desire to work independently. In contrast in collectivist cultures there is likely to be a greater preference to work with others or in groups.
- *Masculinity*: Hofstede distinguishes between 'hard' or 'masculine' values, such as assertiveness and competition and 'soft' or 'feminine' values of personal relations, quality of life and caring for others. In masculine cultures work is valued as a central life interest. By comparison feminine cultures are more likely to stress the value of social rewards.

Based on these dimensions, and a later dimension of time and whether cultures have a long-term vs. a short-term orientation, Hofstede categorized countries into clusters, based on the relative similarities between cultures. If we accept the idea of stereotyping as a common way of perceiving different nationalities, Hofstede's work may be open to criticisms (indeed see the recent debate between Hofstede (2002) McSweeney (2002, 2002a) and Smith (2002) on the recent publication of an updated version of *Culture's Consequences*). For example, there is much argument as to whether cultures can really be thought of as homogenous. However, most writers view the work of Hofstede as important, and as somewhere between a stereotypical description of a national culture and a useful tool for discovering an alien culture. So in that way it can be usefully used as a practical framework for managers to understand potential cross-cultural differences in managing different individuals or in different cultures. To conclude on Hofstede's work, most people would agree that the framework is helpful as a heuristic device to assist the process of learning about a new culture. Hofstede's findings are useful when applied as a general model that requires interpretation of specific circumstances. It is important that culture assessment focuses on the general make up of a nation or culture. This can be thought of as a curve, where most people will be near the 'norm', but there will be people in every society who exhibit characteristics that are distinctly different. Therefore these 'mainstream' cultural traits are best considered as a tendency or describing the behaviour of the average individual, but clearly there is the potential for other individuals to behave differently. Lastly, Hofstede's work is important in suggesting that true convergence in management and organizational practices will never occur due to the varying cultural differences outlined above.

The institutional perspective

The difficulty in operationalizing and making concrete such amorphous notions as tradition and culture has led a variety of writers to shift the analysis more towards social institutions, such as education, vocational training patterns and employee/industrial relations. Ferner (1994: 93) suggests that, 'there is more to national variation than some nebulous notion of "cultural difference"', and as a result, attention should also be paid to more concrete institutional factors. This point is also noted by Tayeb (1994: 431) who recognizes that 'The term "nation" refers not only to culture, but also to other social, economic and political institutions which have a significant bearing on the management style of organizations located in particular countries'. The recognition that culture should not be seen as a synonym for nation and an omnibus variable representing a range of social, historical, political and economic factors, lies at the heart of the institutionalist perspective. The 'harder' institutionalist argument is primarily concerned with structural aspects within society and organizations, such as the division of labour and career, status and reward structures. These features are generated by the institutions of the host country which, as previously noted, will affect elements such as education, training and employee/industrial relations systems. Indeed, it is often the employee/industrial relations system which is most often cited as the least permeable aspect of a host-country environment, as this may often be based on a state regulated legislative framework. Hence, there is likely to be tension between activities carried out by an MNC and the national system of employee/industrial relations in any given host country. This is particularly apparent within countries which have strong regulatory frameworks, which are likely to be a source of rules to which the MNC must comply. For example, an American MNC may ordinarily work without trade unions but in locating in Germany may be forced to recognize and negotiate with trade unions due to the regulatory framework (see Royle 2002 and Royle and

Towers 2002 for an interesting discussion on how McDonald's have sought to override regulatory mechanisms in Europe). In sum, the impact of both the culture and institutions means that a MNC has to consider carefully what HRM policies and practices they can transfer because as Ferner notes (1997: 33):

> ... not all elements [of an MNCs human resource policies] are 'exportable' being too rooted in native cultural assumptions; and second because to varying degrees host countries present obstacles to the 'import' of elements of foreign business systems, and colour the operation of those which are transferred.

Recognition of all of the above variables allows for an assessment of the impact of specific national institutional, legal and cultural frameworks, so as to be able to answer questions about the balance between innovation and adaptation in corporate HR policies.

MNCs and HRM policies and practices in the tourism and hospitality industry

We have recognized that MNCs face choices in both the manner in which they develop their overall approach to IHRM and then how this will determine their approach to international staffing and what HR policies and practices they seek to transfer. Of course, MNCs are likely to want to maintain and develop a degree of consistency in their ways of managing people on a worldwide basis. Equally though in order to be effective locally, they may also need to adapt those ways to the specific cultural and institutional requirements of different societies. We can now briefly assess some of the evidence of how tourism and hospitality MNCs may be seeking to address these issues.

Nankevis and Debrah (1995) report on management practices in a selection of hotels in Singapore and Australia to discuss common and disparate themes within diverse national, cultural, social and labour market environments. The basic premise of Nankevis and Debrah is that the hospitality industry is increasingly looking to HRM to enhance organizational success and competitive advantage. To test this proposition they used a questionnaire with 35 multiple choice questions, which were occasionally supplemented by open-ended follow-up comments for clarification or enlargement. The questionnaire was divided into four major categories: type of hotel; employee details; personnel management/HRM practices and guest feed-back. There were 109 responses (89 from Australia and 20 from Singapore) from 201 questionnaires. In relation to a range of HR issues Nankevis and Debrah found considerable differences in approaches in Singapore and Australia and such dif-ferences were attributable to elements such as national, cultural, social, labour market phenomenon and management styles. Nonetheless their findings did 'also appear to confirm the increasing globalizm of guest market requirements and hotel management responses' (ibid.: 512). This was particularly so in relation to the MNC hotel companies surveyed, leading Nankevis and Debrah (1995: 511) to suggest that, 'A potential consequence of [the high proportion of hotels owned by multinationals] is the standardization of service along with increased efficiency, productivity and thence profitability'.

Similarly, Jansen-Verbeke (1996) reports on research undertaken in hotels (including international hotels, e.g. Hilton International) in Belgium and The Netherlands which suggested a high level of uniformity in managerial practices. Jansen-Verbeke utilized Hofstede's seminal framework to assess the extent to which cultural differences may exist between Belgian and Dutch managers. The research consisted of a written questionnaire, comprising 45 questions asking managers about their everyday practices in hotel management, and the sample consisted of 64 respondents. As Jensen-Verbeke (1996: 547) notes 'The analysis shows that there are only a few differences in the practices of hotel managers in Belgium and The Netherlands'. To explain this convergence Jansen-Verbeke points to a range of factors, such as: the two countries belonging to the same cultural region; the homogenizing effect of organizational culture, reflecting the fact that most MNCs have a strong organizational culture; and the culture of the hotel industry in general, particularly in terms of uniform procedures in guest contact and an emphasis on quality of service. Of these, it is particularly noteworthy that organizational culture and the culture of the industry seem to play such a key role in the process of homogenization and convergence.

Review and reflect

What are some of the potential challenges facing tourism and hospitality MNCs in attempting to transfer their HRM practices across national boundaries?

The above discussion seems to suggest that the continued growth of multinational corporations is likely to lead in the future to greater standardization of services, as organizations seek greater efficiency, productivity and profitability, by utilizing the full range of 'soft' techniques leading to a burgeoning sector wide 'best practice' approach to HRM and quality service (and see also Nickson, 1999). A counter argument though is offered by Mwaura et al. (1998). In their research on the ITT Sheraton Hotel China they found significant evidence of Sheraton's corporate culture being in conflict with several aspects of Chinese culture. For example, Chinese managers and subordinates were not prepared to accept responsibility to ensure responsiveness to the hotel guests. A similar issue was also apparent in attempts to engender a commitment to customer satisfaction via training. Many of the local employees were reluctant to contribute to discussions in training sessions in case they lost 'face'. Similar results were also found by D'Annunzio-Green (2002) in her research on the experience of expatriate managers in Russia. Here the attempts by expatriate managers to engender and maintain high service standards were often thwarted by the different attitudes to service of the Russian staff. Many of the staff, particularly those over 30, still exhibited behaviours which were developed during the previous communist-era Soviet system. Under this system Russians would never complain about service, no matter how bad it was. Resultantly, the lack of a customer orientation is still apparent in a large number of the staff. What the work of Mwaura et al. and D'Annunzio-Green exemplifies is that western management practices cannot always be transferred in the tourism and hospitality industry, due to differing cultural and organizational working environments (and see also Lucas et al., 2004; Zhang and Wu, 2004).

Conclusion

We noted how increasingly tourism and hospitality organizations may be operating on an international or even global basis. It was recognized that in internationalizing organizations face choices in their strategic disposition, for example whether they adopt a broadly ethnocentric or polycentric approach. The overall strategic disposition of a MNC will also impact on how they develop their international staffing. In addressing issues of this nature MNCs may seek to utilize practices only from its home country, imitate practices typical of other countries or increasingly utilize an amalgam of HRM practices drawn from many other companies and countries, especially in pursuit of notions of 'best practice'. We noted how this has led many to talk in terms of whether there is increasing convergence in the manner in which HRM policies and practices are developed. In this view HRM practices are 'culture free' and universalistic and so the transfer of managerial practice is straightforward, particularly if that practice is considered as 'best practice'. On the other hand we also noted the enduring influence of host countries' culture and institutions leading many to argue for divergence. In the latter view HRM practices are 'culture bound' and difficult to transfer because of the primacy of differentiating effects of national culture or the need for MNCs to respond to differing legal and regulatory framework in a number of countries.

References and further reading

Boxall, P. (1995) 'Building the theory of comparative HRM', *Human Resource Management Journal*, 5(5), 5–17.

Branine, M. (1994) 'The cultural imperative of human resource management: a reconsideration of convergence and divergence factors', paper presented to *The Strategic Direction of Human Resource Management: Empowerment, Diversity and Control*, Nottingham Trent University, December.

Brewster, C. (1995) 'National culture and international management', in S. Tyson (ed.) *Strategic Prospects for Human Resource Management*, IPD, 296–308.

Caligiuri, P. and Stroh, L. (1995) 'Multinational corporation management strategies and international human resources practices: bringing IHRM to the bottom line', *International Journal of Human Resource Management*, 6(3), 494–507.

D'Annunzio-Green, N. (1997) 'Developing international managers in the hospitality industry', *International Journal of Contemporary Hospitality Management*, 9(5/6), 199–208.

D'Annunzio-Green, N. (2002) 'An examination of the organizational and cross-cultural challenges facing international hotel managers in Russia', *International Journal of Contemporary Hospitality Management*, 14(6), 266–273.

Ferner, A. (1994) 'Multinational companies and human resource management: an overview of research issues', *Human Resource Management Journal*, 4(2), 79–102.

Ferner, A. (1997) 'Country-of-origin effect and HRM in multinational companies', *Human Resource Management Journal*, 7(1), 19–37.

Gliatis, N. and Guerrier, Y. (1994) 'Managing international career moves in international hotel companies', in C. Cooper and A. Lockwood (eds.) *Progress in Tourism, Recreation and Hospitality Management*, Vol. 5, John Wiley, 229–41.

Guest, D. E. (1990) 'Human resource management and the American Dream', *Journal of Management Studies*, 27(4), 378–397.

Harzing, A. W. (2004) 'Strategy and structure of multinational companies', in A. Harzing and J. Van Ruysseveldt (eds.) *International Human Resource Management*, Sage, 2nd edition, 33–64.

Harzing, A. W. (2004a) 'Composing an international staff', in A. Harzing and J. Van Ruysseveldt (eds.) *International Human Resource Management*, Sage, 2nd edition, 251–282.

Hofstede, G. (1980) *Culture's Consequences: International Differences in Work Related Values*, Sage.

Hofstede, G. (2001) *Culture's Consequences: International Differences in Work Related Values*, Sage, 2nd edition.

Hofstede, G. (2002) 'Dimensions do not exist: a reply to Brendan McSweeney', *Human Relations*, 55(11), 1355–1361.

Hu, Y. (1992) 'Global or stateless corporations are national firms with international operations', *California Management Review*, Winter, 107–126.

Jansen-Verbeke, M. (1996) 'Cross-cultural differences in the practices of hotel managers: a study of Dutch and Belgian hotel managers', *Tourism Management*, 17(7), 544–548.

Lucas, R., Marinova, M., Kucerova, J. and Vetrokova, M. (2004) 'HRM practices in emerging economies: a long way to go in the Slovak hotel industry?' *International Journal of Human Resource Management*, 15(7), 1262–1279.

McSweeney, B. (2002) 'Hofstede's model of national cultural differences and their consequences: a triumph of faith – a failure of analysis', *Human Relations*, 55(1), 89–118.

McSweeney, B. (2002a) 'The essentials of scholarship: a reply to Geert Hofstede', *Human Relations*, 55(11), 1363–1372.

Mayrhofer, W. and Brewster, C. (1996) 'In praise of ethnocentricity: expatriate policies in European multi-nationals', *The International Executive*, 38(6), 749–778.

Mwaura, G., Sutton, J. and Roberts, D. (1998) 'Corporate and national culture – an irreconcilable dilemma for the hospitality manager?' *International Journal of Contemporary Hospitality Management*, 10(6), 212–220.

Nankevis, A. and Debrah, Y. (1995) 'Human resource management in hotels – a comparative study', *Tourism Management*, 16(7), 507–513.

Nickson, D. (1999) *A Review of the Internationalization Strategies of Three Hotel Companies with a Particular Focus on Human Resource Management*, unpublished PhD Thesis, University of Strathclyde.

Nickson, D. and Warhurst, C. (2001) 'From globalization to internationalization to Americanization: the example of "Little Americas" in the hotel sector', in M. Hughes and J. Taggart (eds.) *Multinationals in a New Era – International Strategy and Management*, Palgrave, 207–225.

Olie, R. (1995) 'The culture factor in personnel and organisational policies', in A. W. Harzing and J. Van Ruysseveldt (eds.) *International Human Resource Management*, Sage, 124–143.

Paauwe, J. and Dewe, P. (1995) 'Organizational structure of multinational corporations, in' A. W. Harzing and J. Van Ruysseveldt (eds.) *International Human Resource Management*, London: Sage, 51–74.

Perlmutter, H. (1969) 'The torturous evolution of the multinational corporation', *Columbia Journal of World Business*, 4(1), 9–18.

Roper, A., Brookes, M. Price, L. and Hampton, A. (1997) 'Towards an understanding of centricity: profiling international hotel groups', in N. Hemmington (ed.) *Proceedings of the Sixth Annual Council for Hospitality Management Education (CHME) Research Conference*, Oxford Brookes University, 370–388.

Roper, A., Doherty, L., Brookes, M. and Hampton, A. (1998) '"Company Man" meets international hotel customer', in D. Litteljohn (ed.) *Proceedings of the Seventh Annual Council for Hospitality Management Education (CHME) Annual Conference*, Glasgow Caledonian University, 328–343.

Royle, T. (2002) 'Just say no! Union busting in the European fast food industry: the case of McDonalds', *Industrial Relations Journal*, 33(3), 262–278.

Royle, T. and Towers, B. (2002) *Labour Relations in the Global Fast Food Industry*, Sage.

Schuler, R., Dowling, P. and De Ceiri, H. (1993) 'An integrative framework of strategic international human resource management', *International Journal of Hunan Resource Management*, 4,(4), 717–765.

Smith, P. (2002) 'Culture's Consequences: something old and something new', Human Relations, 55(1), 119–135.

Smith, C. and Meiksins, P. (1995) 'Systems, society and dominance effects in cross-national organizational analysis', Work, Employment and Society, 9(2), 241–267.

Tayeb, M. (1994) 'Organizations and national culture: methodology considered', Organization Studies, 15(3), 429–446.

Torrington, D. (1994) International Human Resource Management – Think Globally, Act Locally, Prentice Hall.

Van Maanen, J. and Laurent, A. (1993) 'The flow of culture: some notes on globalization and the multinational corporation', in S. Ghoshal and D. Westney (eds.) Organization Theory and the Multinational Corporation, St Martins Press, 275–312.

Zhang, H. and Wu, E. (2004) 'Human resource issues facing the hotel and travel industry in China', International Journal of Contemporary Hospitality Management, 16(7), 424–428.

Websites

http://www.eiro.eurofound.eu.int/is the website of The European Industrial Relations Observatory (EIRO). The site offers news and analysis and up-to-date information on key developments in industrial relations in Europe.

The International Labour Organization is a specialized agency of the United Nations responsible for labour issues globally http://www.ilo.org/

Chapter 3
Organizational culture

Chapter objectives

This chapter considers the increasing importance of organizational culture to tourism and hospitality organizations. The objectives of this chapter are:

- To assess debates about the manageability of culture.
- To consider the various aspects of organizational culture.
- To recognize the role of organizational culture in a broader HRM strategy.

Introduction

We recognized in the previous chapter the importance of national culture and particularly the manner in which it is likely to have an impact on workplace behaviour. The same is also true within organizations. All organizations will have a culture which will have an impact on the way employees behave within the organization. As we have already recognized in Chapter 1 within human resource management employees are seen as a key resource. Our core definition of HRM from Storey talked about cultural aspects of HRM, so part of the way in which employees, as a key resource, can be managed is through the use of organizational culture to generate commitment to the organization and its values. Thus, as Ogbonna (1992: 80) notes, 'the achievement of HRM objectives requires the management of the organizational value system (culture) and this requires skilful implementation'.

Often within tourism and hospitality such values will be concerned with encouraging employee buy in to the customer care and service quality initiatives, which organizations see as a form of competitive advantage in the crowded marketplace. This process of seeking buy in from employees is likely to have a significant impact on a range of human resource practices, such as recruitment and selection, training and remuneration. For example, tourism and hospitality organizations may look to recruit and select those who are considered to 'fit' in with the culture. However, whilst many organizations and managers within the tourism and hospitality industry now see the management of organizational culture as a potential source of competitive advantage, there are others who caution against the overly optimistic claims made for organizational culture. Recognizing these competing views on organizational culture this chapter will aim to offer a balanced assessment of the place of organizational culture within a broader human resource strategy. Specifically, in examining organizational culture there are three key questions that need to be addressed:

1 What is organizational culture?
2 How can we study it?
3 What role does organizational culture play in organizational success?

In search of a definition

Before we begin to move towards a definition it is important initially to recognize debates about the terminology employed to describe the manner in which organizations attempt to use culture as a device to create integration and cohesion across the organization. Central to this debate is the key question of the manageability or otherwise of culture (Legge, 1994). Commonly in books or articles the terms organizational and corporate culture may be used interchangeably. Legge (1994) cautions against this uncritical use of the two terms. For example, she argues that 'in using the term "corporate" culture, many writers seem to be imputing a culture created by senior management for the lower orders to swallow' (p. 407). In this view 'corporate' culture is something an organization *has*. Consequently, it can clearly be managed for the benefit of the organization and its members. On the other hand, the use of the term organizational culture reflects the manner in which culture emerges from social interaction amongst organizational members; something that an organization *is*. In the latter view culture may be difficult to manipulate, change or manage. Given some of the claims that are made about the link between organizational or corporate culture and organizational success this is an important caveat from Legge and one that should be borne in mind throughout the chapter.

Notwithstanding debates about whether the preferred terminology should be organizational or corporate culture, we should attempt to define the concept. Brown (1998: 7–8) recognizes the multiplicity of definitions of organizational culture and the differing intellectual traditions that they come from. Based on these various definitions Brown (1998: 9) offers his own: 'Organizational culture refers to the pattern of beliefs, values, and learned ways of coping with experience that have developed during the course of an organization's history, and which tend to be manifested in its material arrangements and in the behaviour of its members'. For many this can be succinctly summarized as, 'The way we do things around here' (Deal and Kennedy, 1988: 4). As we noted earlier all organizations have their own unique culture and in recent years attention has focused on the manner in which organizations can potentially use culture to unlock the commitment and enthusiasm of employees. This process of unlocking commitment and enthusiasm is by no means straightforward or uncontested (Thompson and McHugh, 2001). For example, we should be aware of the notions of sub-cultures, such that all organizational members might not subscribe to the organizational vision. Recognition of the potentially contested nature of organizational culture is important because it points to the manner in which there may be a disjuncture between the rhetoric and reality of organizational culture. Brown (1998) expresses this point as the espoused culture and the culture in practice. The former may be the positive view that is presented for public consumption, whilst the latter may allow for a more critical reading of any given organizational culture and to further appreciate this point the chapter now considers competing views of organizational culture.

Competing views on organizational culture

The discussion above points to the debate about whether culture is, in fact, manageable and to recognize some of the competing claims made about culture we should acknowledge the useful work of Ogbonna and Harris (2002). In reviewing organizational culture they attempt to categorize the range of work into three broad labels, 'the optimists', 'the pessimists' and 'the realists'.

Optimists

A key aspect of the optimists position is that culture can be used as a mechanism to facilitate organizational unity and cohesion. Thus, 'the key works of key "cultural optimists" show that this perspective not only assumes the existence of unitary cultures in organizations but it also implies that cultural control by top management is possible and desirable' (p. 35). Indeed, Ogbonna and Harris suggest that in recognizing the manageability of culture optimists, 'generally argue that those organizations that fail to control their cultures will be missing an opportunity to harness their human resources' (p. 35). The optimists view relies on a lot of assumptions, not least that the interests of senior managers are shared by others in the organizational hierarchy. This type of thinking was particularly prevalent in much of the research and writing about organizational culture in the 1970s and 1980s, most obviously exemplified by the excellence genre, or what Thompson and McHugh (2001) refer to as the 'corporate culture merchants', such as Peters and Waterman (1982). Optimists also argue that there is a potentially positive relationship between organizational culture and business performance (and see HRM in practice 3.1).

Pessimists

Ogbonna and Harris note that academics tend to predominate in this group and often approach the issue from largely theoretical perspectives. In that sense pessimists seek to develop the 'explanatory power of the culture concept rather than in

HRM in practice 3.1   Strong culture at the Regent Hotel

Kemp and Dwyer (2001) reflect an optimistic view of organizational culture in their research undertaken in the Regent Hotel, Sydney. The starting point of Kemp and Dwyer's research is that culture is viewed as an integrating, unifying phenomenon, shared by all organizational members. In this manner culture can be used to integrate and bind organizational members; it becomes a normative 'glue'. The authors believe that a 'strong' culture is an important enabling force in strategy formulation and ultimately is a major aspect of enhancing organizational performance. Drawing on interviews with 45 managers and employees of the hotel, Kemp and Dwyer recognize a variety of ways in which cultural aspects are integral to the development of HRM practices. For example, they suggest that within the hotel control is primarily through attempts to ensure that the employees offer quality service and exceed guests' expectations. Thus, 'Behavioural control is exerted through hotel training. Staff are taught how to enjoy their job and that they should greet guests at all times with a smile. In the attitude workshop staff are told that "smiles are what count". These smiles need to be as crisp as their daily dry-cleaned uniforms' (p. 87). Even before the extensive attitudinal and behavioural training though control is exerted through recruiting the 'right' kind of people, who identify with the corporate objectives. It is also suggested that control is not too tight, but rather the Regent Way corporate culture encourages the 'right' kind of behaviour. If employees exhibit the right kind of behaviour this is recognized in formal celebrations of cultural values, often in the form of ceremonies which celebrate an aspect of the organizational culture. To illustrate this point Kemp and Dwyer recognize how the Regent Hotel rewards staff who exceed expectations in some way with a formal presentation in front of their peers, arguing that, 'These ceremonies are extremely motivating and serve to ensure a repeat of the superior performance by the staff member' (p. 84).

Culture, it is suggested, permeates every aspect of operations at the Regent Hotel, shaping the employees' responses to guests and also management's responses to their most important asset, their human resources. According to Kemp and Dwyer, the Regent Hotel exemplifies a strong culture in which top management set the game plan and then individuals throughout the organizational hierarchy have responsibility for operationalizing the plan. The cultural approach of the Regent Hotel has resulted in breaking down the barriers between the thinker and doers. It is suggested that staff at the Hotel share a strong awareness of the corporate mission and philosophy. They all know that the 'Regent Way' encourages 'Regent People' to be innovative and creative.

HRM in practice 3.2   Culture as an Orwellian mechanism

One of the more pejorative critiques of 'corporate culturism' is that offered by Wilmott (1993). Wilmott talks about the Orwellian nature of corporate culture, with its nascent totalitarianism and 1984-style doublethink which attempts to create 'governance of the employee's soul'. He suggests that corporate culture is largely interested in creating a mono-culture where alternative views or competing cultures are not tolerated. By excluding those considered as inappropriate in the recruitment and selection process and eliminating any alternative values by training, corporate culture aims to strengthen core organizational values. Any attempt to challenge the prevailing culture is considered a 'crime against the culture'. Consequently corporate culture is *'a totalitarian remedy for the resolution of indeterminacy and ambiguity: thought control through uniform definition of meaning* ... In Orwell's Oceania, *"freedom is slavery"* and *"ignorance is strength"*. In the world of corporate culture, *"slavery is freedom"* and *"strength is ignorance"'* (p. 527, emphasis in original).

identifying its practical utility for managers of organizations' (p. 36). Thus, and arguably in response to the excellence genre, much of the research and theorizing from the 1980s onwards has frequently questioned the extent to which organizations can manage culture successfully. The main thrust of the pessimists critique is that such a complex issue as culture has been overly simplified by the optimists; 'it is argued that that culture is located at the deepest level of human consciousness, of which neither researchers nor managers have sufficient knowledge to influence' (p. 36). A second strand to the critique is the unitary assumptions that underpin the optimists position on culture. Pessimists would point to the potential for conflict and contradiction in organizations which may be at odds with what the leaders and managers in an organization think (see HRM in practice 3.2).

Realists

The last category suggested by Ogbonna and Harris are the realists. Increasingly many researchers and writers are seeking a middle-way between the optimists and the pessimists and this has led to the emergence of a realist research agenda. Realists recognize that potentially culture can be changed. Equally, though, they eschew the idea that this process will always be controlled by top management. Consequently, 'realists are neither in support nor against the management of organizational culture. Rather, they advocate fuller explorations of the application of the concept, in order to develop greater understanding of the dynamics of cultural change' (p. 37). For example, Ogbonna and Harris note how culture change is more likely to occur during the formation of the organization, periods of crisis or during leadership turnover. In sum, the realist position, which is advocated by Ogbonna and Harris, is one which aims to merge theoretical rigour with contributions to the practicality of how organizational culture may be usefully used within a specific organizational context.

Review and reflect

Using an organization with which you are familiar consider the extent to which you would adopt either the optimistic, pessimistic or the realistic perspective to describe its culture.

How can we study organizational culture?

Brown (1998) suggests that a number of different aspects or elements of culture have been identified and all of these various aspects are useful in attempts to study organizational culture:

- material objects;
- corporate architecture and corporate identity;
- symbols;
- language;
- metaphors;
- stories;
- myths;
- heroes;
- ceremonies, rites and rituals;
- norms of behaviour;
- values, beliefs and attitudes;
- basic assumptions;
- ethical codes;
- history.

As Brown recognizes there may be a degree of overlap between the above elements, a point we return to below. Another key theme running through these various aspects of an organization's culture is the extent to which they may be manifest or visible. Schein (1985), for example, offers a well-known model which describes three levels of cultural phenomenon in organizations: visible manifestations, values and the deepest level of basic underlying assumptions. The first level consists of artefacts and creations that construct the physical and social environment of the organization. This level is the most superficial manifestation of culture and includes things like corporate logos, dress codes and written and spoken language used in the organization. The second level is concerned with values, beliefs and attitudes, which become prominent in the manner in which individual organizational members justify their actions and behaviour. As Lashley and Lee-Ross (2003: 154) note 'The extent to which members hold these core values and norms as unquestionable determines whether the organizational culture is "strong" or "weak"'. The last level is the most fundamental and relates to basic and tacit assumptions which impact on how organizational members perceive, think and feel. Schein (1985: 18) suggests that 'Basic assumptions … have become so taken for granted that one finds little variation within a cultural unit. In fact, if a basic assumption is strongly held in a group, members would find behaviour based on any other premise inconceivable'. To further consider the manifest and not so manifest levels of culture the chapter now returns to some of Brown's elements of culture.

Material objects, corporate architecture and corporate identity and symbols

These aspects of an organization's culture provide a visible and manifest way in which it can be assessed. For example, mission statements are an obvious manifestation of material objects within organizations. Sufi and Lyons (2003) note how mission statements are now considered an important part of any company's strategic planning processes. The same authors note how mission statements can act as an important tool for tourism and hospitality organizations to communicate to organizational members and those outside the organization, such as customers and suppliers. A good mission statement should have some of the following components (Sufi and Lyons, 2003: 258): concern for the customer, purpose, identity/image, differentiation factors, corporate values, products, markets, concern for survival, growth, profitability, company philosophy and employee and social concern.

Beyond mission statements service organizations are also increasingly aware of how they portray their corporate image, both in terms of attempts to offer aesthetically pleasing 'hardware' and 'software' (Nickson et al., 2001). Aesthetics are a sensory experience through which objects appeal in a distinctive way. This appeal does not necessarily have to be beautiful but rather and more simply expressive. Materializing the concept of a company requires the transformation of an abstractly defined identity into the adoption of a style; in practice, the production of an aesthetic experience. Aesthetics have always been important to companies. Companies past and present use aesthetics to express corporate identity. These expressive forms are most obvious in the 'hardware' of organizations, such as marketing material (internal and external), product design and the physical environment of workspaces/offices (Witz et al., 2003). Three points are worth noting with regard to the expression of corporate identity.

Firstly, as symbols and artefacts, these aesthetics are intended to influence the perception of people as either customers or clients: organizations 'use these symbols in a vivid, dramatic and exciting way, because they know that symbols have power to affect the way people feel'. Secondly, they are intended to add value to the company. 'Generally speaking, when companies use identity expressed through design, they use it as a commercial tool; their purpose is to make greater profit out of what they do in the short term'. Thirdly, in highly competitive markets with little to differentiate most goods and services, aesthetics contribute to organizational distinctiveness: 'intangible, emotional. The name and visual style of an organization are sometimes the most important factors in making it appear unique' (Olins, 1991: 53, 71 & 75). Here we could think of McDonald's Golden Arch, for example (and see also Bryman, 2004 for a more general discussion of theming in other tourism and hospitality settings).

With regard to 'software' service organizations are becoming increasingly concerned to regulate the appearance of their staff, through the use of uniforms, dress codes and appearance standards. Rafaeli (1993), for example, considers how the dress and behaviour of customer contact employees' shapes customer perceptions of service quality. As she suggests:

… the thrust of organizational management of employees' dress is that the appearance of employees communicates something about the organization.

The assumption is that what employees wear while at work, and how they appear when interacting with customers, can influence customers' feelings about the organization and the service that it provides (p. 182).

Disney, for example, has a 36 page cast members' appearance guide detailing length and style of hair and the colour and quantity of cosmetics (Henkoff, 1994; and see also Bryman, 2004). Some of the implications arising from how organizations are increasingly seeking competitive advantage via employees appearance or their 'aesthetic labour' (Nickson et al., 2001) are further considered in Chapter 5.

Language and metaphors

Bryman (2004) recognizes that increasingly service organizations aim to create performativity in the service encounter through the use of performative labour. Such labour is described as 'the rendering of work by managements and employees alike as akin to a theatrical performance in which the workplace is construed as similar to a stage' (p. 103). The use of a dramaturgical or theatrical metaphor is one that has often been used with regard to the manner in which service employees perform emotional labour (Hochschild, 1983). As Burns (1997: 240) notes the emotional demands made of front-line tourism and hospitality employees is that they should 'constantly be in a positive, joyful and even playful mood'. Brown (1998) recognizes how language and metaphors aim to construct a common understanding in organizations so that abstractions such as 'good service', 'high quality' and 'excellence' are made meaningful. HRM in practice 3.3 and 3.4 offer examples of how two organizations respectively use language and metaphor, explicitly drawing on notions of performativity, to create the right type of behaviour in their front-line employees.

Review and reflect

To what extent should tourism and hospitality organizations be able to use aesthetic and emotional labour to exert control over the manner in which employees behave? What are the likely challenges of using these types of cultural controls?

HRM in practice 3.3   The use of language in Disney

Everyday terms	Disney speak
HR department	Casting office
HR manager	Casting rep
Theme park visitor customer	Guest
Employee	Cast member
Front-line employee	Host or hostess
Public areas	Onstage
Restricted areas	Backstage
Theme park ride or show	Attraction
Hiring for a job	Casting
Job	Role
Foreman	Lead
Uniform	Costume
Job interview	Audition
Accident	Incident
Queue/line	Pre-entertainment area
Attraction designer	Imaginer
Talking robot	Audio-animatronic figure

Derived from Bryman (2004) IRS (2003).

Stories, myths, heroes and history

Deal and Kennedy (1999) note how stories are an important part of an organization's culture due to their ability to transmit cultural values. Corporate stories will often focus on exemplifying core values in the organization, often with recourse to the achievements and daring do of cultural heroes, such as the founder of an organization. In an earlier work Deal and Kennedy (1988) suggested that these heroes personify the organizational values and epitomize the strength of the organization. In becoming a 'John Wayne in pinstripes' heroic figures in organizations' become role models for employees to follow. For example, Herb Kelleher co-founder and long-time chief executive officer (CEO) of Southwest Airlines is well known for his attempts to generate a sense of fun in the workplace. Known as the

HRM in practice 3.4   Warm fuzzies and cold pricklies: the use of metaphor in Pizza Hut

Bate (1995: 44–45) notes that during the 1980s and early 1990s Pizza Hut's employee induction programme made use of a booklet called *Feelings*. The booklet attempted to set out what employees should feel and particularly how they should display warm feelings, or what were termed 'warm fuzzies', during their work. Negative feelings were characterized as 'cold pricklies'. These two feelings were anthropomorphized into two cartoon characters: a malevolent, spiky haired, spiky-bearded dwarf (cold prickly) and an appealing, round-eyed cuddly powder puff creature (warm fuzzy). Warm fuzzies were shown helping old ladies and giving out 'positive strokes' to everybody. In contrast, cold pricklies were seen getting wet and angry under black storm clouds and showing hostility to customers. The coldest of cold pricklies was the Big Fat Zero, who kept customers waiting, refused to smile and ignored people altogether. Warm fuzzies were represented in the booklet booting out cold pricklies and smiling no matter how hectic things became. In attempting to create the right kind of emotional labour the company aimed to ensure Pizza Hut employees saw themselves as warm fuzzies and act accordingly by demonstrating the right kind of positive feelings towards customers, even when they did not necessarily feel like doing so.

'High Priest of Ha-Ha' Kelleher was integral in creating a corporate culture premised on fun. He believed in encouraging Southwest's flight attendants to joke and kid with passengers. Sunoo (1995) suggests that this strategy to hire the best people, treat them with respect, and give them the freedom to make decisions and to have fun just being themselves has created some of the most loyal employees in the airline industry. Indeed, Bearden (2001) notes that in the immediate aftermath of 9/11 each of Southwest's 32 000 employees agreed to give back some of their pay to ensure company stability in a turbulent business environment (and see also HRM in practice 3.5).

Norms of behaviour, values, beliefs and attitudes, and basic assumptions

Our earlier discussion of aspects such as performative labour and the mechanisms utilized by tourism and hospitality organizations to engender the right kind of emotional labour points to the manner in which they strive to achieve appropriate

HRM in practice 3.5   Stories and myths from some of the great hospitality entrepreneurs

Nickson (1997) argues for the importance of appreciating the need for an understanding of history in reviewing the auto/biographies of Charles Forte, Conrad Hilton, Kemmons Wilson (the founder of Holiday Inn) and Bill Marriott (senior). Nickson notes the manner in which the stories and myths surrounding these famous hospitality entrepreneurs play an integral part in creating a corporate aura and values. For example, the three American 'giants' are suggested to exemplify the American Dream, which sees America as a land of opportunity, where individuals by hard work and self-improvement can achieve great success. A key element of this is respect for 'rugged individualism' (Guest, 1990: 390) and a willingness of individuals to grasp their opportunities by pushing back the frontiers, both literally and metaphorically. In a literal sense, Hilton was brought up in the 'half civilized country' of New Mexico, where his father nearly became a victim of his own pioneering spirit as he was only one of two men to survive an attack by Apache Indians, an attack that left five others dead. The young Bill Marriott also demonstrates his frontier spirit on a camping trip in killing a deadly snake – naturally 'the biggest rattler anyone could remember' (O'Brien, 1977: 52–53) and two menacing brown bears. In a metaphorical sense some of this frontier spirit is evidenced in the notion of the self-reliant small businessman who sets up their own business and makes it successful. A common theme which in the accounts is the humble beginnings of the subjects' organizations. Hilton, for example, famously described his first hotel, the Mobley, purchased in Cisco, Texas in 1919 as 'a cross between a flop house and a gold mine' (Hilton, 1957: 109). Bill Marriott's early business career began with an 'A and W' root beer franchise which he acquired in 1927 and Charles Forte's move into business came with the opening of a milk bar in 1934. From such beginnings the nascent organizations quickly flourished and many of the operating procedures and management styles described in those early years can to some extent still be observed in the contemporary hospitality industry. For example, Hilton is credited with being the 'founder' of internationalization in the hotel sector and many aspects of the present Marriott philosophy, such as empowerment, can be seen to trace their history to Bill Marriott senior's way of doing business.

behaviour. Many tourism and hospitality organizations may well recognize that attempting to connect with their employees to generate a more fundamental level of engagement in the appropriate values, beliefs and attitudes or even basic assumptions in the organizations, may be doomed to failure. In this sense the ability of tourism and hospitality organizations to achieve cultural change at the deepest levels of basic assumptions may well be impossible. Of course, employers will use a variety of mechanisms to create the right kind of behaviour. Some of these may be cultural mechanisms as described above; others may simply be about the use of other means of control. For example, whilst some might claim that the 'strong' culture at McDonald's is largely created by the prevailing organizational culture, more critical authors would point to aspects such as deskilling and the use of non-human technology (Ritzer, 2004). Even cultural mechanisms may be underpinned by more rigid control mechanisms. Ogbonna and Wilkinson (1990) report the example of one supermarket that as part of a culture change programme encouraged employees to smile more when engaging with customers. However, the company went one step further in introducing 'smile supervisors' who were tasked to assess whether employee smiles were genuine. If smiles were felt not to be genuine employees were reprimanded by the smile supervisors. Needless to say this approach created a good deal of employee resentment. In reality, most organizations will simply settle for the right kind of outward behaviour being manifested by their employees, without recourse to smile supervisors, even if such a performance is simply a manifestation of resigned behavioural compliance.

Clearly, then, there are a number of functions that organizational culture will play. In this normative view of corporate culture, it attempts to foster social cohesion, so that it becomes the 'cement' or 'glue' that binds an organization together so it may offer co-ordination and control, reduction of uncertainty, a means to motivate staff and ultimately competitive advantage. Throughout this chapter though we have alluded to some of the potential difficulties in sustaining this normative view of culture. Beyond this point there is also a need to recognize the debate about whether there really is any evidence to support a relationship between organizational culture and performance, particularly whether culture can enhance the effectiveness of an organization's performance. Alvesson (2002: 53–54) suggests that there are four views on the relationship between organizational culture and performance:

1 *The so-called strong culture thesis*. In this view employees are assumed to be inculcated into a strong organizational culture and resultantly demonstrate a high level of commitment to the organization and its values. Within the strong culture thesis it is assumed that the strength of the culture will be directly correlated with the level of profits in a company.

HRM in practice 3.6   A failure to adapt?

The failure of a culture to adapt may arguably partially explain the inability of Forte to resist the hostile takeover mounted by the Granada organization. Nickson (1997) notes the important role played by Lord Forte, the founder of the company, and how his influence was pervasive on the culture. In time, Lord Forte was succeeded by his son, Rocco Forte, though many foresaw the difficulties of succeeding Lord Forte. Lashley and Lee-Ross (2003) note how the strong power/role culture created in the Forte group was anachronistic and uncompetitive and left the company vulnerable to the takeover. Several pieces written during the height of the take-over battle seemed to question the extent to which Rocco Forte could carry on his father's legacy, especially if the previously strong culture was creating rigidity and group think in the organization.

2 *A reverse relationship between culture and performance*. In this view it is suggested that high-performance leads to the creation of a strong corporate culture. Organizational success creates common orientations, beliefs and values and an acceptance of the 'way of doing things'.

3 *A contingent view of culture*. In particular circumstances or conditions a particular type of culture is appropriate or even necessary and is likely to contribute to efficiency.

4 *The need for adaptive cultures*. Cultures that are able to respond to changing circumstances or a change in the business environment are the key to good performance (and see HRM in practice 3.6).

Ultimately in considering the relationship between culture and performance Alvesson (2002: 54) notes that, 'the relatively few systematic studies on the culture-performance link lead us to conclude that none of these four ideas have received much empirical support'. For example, much of the earlier work on culture, as exemplified by Peters and Waterman (1982), was often underpinned by support for the strong culture thesis. Thompson and McHugh (2001), amongst others, question the evidence offered by Peters and Waterman and others supporting the strong culture-enhanced performance thesis. As they suggest, 'The tenuous link between cultures, excellence and performance turned out to be highly fragile' (2001: 199). Generally, then, the case for whether a 'strong' organizational or corporate culture is integral to the success of an organization remains unclear. More broadly, whilst it might seem intuitively true that, for example, adaptive cultures are self-evidently superior, again the evidence seems sparse, as far as Alvesson is concerned.

Organizational culture and HRM: a reprise

Throughout this chapter, we have considered the relationship between cultural mechanisms and HRM strategies. Equally, we have also recognized debates about the manageability of culture or whether organizational culture can be causally related to enhanced effectiveness or performance in organizations. Ultimately, as we have already recognized there are no easy answers to these issues and there is a need to recognize the many competing claims or views about the nature of organizational culture. That said, Ogbonna and Harris' espousal of the realist position is one that attempts to reconcile some of these debates. If we accept the realist position then there may be instances were culture may be managed or changed in support of organizational aims. As a corollary attempts to manage culture in support of organizational aims will mean the adoption of certain HRM practices. Specifically, we recognized that attempts to sustain a degree of cohesion through cultural mechanisms is likely to mean that organizations will look to recruit those individuals who are deemed to 'fit' in with the prevailing culture. Once recruited employees will then undergo an intense period of induction and socialization to be fully inculcated into the organizational culture. This process of inculcation is further reinforced through training and development activities, which as we noted within hospitality and tourism, will often be directed towards enhancing quality service. Lastly, organizations may chose to reward those who are seen to have internalized the values of the organization through enhanced financial rewards, such as those described in Kemp and Dwyer's case study of the Regent Hotel.

Review and reflect

What are some of the likely challenges facing tourism and hospitality organizations who are seeking to use organizational culture as a unifying device as part of their broader HRM strategy?

That said, there is a need to consider some of the potential contradictions and dilemmas in managing culture. Some of the contradictions and dilemmas may well be posed by the sectoral context in which an organization operates. For example, with regard to tourism and hospitality, Ogbonna and Harris (2002: 39–40) note how:

> ... the tensions between the key employment features of the industry – such as labour flexibility, low pay, poor terms and conditions, casualization and feminization – and the traditional 'high commitment' objectives of culture management programmes make this an important industry for the study of organizational culture.

Recognizing this point they go on to recognize some of the limitations in the extent and manner of cultural intervention in the case study companies reported in their study. For example, Ogbonna and Harris remain sceptical of the ability of tourism and hospitality organizations to achieve cultural change at the deepest levels of basic assumptions across the organizational hierarchy. The ability to achieve deeper levels of cultural transformation may be problematic due to working conditions and terms of employment, such as unsocial working hours and low pay. Equally, the managers interviewed in Ogbonna and Harris' case study organizations recognized the difficulties of gaining significant commitment from peripheral workers (and see also Figure 3.1).

Ideal HRM goals	Contradictions and dilemmas
Tight 'fit' between organization and individual	Labour shortages, competition for labour, ad-hoc recruitment and selection
Quality and service	Difficult customers
High trust and commitment	Surveillance, tight control, low pay
Strong internal labour market	High labour turnover, high percentage of part-time employees

Adapted from Ogbonna (1992).

Figure 3.1 HRM and culture: contradictions and dilemmas

Ultimately, in considering the implications for practitioners Ogbonna and Harris suggest that their findings point to how culture can best be managed. Crucial to this point is the need to recognize that a differentiated approach is likely to work best, reflecting the core and peripheral workforce in the tourism and hospitality industry. In that sense core staff, who are long serving and exposed to extensive and intensive culture programmes, may well be inculcated to a large degree into the organization's culture. However, for peripheral workers, 'practitioners may well focus their attention on ensuring behavioural compliance and appropriate emotional displays' (p. 50). Clearly then this points to the need for organizations to consider differentiated, complex and sensitive change programmes as these are more likely to be successful in gaining buy in to the culture from organizational members.

Conclusion

Alvesson (2002) suggests that too much organizational culture thinking has been grounded in assumptions about the potentially positive consequences of culture, a trend which arguably emerged with the panacean nature of the excellence genre, which captured the managerial imagination when it first emerged in the early 1980s. Over time more reflective and critical accounts have sought to temper some of this initial enthusiasm for the role that culture can play within the organization. Ogbonna and Harris' characterization of 'optimists', 'pessimists' and 'realists' neatly captures the evolving nature of the debate about organizational culture and its ability to enhance commitment amongst organizational members. In adopting a realist position Ogbonna and Harris attempt to recognize that culture can be managed, though the extent to which this process may be successful remains contingent. The nature of the industry, organization, occupation, employment status within the organization and many other things beside are all likely to impact on the extent to which organizational members ultimately immerse themselves in the basic assumptions of the organization, or simply manifest resigned behavioural compliance.

References and further reading

Alvesson, M. (2002) *Understanding Organizational Culture*, Sage.
Bate, P. (1995) *Strategies for Cultural Change*, Butterworth-Heinemann.

Bearden, T. (2001) 'High flyer', *PBS News*, November 28, http://www.pbs.org/newshour/bb/transportation/july-dec01/southwest_11-28.html (accessed 8 August 2005).

Brown, A. (1998) *Organizational Culture*, Pitman, 2nd edition.

Bryman, A. (2004) *The Disneyization of Society*, Sage.

Burns, P. (1997) 'Hard-skills, soft-skills: undervaluing hospitality's "service with a smile"', *Progress in Tourism and Hospitality Research*, 3, 239–248.

Deal, T. and Kennedy, A. (1988) *Corporate Cultures: The Rites and Rituals of Corporate Culture*, Penguin.

Deal, T. and Kennedy, A. (1999) *The New Corporate Cultures: Revitalizing the Workplace after Downsizing, Mergers, and Reengineering*, Perseus.

Guest, D. E. (1990) 'Human resource management and the American Dream', *Journal of Management Studies*, 27, 4, 378–397.

Henkoff, R. (1994) 'Finding and keeping the best service workers', *Fortune*, 3 October, 52–58.

Hilton, C. N. (1957) *Be My Guest*. Englewood Cliffs, New Jersey: Prentice-Hall.

Hochschild, A. (1983) *The Managed Heart*, University of California Press.

Industrial Relations Services (2003) 'The mouse trap: company culture at Disney World', *IRS Employment Review*, 783, 3 October, 21–23.

Kemp, S. and Dwyer, L. (2001) 'An examination of organizational culture – the Regent Hotel, Sydney', *International Journal of Hospitality Management*, 20, 77–93.

Lashley, C. and Lee-Ross, D. (2003) *Organization Behaviour for Leisure Services*, Butterworth-Heinemann.

Legge, K. (1994) 'Managing culture: fact or fiction', in K. Sisson (ed.) *Personnel Management: A Comprehensive Guide to Theory and Practice in Britain*, Blackwell, 397–433.

Nickson, D. (1997) 'Colorful stories' or historical insight? A review of the auto/biographies of Charles Forte, Conrad Hilton, J.W. Marriott and Kemmons Wilson, *Journal of Hospitality and Tourism Research*, 21(1), 179–192.

Nickson, D., Warhurst, C., Witz, A. and Cullen, A.M. (2001) 'The importance of being aesthetic: work, employment and service organization', in A. Sturdy, I. Grugulis, and H. Wilmott (eds.) *Customer Service – Empowerment and Entrapment*, Palgrave, 170–190.

O'Brien, R. (1977) *Marriott: The J Willard Marriott Story*, Desert Book Company.

Ogbonna, E. (1992) 'Organizational culture and human resource management', in P. Blyton and P. Turnbull (eds.) *Reassessing Human Resource Management*, Sage, 74–96.

Ogbonna, E. and Harris, L. (2002) 'Managing organizational culture: insights from the hospitality industry', *Human Resource Management Journal*, 12(1), 33–53.

Ogbonna, E. and Wilkinson, B. (1990) 'Corporate strategy and corporate culture: the view from the check out', *Personnel Review*, 19(4), 9–15.

Olins, W. (1991). *Corporate Identity*, Thames and Hudson.

Peters, T. and Waterman, R. (1982) *In Search of Excellence: Lessons from America's Best-run Companies*, Harper and Row.

Rafaeli, A. (1993) 'Dress and behaviour of customer contact employees: a framework for analysis', *Services Marketing and Management*, 2, 175–211.

Ritzer, G. (2004) *The McDonaldization of Society*, Pine Forge Press, Revised New Century Edition.

Schein, E. (1985) *Organizational Culture and Leadership*, Jossey-Bass Publishers.

Sufi, T. and Lyons, H. (2003) 'Mission statements exposed', *International Journal of Contemporary Hospitality Management*, 15(5), 255–262.

Sunoo, B. (1995) 'How fun flies at Soutwest Airlines', *Personnel Journal*, June, 62–73.

Thompson, P. and McHugh, D. (2001) *Work Organizations: A Critical Introduction*, MacMillan Press, 3rd edition.

Van Maanen, J. (1990) 'The smile factory: work at Disneyland', in P. Frost, L. Moore, M. Louis, C. Lundberg and J. Martin (eds.) *Reframing Organizational Culture*, Sage Publications, 58–76.

Wilmott, H. (1993) 'Strength is ignorance; slavery is freedom: managing culture in modern organizations', *Journal of Management Studies*, 30(4), 515–552.

Witz, A., Warhurst C. and Nickson, D. (2003) 'The labour of aesthetics and the aesthetics of organization', *Organization*, 10(1), 33–54.

Woods, R.H. (1989) 'More alike than different: the culture of the restaurant industry', *Cornell Hotel and Restaurant Administration Quarterly*, 30(2), 82–98.

Websites

There are a number of useful weblinks and case studies which can be found at http://www.new-paradigm.co.uk/Culture.htm

Southwest Airlines has a unique culture which stresses the fun nature of the business and details can be found at http://www.southwest.com/about_swa/

Edward de Bono and Robert Heller are well know management gurus and they have some interesting thoughts on organizational culture which can be found at http://www.thinkingmanagers.com/business-management/corporate-culture.php

Chapter **4**
Labour markets

Chapter objectives

This chapter considers the nature of labour markets in the tourism and hospitality industry. Specifically, the objectives are:

- To appreciate the different levels of analysis in understanding labour markets.
- To understand the particular sectoral characteristics that determine the tourism and hospitality labour market.
- To consider debates about the use of flexible labour strategies within tourism and hospitality organizations.

Introduction

We should start by asking a key question; what do we mean when we talk about labour markets? At any one time people will be trying to either change their job or acquire a job and employers will be looking for employees, and this means that, in principle, in the external labour market all workers are assumed to be competing for all the jobs all the time. In reality, of course, this may not be the case and we can appreciate this by disaggregating different types of labour markets. Within this process there is also a need to have some awareness of a range of macro-economic issues, political and social factors and their impact on the external and internal labour markets, which will change and affect the work of HR practitioners directly and visibly, in terms of issues like employee/industrial relations, recruitment, training and development and pay. It should also be recognized that the nature of labour supply is equally important and as the Cabinet Office (2003) has recently noted demographic changes are having a significant impact on labour supply. In that sense the Cabinet Office recognizes that most established European Union (EU) member states are experiencing to a greater or lesser extent a number of challenges with regard to labour supply. Specifically within a UK context:

- Declining birth rates mean that by 2011 under 16s will make up only 18 per cent of the population in the UK.
- Increases in longevity, plus more young people into higher education, mean that the 'greying' of the workforce – in 2006, 45–59 year olds formed the largest group in the workplace.
- The workforce is becoming increasingly 'feminized' – by 2011, 82 per cent of extra jobs will be taken by women.
- The role of people from ethnic minorities is likely to become increasingly significant – they could account for no less than 50 per cent of growth in the working population over the next decade.
- Migrant workers already make up much of the labour shortfall and are likely to continue to do so.

Levels of analysis in the labour market

To further appreciate some of the points discussed above we can develop an understanding of labour markets by recognizing several different levels of analysis, encompassing both the external and internal labour market. We begin with understanding the external labour market; that is the labour market outside of the organization and initially consider the idea of a transnational labour market.

Transnational labour market

Throughout time economic migration has meant that people have been willing to move to find work or better paying jobs. In a more contemporary vein one of the key drivers of an increasingly transnational and international labour market is the role of multinational companies (MNCs). We have already noted in Chapter 2 how the continuing growth of world markets, increased availability of management and technological know-how in different countries, global competition and international customers, advances in telecommunications, and greater regional political and economic integration have all increasingly pushed MNCs down the road to seeking a more global orientation. Equally, we also noted how MNCs face choices in how they staff their overseas units, including the use of expatriate managers and how the use of such managers is commonplace in the tourism and hospitality industry. Expatriate managers can be seen as denoting a rather more strategic use of HR by MNCs. In addition to this more strategic movement of individual managers, individuals may also choose to move internationally in their search for work or enhanced career development.

A further aspect which has already been alluded to is the creation of regional trading blocs. It is widely recognized that the EU is the most developed trading bloc and already evidences a high degree of economic and social integration. With regard to employment a key issue has been the commitment to sustain the free movement of labour between member states. More recently the EU has seen the accession of 10 new member states (Poland, Czech Republic, Hungary, Slovakia, Lithuania, Latvia, Slovenia, Estonia, Cyprus (Greece) and Malta) from 1 May 2004 and some of the employment implications of the increase from 15 to 25 countries within the EU are considered in HRM in practice 4.1.

National labour market

At the national level the government has a major influence on the labour market and the manner in which policy is developed with regard to employment and economic

HRM in practice 4.1   EU expansion: A solution to labour and skill shortages in tourism and hospitality?

The accession of the 10 new states from Central and Eastern Europe meant another 74 million people joined the world's largest single market. Whilst there has been some concern at the notion of large numbers of people seeking to move from Eastern to Western Europe with the new immigrants proving a strain on existing member states, in reality, the movement across Europe has been relatively small. In part, this is explicable by the fact that initially only the UK, Irish and Swedish Governments allowed people from the new accession states to work, as long as they register. The other 13 EU countries agreed to impose restrictions on immigration from the east until at least 2006, and possibly till 2011. The decision of the British Government was largely driven by the recognition of significant labour and skill shortages in a number of industries, including hospitality and tourism, a situation likely to be exacerbated with the recognition that over 500 000 new jobs are expected to be created to 2010. Many of those moving from the new member states are young, well educated, highly motivated and seeking work in tourism and hospitality. Employers in tourism and hospitality are already recognizing this new source of labour and migrant workers seem to be viewed in a positive manner by employers. Jean Urquhart, owner of the Cellidh Place, an arts hotel in Scotland, is quoted as saying, 'The whole tourism industry would collapse without them'. Similarly a manager from Pizza Hut in Inverness suggests that his five Polish workers were 'never sick, never late, they just work away and we value them very, very highly', even to the extent of suggesting that they are better than Scottish workers. Corus Hotels is another company which has taken advantage of the wider talent pool and targeted more workers from Eastern Europe by recruiting over 30 new employees from Poland.

Derived from Cottell (2005), Gunn (2004), Meiklem (2004) and Warren (2004).

issues will clearly impact on the nature of the national labour market. Generally speaking when governments come to develop their labour market policy they face a choice in terms of the extent to which they will seek to regulate employment policies and practices. For example, it is often argued that there is a distinct difference between a European approach to labour markets, which is often described as the European social model; and the so-called Anglo-Saxon approach, which is represented by the US, and to an extent the UK. In simple terms it is suggested that the European social model has tended to offer much greater regulation to achieve a balance in interests between capital and labour, whilst in the US especially the approach has relied much less on regulation and instead has operated on a free market basis. Of course, this is something of an oversimplification, though it is useful to delineate differing approaches and in more recent years the UK has sought a balance between these two approaches with the so-called 'third way', which seeks both a degree of regulation and flexibility. To appreciate why this is the case it is worthwhile briefly considering recent labour market developments in the UK, within the context of the discussion above.

In recent years there has been something of a change in policy within the UK. In the period 1979–1997 the Conservative Governments of Margaret Thatcher and John Major felt that there was too much regulation and the key thrust of much of their policy towards the labour market was to remove what they viewed as rigidities in the labour market. By espousing a free market with little regulation, the Conservative Governments argued that employers had greater freedom in developing their employment policies and practices and that this was important for wealth creation. The shift towards much less regulation in the labour market was felt to be especially important for small businesses who often complain about the deleterious impact of too much regulation on their business. As part of a whole series of legislation such as the *Wages Act 1986, Trade Union and Labour Relations Consolidation Act 1992* and the *Trade Union Reform and Employment Rights Act 1993* the Conservative Governments sought to limit and restrict the autonomy and influence of trade unions as well as allowing employers much greater latitude in areas such as hiring and dismissing workers and pay setting.

Since 1997 the Blair Governments have attempted to keep many elements of the flexible approach advocated by the previous government though they have, at the same time, introduced some measures to regulate employment. Firstly, they signed up to the enlarged EU Social Chapter in 1997. Although the Social Chapter is not a legislative programme it does provide mechanisms for harmonizing minimum standards of employment and social provision across the EU. The previous UK Conservative Government (1992–1997) had negotiated an opt-out, but with the Labour Government signing up to the Social Chapter a number of HRM policies were affected.

From a labour market point of view the most important impact was the introduction of Directives on parental leave, working time and part-time employees. The Parental Leave Directive allows parents to take up to 3 months unpaid leave after the birth of a child, up to their 8th birthday (and see HRM in practice 4.2).

HRM in practice 4.2   Female friendly? How do countries compare?

There is much debate about how best to respond to greater feminization in the labour market and how best to balance work and family. A key issue within this broader debate is the support from the state to women in providing maternity leave and pay and facilitating a return to work. Practices vary significantly between countries and this is a good indicator of the extent to which governments are willing to intervene in a key labour market issue. For example, in the UK women have the right to return to work after 26 weeks paid maternity leave. Employers also have to 'seriously consider' requests from parents for more flexible working. This is in contrast to the US where there is no nationwide policy on parental rights and no national provision for maternity leave, paid or otherwise. The same is also true for Australia where maternity leave is unpaid and only available to employees who have been on the payroll for 12 months prior to the birth. The most family-friendly countries are arguably Sweden and Norway. For example in Sweden both parents are entitled to 18 months off work and in Norway a year's leave is paid at 80 per cent of salary.

Derived from Groskop (2006).

The Working Time Regulations are considered more fully in Chapter 11. Lastly, the regulations on part-time employees require employers to treat them no less favourably than full-time employees. For example, part-time staff should receive the same pay and benefits, on a pro-rata basis, as full-time employees. As we have already noted in Chapter 1, hospitality and tourism is particularly reliant on part-time workers and it was felt that this and the other Directives would be potentially harmful to the viability of many businesses, particularly small business. In reality, though, the impact has been less than feared, in part because employers have been able to water down the regulations to lessen their impact (see for example Hurrell, 2005). In addition to signing up to the Social Chapter, the Blair Governments have also introduced a range of employment-related legislation. Most noteworthy are the *National Minimum Wage Act 1998, Employment Relations Act 1999* and *Employment Act 2002.* These acts established minimum employment standards in areas such as pay, dismissal and trade union recognition.

Whilst all of these aspects have certainly added some regulation to the labour market and impacted on tourism and hospitality employers HRM policies, in reality the UK is felt to have a relatively unregulated labour market compared to most other EU countries. Indeed, the UK Prime Minister Tony Blair still regularly claims that the UK remains the most lightly regulated labour market of any of the leading economies. What much of the above discussion points to is the recognition of the impact of government policy on employment policy and HRM practices in organizations. Thus, it is important to understand that this is an important environmental and contextual feature in terms of how firms will plan their labour market policies.

Sectoral labour market

To consider the nature of the sectoral labour market in tourism and hospitality, we should remind ourselves again what kind of industry tourism and hospitality is. As we have already noted the tourism and hospitality industry can be taken to include a wide variety of organizations encompassing areas like hotels, guest-houses, bed and breakfast, farm houses, holiday parks, restaurants, pubs and cafes, airlines, cruise ships, travel agencies, tour companies and so on. Equally, we also recognized that it would be wrong to imagine that the industry can be thought of as homogenous (an obvious example is the spread of different types of organizations in the industry, from the local chip shop to huge multinationals with a presence all over the world). Despite this growth in larger chains most sectors of the industry are still dominated by small, usually owner-managed units consisting of family labour and a small number of helpers. Clearly, then, the sector is better conceptualized as heterogeneous. However, whilst there is great heterogeneity in the types and size of organizations there may be certain recurring features in large parts of the tourism and hospitality industry, which are outlined below:

- Large numbers of individual units of varying size and many different types are located throughout the whole of the country and internationally.
- Many units operate 24 hours a day, 7 days a week, 365 days a year.
- There are high fixed costs, a fixed rate of supply, but a fluctuating, seasonal and often unpredictable demand.
- It is both a production and service industry.
- There is a wide variety of customers seeking to satisfy a variety of needs and expectations. For example, leisure, business, conference and so on.

- Services are supplied direct to the customer on the premises and the customer usually leaves with no tangible product.
- Managers are expected to demonstrate proficiency in technical and craft skills as well as in management areas.
- Many different skills are required but there are relatively large numbers of semi- and unskilled staff.
- The majority of staff are low paid.
- Staff are often expected to work long and unsociable hours.
- There is a large proportion of female, part-time, casual, student and migrant labour.
- Generally trade union membership is low.
- There is high labour mobility within the industry, and a high turnover of staff joining and leaving the industry.
- The industry is labour intensive.

Perhaps the single biggest influence on the nature of labour markets in the tourism and hospitality industry is the recognition that there are often wide fluctuations in short-term demand for the product, which has major and obvious implications for the staffing of an organization (and see Table 4.1).

Allied to this demand unpredictability is the fact that the industry is labour intensive, which means labour is a high cost in the total costs of tourism and hospitality businesses. Therefore many employers have tried to minimize labour costs. This has meant that traditionally the industry has been staffed with what Wood (1997) calls the so-called 'marginal workers', namely: women, young people, students, migrant workers and ethnic minorities. Resultantly, it is argued by many that these workers form the basis of a casualized, part-time workforce. This workforce finds themselves in a low-skill job characterized by relatively low pay, which leads to a lack of motivation and commitment on the part of employees, who may perceive they are in a job which is often stereotyped as being about servility. Of course, as we noted in Chapter 1, this description may be over generalizing the employment experience of many working in tourism and hospitality, and this characterization is unlikely to be true for all organizations, or reflect the circumstances for all workers. For example, for many women working part-time will allow them to match domestic and employment responsibilities. Equally, there may well be skilled craft jobs which require some formal training or education, as opposed to unskilled work which is just learnt on the job (and see HRM in practice 4.3).

Table 4.1 Hotel demands variability

	Examples of hotel demand variability
Daily	Morning rush hour guest check-out and evening check-in peak demands for restaurant services during meal time: breakfast (7–10 a.m.), lunch (12–2 p.m.) and dinner (7–10 p.m.).
Weekly	High occupancy during mid-week for business hotels, but low in weekends. More restaurant reservations at the weekend.
Seasonal	Winter closure of beach resorts. High occupancy rate in ski chalets during the winter.
Ad hoc	Flight cancellation leading to unpredictable demand for hotel rooms and meal services. 'Chance' guest bookings.

Source: Lai and Baum (2005). Reprinted by permission of Emerald Group Publishing Ltd.

HRM in practice 4.3   Working in paradise

Patricia and Peter Adler (2004) offer an interesting example of how within luxury hotels in Hawaii different types of employees are likely to have very different employment experiences. Based on a near-10-year ethnographic study, *Paradise Laborers* is an attempt to understand what goes on behind the scenes in five luxury hotels in Hawaii. Specifically, Adler and Adler offer an in-depth analysis of the complex organizational and social systems of the hotels and how this impacts on the experiences of those working there; and why, for many, working in the hospitality industry in Hawaii is akin to paradise. At the heart of the book lies Adler and Adler's typology of four different types of worker: new immigrants, locals, seekers and managers. New immigrants are those who fill the most menial, psychically demanding jobs in areas such as housekeeping and stewarding, positions which are considered undesirable by indigenous Americans. This characterization of the new immigrants might suggest a life of hardship, drudgery and exploitation for this group of workers. However, Adler and Adler note how the new immigrants were 'highly valued, even crucial, workers in the hospitality and other local industries. While others have depicted globalized workers as transient, our new immigrants became heavily tied to and invested in their new country by opportunity, family, community, work, and fierce loyalty' (p. 217). Locals are equally tied to Hawaii – indeed Adler and Adler characterize new immigrants and locals as being 'trapped', by choice, by the vicissitudes of the local labour market. For many locals though, work in the resorts in regarded as being desirable, unsurprising perhaps when travel and tourism provides over 20 per cent of employment within Hawaii. Locals tended to occupy those jobs immediately above the entry jobs taken by new immigrants in positions such as valets and bellmen and tended to approach work with a 'work to live' attitude as 'they did not want to live in paradise if the cost was they could not enjoy it' (p. 60). The latter two groups of seekers and managers are characterized as being transient and primarily are affluent, middle-class, male, mainland Americans who are usually just passing through Hawaii. Unlike new immigrants and locals, seekers and managers are able to draw on their inherent cultural capital, such as their education, which allows them greater occupational choice. However, whilst managers are aiming to make a career in hospitality management and often work long hours for relatively low rewards; seekers, or 'drifter workers' (p. 81), are attracted to Hawaii to experience a much more hedonistic lifestyle, where leisure is foregrounded over work, and work becomes a means to a recreationally focused end.

HRM in practice 4.4   Re-considering skill

Baum (2002) considers the nature of skill in the tourism and hospitality industry and argues the need for more expansive thinking about the issue. Whilst broadly accepting Riley's characterization, Baum also points to the need to consider the changing nature of skills in tourism and hospitality, with the emergence of aspects such as emotional and aesthetic labour. These 'softer' skills are harder to classify and locate within traditional debates about the meaning of skill, dominated as they often are by the understanding of skills being 'hard', technical skills, often accredited by qualifications or an apprenticeship. Resultantly, the tendency towards describing much tourism and hospitality work as unskilled may be increasingly oversimplified. Relatedly, Baum also questions the overwhelmingly western centric view of skills, something that is inappropriate in a developing country context. Here many of the softer skills coming under the rubric of emotional or aesthetic labour may be highly valued.

With regard to skill, Riley (1996) estimated that the skill composition in a typical unit in the hospitality industry would consist of 6 per cent managerial, 8 per cent supervisory, 22 per cent skilled craft workers and 64 per cent semi- or unskilled operative staff, though see also HRM in practice 4.4.

In sum, then, the tourism and hospitality labour market is characterized by:

- A relatively large proportion of unskilled occupations.
- Transferability of skills at any level between a broad range of establishments.
- Often, but not inevitably, high levels of labour turnover.
- Relatively low levels of pay, particularly for unskilled workers.

All of the above points mean that many organizations compete in what is often described as the secondary labour market.

The internal labour market and the utilization of flexible labour

Whilst the description of the broader context, as represented by the transnational, national and sectoral labour markets, is important, we should also consider some of the choices that organizations themselves will make in developing their internal labour market. Riley (1996: 12) describes the internal labour market in the following manner:

> The concept of the internal labour market is based on the idea that sets of rules and conventions form within an organization which act as allocative mechanisms governing the movement of people and the pricing of jobs. Such rules are about promotion criteria, training opportunities, pay differentials and the evaluation of jobs, but most importantly, they are about which jobs are 'open' to the external labour market.

Traditionally many tourism and hospitality organizations have failed to develop strong internal labour markets, where skills are developed maximally via internal promotion and upgrading, and managers have relied instead on the external labour market, which is cheaper because labour is plentiful. Another aspect of the internal labour market is the choices that organizations may face in their use of various form of flexibility.

As we noted above the aim of much of the legislation of the Conservative Governments of the 1980s and 1990s was to increase the flexibility of the labour market. As Kelliher and Riley (2003: 99) note, 'Flexibility was seen as a means of enhancing competitiveness and adapting to changes in the business environment'. Much of the debate generated about the nature of flexibility in organizations was developed with recourse to the highly influential work of Atkinson (1984), which proposed the 'flexible firm' model. Although subsequently heavily criticized, the model does usefully distinguish between 'core' and 'peripheral' employees. The former group are characterized as being permanent, usually full-time, staff that are viewed as a valuable resource, likely to be multi-skilled and enjoying employment security and career progression. By contrast, the latter group are likely to be part-time or casual, enjoy little employment security, have fewer skills and be easily disposable, reflecting Wood's view of marginal workers described earlier. In reality, as with other ideal types described in this book, these descriptions tend to oversimplify the nature of core and peripheral staff in hospitality and tourism (Deery and Jago, 2002). For example, Walsh (1990) has described how staff that would be thought of as 'peripheral' will often be integral to the running of a hotel and may be equally committed to the organization as core staff. Nevertheless, the notion of core and peripheral workers is useful in pointing to the types of labour flexibility utilized by tourism and hospitality organizations, two of the most prominent being functional and numerical flexibility.

Functional flexibility

Functional flexibility is seen as the employer's ability to deploy employees, and more specifically core employees drawn from the primary labour market, between activities and tasks. In increasing the range of tasks that an employee can undertake employers will expect employees to be capable of working in different functions within the same department, or even work between departments. Such an approach can lead to increased skills, job satisfaction, more meaningful work and enhanced career prospects for employees. Many descriptions of functional flexibility in the tourism and hospitality sector, though, have pointed to a rather ad hoc approach, which may be more about covering short-term problems rather than creating a genuinely multi-skilled employee. This point has led Riley (1992) to describe true functional flexibility within tourism and hospitality as being a 'Cinderella idea'. However, Kelliher and Riley (2003) report research from four case study organizations in the hospitality industry who had enjoyed benefits to both employers and employees in introducing functional flexibility. Employers reported more efficient use of labour, lower labour costs, better operational functioning, improved customer service, reduced levels of labour turnover and an improvement of their position in the local labour market. Employees also reported increased job satisfaction, greater job security and enhanced remuneration (and see also HRM in practice 4.5).

HRM in practice 4.5   Marriott Marble Arch: Aiming to multi-task and multi-skill

Lowe (2002) recognizes that, as with every other tourism and hospitality organization, the London Marriott Marble Arch hotel has to cope constantly with staff recruitment, retention and motivation to maintain high standards of customer services. The four-star hotel introduced a cross-training scheme to improve the skills of its employees to help them cope with the requirements of their job roles.

To improve their staff recruitment and retention, the Marble Arch hotel set up its cross-training Discovery scheme. The programme was designed to increase staff skills and to ease career promotions into higher or sideways positions through developing employee skills in other areas. Last but not least, it also endeavoured to base labour scheduling on a flexible, multi-skilled workforce, allowing the hotel to use its employees in the most cost-effective manner. The scheme was targeted at every employee and was completed during normal working hours. Overall, it took more than 320 hours, spread over 40 one-day sessions, for the hotel to complete their Discovery cross-training. At the end of the formal training each participant received individual feedback and a certificate of achievement. The HR department was involved in co-ordinating the scheme, liaising with heads of departments and getting constructive feedback from participants in order to control and modify the scheme. Parallel to this, further developments were introduced, such as a 2-week critical cross-training session was added to new associates' 90-day induction plan in order to make them develop skills within their critical departments. For instance, new restaurant employees were supposed to spend time in the kitchen, bar and banqueting areas. In addition, the programme was made available all the year and HR ensured employees had completed their cross-training before letting them move within departments.

The Discovery scheme led to substantial improvements. It impacted positively on two performance measures. First, the programme improved the Balanced Score Card, a tool used for measuring and communicating hotel performance at Marriott hotels.

Second, the results of an annual employee survey significantly improved. Employees felt that training to carry out daily tasks improved, raising its score from 21 to 87 per cent. They also believed their opportunities to develop their career had increased by 4 per cent and 84 per cent felt that they had accessible job opportunities compared to only 9 per cent before the introduction of the scheme. As Lowe, HR manager at the hotel, comments, 'The initiative has proved invaluable to the London Marriott Marble Arch hotel. It is a concept that could easily be adapted to other businesses to help meet the constant challenge of staff recruitment and retention' (p. 14). Indeed, the hotel was awarded the large establishment category prize at the large annual Excellence through People Awards held by the British Hospitality Association in 2002.

Numerical flexibility

Numerical flexibility refers to the capacity of employers to adjust labour supply to fluctuations in business demand, which may equal less job security, low pay, lack of opportunities for training and career advancement for employees. Unsurprisingly given this description the peripheral workforce is most often associated with numerical flexibility. In pursuing numerical flexibility employers can look to either internal or external means (Lai and Baum, 2005). Internal means are largely concerned with the use of 'non-standard employment contracts', such as part-time and shift working and the use of temporary and casual workers. External means include aspects such as contracting out services, for example a hotel contracting out its leisure facilities, and the use of agency staff (and see HRM in practice 4.6).

In addition to functional and numerical flexibility, tourism and hospitality organizations can also use temporal flexibility, such as annual hours contracts and job sharing; and pay flexibility, for example enhanced payments in return for being functionally flexible.

It is interesting here to briefly think about the descriptions of flexibility within our earlier discussion of hard and soft HRM. As we noted in Chapter 1 hard and soft HRM allow us to appreciate that the reason for organizations adopting certain HR practices may vary. Based on our description of the two approaches we could, rather crudely, characterize numerical flexibility as being largely about hard HRM. This hard approach emphasizes the use of labour which is aimed at reducing labour costs, either by the most efficient use of labour or alternatively its most

HRM in practice 4.6 Just in time labour supply in the hotel sector

Many four- and five-star hotels will often rely on agency staff recruited from employment agencies, particularly in areas such as housekeeping. Research by Lai and Baum (2005) suggests that hotels can reduce labour costs by utilizing agency staff thus avoiding having to pay fringe benefits such as sickness cover, pension contributions, maternity leave payments and holiday entitlements, all of which are covered by the employment agency. Additionally, HR activities such as recruitment and selection, induction and training are often undertaken by the agencies. Lai and Baum suggest that one hotel in their research saved up to £500 000 a year in housekeeping payroll costs. In addition to cost savings, Lai and Baum also found that agency staff had often worked for the same hotel for a number of years with the consequence that quality and performance were improved.

effective exploitation. In this view approaches to flexibility will be concerned with minimizing labour costs and ensuring the size and mix of labour inputs is adjusted to changes in product demand. On the other hand, the soft approach is more concerned with broadening employees' skills through training to create workforces which are flexible. Such a description is more concerned with functional flexibility.

As we have seen the most frequently utilized method of flexibility in the tourism and hospitality industry is numerical flexibly, which is often characterized by low-paid, low-skill, casual and part-time operative level work. An example of such an approach would be a pool of available staff that could be called in at short notice to work in the organization, for example, in the banqueting department of a hotel. Indeed, many have argued that talk of flexibility and core and peripheral workers induces nothing more than an ominous sense of déjà vu within the tourism and hospitality industry. Due to the nature of the industry, patterns of employment within tourism and hospitality have largely been arranged in a way that promotes a high degree of employment flexibility, through the use of employment practices that have often left individual workers with limited opportunities for advancement and low job security. Wood (1997: 168), for example, argues that, 'Flexible working practices in the commercial hotel and catering sector are not new to the industry, the use of part-time casual and part-time workers and multi-skilled staff being a common and arguable defining feature of labour organization in some sectors, most notably small hotel business'.

Conclusions

We have outlined a fairly bleak scenario of what traditionally the organizational characteristics of the tourism and hospitality industry have meant for those working in the industry. The tendency to short termism and ad hocism is the key feature of labour markets in the industry. Management responses to these issues are also similarly short term and ad hoc, with their role often being one of responding to situations and unanticipated crises, or trying to cope with varying demand. This, of course, leaves us with an obvious paradox, namely how can the tourism and hospitality industry compromise the need for staffing flexibility with the attainment and maintenance of a quality service and product to the customer? There are no easy answers to this conundrum and even a cursory understanding of the nature of labour markets in tourism and hospitality allows us to appreciate this point.

References and further reading

Adler, P. and Adler, P. (2004) *Paradise Laborers: Hotel Work in the Global Economy*, Cornell University Press.

Atkinson, J. (1984) 'Manpower strategies for flexible organizations', *Personnel Management*, 16(8), 28–31.

Baum, T. (2002) 'Skills and training for the hospitality sector: a review of issues', *Journal of Vocational Education and Training*, 54(3), 343–363.

Cabinet Office (2003) *Ethnic Minorities and the Labour Market*, Cabinet Office.

Cottell, C. (2005) 'An industry in need of serving suggestions', *Guardian Work*, 26 March, 21.

Deery, M. and Jago, L. (2002) 'The core and periphery: an examination of the flexible workforce model in the hotel industry', *International Journal of Hospitality Management*, 21(4), 339–351.

Groskop, V. (2006) 'Mamafesto', *New Statesman*, 17 July, 26–28.

Gunn, J. (2004) 'New EU states workers could ease jobs crisis', *Caterer and Hotelkeeper*, 5 August, 7.

Hurrell, S. (2005) 'Dilute to taste? The impact of the working time regulations in the hospitality industry', *Employee Relations*, 27(5), 523–546.

Kelliher, C. and Riley, M. (2003) 'Beyond flexibility: some by-products of functional flexibility', *Service Industries Journal*, 23(4), 98–113.

Lai, P. and Baum, T. (2005) 'Just-in-time labour supply in the hotel sector: the role of agencies', *Employee Relations*, 27(1), 86–102.

Lowe, C. (2002) 'Marriott's cross-training', *Leisure and Hospitality Business*, 29 November, 14.

Meiklem, P. (2004) 'Highland hospitality … courtesy of Eastern Europeans', *Sunday Herald*, 14 November, 9.

Riley, M. (1992) 'Functional flexibility in hotels – is it feasible?', *Tourism Management*, 13(4), 363–367.

Riley, M. (1996) *Human Resource Management in the Hospitality and Tourism Industry*, Butterworth-Heinemann, 2nd edition.

Walsh, T. (1990) 'Flexible employment in the retail and hotel trades', in A. Pollert (ed.) *Farewell to Flexibility*, Blackwell, 140–150.

Warren, C. (2004) 'Continental drift', *People Management*, 6 May, 28–33.

Wood, R. C. (1997) *Working in Hotels and Catering*, International Thomson Press, 2nd edition.

Websites

The International Labour Office produces an annual labour market indicator and details of this and other aspects of their work on labour markets can be found at http://www.ilo.org/public/english/employment/strat/kilm/

The European Foundation for the Improvement of Living and Working Conditions has some interesting material and other links at http://www.eurofound. eu.int/areas/labourmarket/index.htm/

The UK Government's official statistics website http://www.statistics.gov.uk/cci/nscl.asp?id=5006 has some interesting labour market statistics.

Chapter 5
Recruitment and selection

Chapter objectives

This chapter addresses recruitment and selection in the tourism and hospitality industry. In particular the chapter aims:

- To understand the differences between, yet complementary nature of, recruitment and selection.
- To appreciate the importance of job descriptions and person specifications/competency profiles in recruitment and selection.
- To recognize the type of people and skills that tourism and hospitality organizations are seeking.
- To consider the range of selection techniques available to tourism and hospitality organizations.

Introduction

Generally recruiting and selecting people to fill new or existing positions is a crucial element of human resource activity in all tourism and hospitality organizations, irrespective of size, structure or activity. Although we have noted how the importance of service quality has increased the pressure on organizations to select the 'right' kind of individual, it is often widely suggested that too often decisions are made in an informal, ad hoc and reactive manner. This point may be especially true in smaller organizations that may not have well developed HRM functions or recruitment and selection systems, and may recruit irregularly with heavy reliance on informal systems and methods (Jameson, 2000). Indeed, within the context of the hospitality sector, Price (1994) found that of 241 hotels sampled in her research, a third never used job descriptions or person specifications. More recently, Lockyer and Scholarios (2005) surveyed over 80 hotels and again found a general lack of systematic procedures for recruitment and selection. This lack of systemization may seem strange when many writers would point to the cost of poor recruitment and selection being manifested in such things as:

- expensive use of management time;
- retraining performers;
- recruiting replacements for individuals who leave very quickly;
- high-labour turnover;
- absenteeism;
- low morale;
- ineffective management and supervision;
- disciplinary problems;
- dismissals.

Clearly then it is important for organizations to consider how they can approach recruitment and selection to increase the likelihood of a successful appointment/decision and in a cost effective manner. Reflecting this latter idea of cost effectiveness it is important to recognize the contingent nature of recruitment and selection. Thus, although there may be good practice approaches to recruitment and selection these are not going to be appropriate for all positions available in an organization. For example, for a management traineeship in a major hotel the company may use a variety of sophisticated and costly mechanisms culminating in an assessment centre. On the other hand for a part-time seasonal position in a fairground the company may recruit an employee based on word of mouth. Indeed, in considering why it may be difficult for tourism and hospitality companies to aim for best practice in recruitment and selection Lockyer and Scholarios (2005) recognize that the lack of formality can often be overcome by effective use of local networks in recruiting employees. For example, they suggest that the person responsible for selection should have a good knowledge of the local labour market and be able to make the best use of informal networks to find suitable employees.

A further point to consider by way of introduction is the notion of 'fit' between the individual and the organization who are seeking to attract and admit those who are considered 'right' for the organization, in terms of issues like commitment, flexibility, quality, ability to work in a team and so on. Thus, the match between the individual and organization may be 'loose', that is applicants having the ability to do the job; or 'tight', where the individual has to demonstrate not only technical competence but whether they have a specific personality profile to 'fit' the organizational culture, as discussed in Chapter 3. In such circumstances clearly there is the possibility to see the notion of tight fit between organization and individual in a slightly sinister way and we will consider this point throughout the chapter. Relatedly, there is the idea of discrimination being a key issue within the recruitment and selection process. Of course, at one level recruitment and selection is inherently discriminatory as, at times, organizations will have to choose between two or more applicants for a job, particularly for managerial positions. Crucially though such discrimination should be based on the applicants ability to do the job. Thus companies are discriminating all the time

HRM in practice 5.1   Skills involved in the recruitment and selection process

The recruitment and selection process	The skills required
Job description	Evaluation of the vacancy
Person specification	Drafting the criteria
Advertisement	Summarising
Shortlist	Fair discrimination
Interview	Questioning skills
Selection tests	Listening skills
References	Assessment skills
Decision	Evaluation

on the basis of whether or not candidates have the attributes and skills to do the job, but this should not contravene statutes in areas such as race, sex and disability (and see Chapter 6). One final point by way of introduction is to recognize the range of skills which managers need in the recruitment and selection process. As many line managers in tourism and hospitality, as well as human resource specialists, are increasingly involved in recruitment and selection it is important that they should recognize the skills required in such a process (and see HRM in practice 5.1).

Recruitment

Recruitment is defined by Heery and Noon (2001: 298) as 'the process of generating a pool of candidates from which to select the appropriate person to fill a job vacancy'. In essence, in the recruitment process organizations are seeking to attract and retain the interest of suitable candidates, whilst at the same time also seeking to portray a positive image to potential applicants. Of course, recruitment is a dynamic process as within organizations people are constantly retiring, resigning, being promoted or, at times, being dismissed. Equally, changes in technology, procedures or markets may all mean that jobs are re-configured and become available to the external labour and thereby trigger the recruitment and selection process. Having decided to recruit, organizations will ordinarily consider a range of question to determine how they might approach filling the vacancy. Specifically, they might ask themselves the following questions:

- What does the job consist of?
- What are the aspects of the job that specify the type of candidate?
- What are the key aspects of the job that the ideal candidate wants to know before applying?

Conventionally the answers to these questions will be provided by job analysis, the job description and person specification, which allow the candidates to gauge their chances of being appointed.

Job analysis

Armstrong (1999: 190) defines job analysis as 'the process of collecting, analysing and setting out information about the contents of jobs in order to provide the basis for a job description and data for recruitment, training, job evaluation and perform-ance management'. Marchington and Wilkinson (2005) suggest that undertaking a job analysis may not be necessary for every time a vacancy arises, especially in organizations that have high levels of labour turnover. However, they do recognize that job analysis does allow for an examination of whether existing job descriptions and person specifications/competency profiles are appropriate for future needs. The same authors also recognize that there is likely to be variation in terms of the sophistication, cost, convenience and acceptability of job analysis and this will also determine the methods utilized to analyse a job. Organizations may use one or more of the following methods: observation of the job, work diaries, interviews with job holders and questionnaires and checklists. The output from such job analysis is the job description and person specification.

Job description

Heery and Noon (2001: 186) describe the job description as, 'A document that out-lines the purposes of the job, the task involved, the duties and responsibilities, the performance of objectives and the reporting relationships. It will give details of the terms and conditions, including the remuneration package and hours of work'. In many respects the job description can be thought of as a functional document which outlines the 'what' elements of a job. It should aim to provide clear infor-mation to candidates about the organization and the job itself, such that it acts as a realistic preview of the job. Importantly, as well as offering a realistic description of the nature of the job, the job description should also act as a marketing docu-ment that seeks to make the job look attractive to potential applicants.

Person specification/competency profile in the recruitment context

Whilst the job description considers the 'what' aspects of the job, the person spec-ification is concerned with the 'who'. In this way the person specification should aim to provide a profile of the 'ideal' person for the job. In reality, the ideal person may not exist, but the person specification provides a framework to assess how close candidates come to being the ideal. Conventionally the person specification is a document which describes the personal skills and characteristics required to fill the position, usually listed under 'essential' and 'desirable' headings. In that sense essential criteria form the minimum standard expected for any given job and will form the basis for potentially rejecting applicants. For example, if an advert for a tour company manager stipulates a degree in a travel and tourism-related area, then non-degree holders would be automatically excluded. On the other hand the desirable criteria are those things which are considered over and above the minimum and should provide the basis for selection. For example, an organization may stipulate that for the same managerial job we have just outlined that a foreign language is desirable. If a candidate had a foreign language they may be at an advantage to other candidates who do not, though ultimately the company may appoint somebody who does not have a language.

The two most important person specification models are those provided by Alec Rodger in 1952 and John Munro Fraser in 1954 (Torrington et al., 2005).

Rodger seven-point plan

1 *Physical characteristics* – such as the ability to lift heavy loads or appearance, speech and manner.
2 *Attainments* – educational/professional qualifications, work experience considered necessary for the job.
3 *General intelligence* – such as the ability to define and solve problems.
4 *Special aptitudes* – skills, attributes or competencies relevant to the job.
5 *Interests* – work related or leisure pursuits that may have a bearing on the job.
6 *Disposition* – job-related behaviours, for example demonstrating friendliness.
7 *Circumstances* – for example domestic commitments or ability to work unsocial hours.

Munro Fraser five-fold grading system

1 *Impact on other people* – similar to Rodgers physical make-up.
2 *Qualifications and experience* – similar to Rodgers attainments.
3 *Innate abilities and aptitude* – similar to Rodgers general intelligence.
4 *Motivation* – a person's desire to succeed in the workplace.
5 *Adjustment* – personality factors that may impact on things like ability to cope with difficult customers.

More recently, Marchington and Wilkinson (2005) note how many companies now use competency frameworks to outline the type of person that they are seeking. The focus of competency frameworks is on the behaviours of job applicants and they are useful as they can also set a framework for other subsequent HR practices, such as performance management and pay. Marchington and Wilkinson (2005: 169) also note how, 'the competencies can be related to specific performance outcomes rather than being concerned with potentially vague processes, such as disposition or interests outside of work'. The use of competencies tends to focus on areas such as team orientation, communication, people management, customer focus, results orientation and problem-solving.

Regardless though of whether organizations are using person specifications or competency frameworks, tourism and hospitality organizations are now seeking employees, especially those who will interact with customers, with certain types of skills.

Review and reflect

What are the types of skills that tourism and hospitality organizations are likely to seek in their front-line staff? How can these skills be discerned in the recruitment and selection process?

The 'ideal' front-line tourism and hospitality employee

With the shift to a service economy the type of skills demanded by employers has also shifted. Employers in hospitality and tourism in both the UK and elsewhere increasingly desire employees with the 'right' attitude and appearance (Chan and Coleman, 2004; Nickson et al., 2005). The right attitude encompasses aspects such as social and interpersonal skills, which are largely concerned with ensuring employees are responsive, courteous and understanding with customers, or in simple terms can demonstrate emotional labour. However, it is not only the right attitude that employers seek. Nickson et al. (2001) have developed the term 'aesthetic labour' – the ability to either 'look good' or 'sound right' (Warhurst and Nickson, 2001) – which points to the increasing importance of the way in which employees are expected to physically embody the company image in tourism and hospitality.

In an analysis of 5000 jobs advertisements across a number of different occupations and sectors in the UK, Jackson et al. (2005) found that the skills stated as necessary by employers are 'social skills' and 'personal characteristics'; only 26 per cent of organizations mentioned the need for educational requirements. Within personal services this figure was less than 10 per cent. Furthermore Jackson et al. found numerous instances of front-line service jobs asking for attributes that referred less to what individuals could *do* than to what they were *like*, such as being 'well-turned out' or 'well-spoken', or having 'good appearance', 'good manners', 'character' or 'presence'.

Nickson et al. (2005) also report evidence from a survey of nearly 150 employers in the retail and hospitality industry. On the question of what employers are looking for in customer facing staff during the selection process, Nickson et al. found that 65 per cent suggested that the right personality was critical, with the remainder of respondents suggesting this aspect was important. Equally, 33 per cent of the employers surveyed felt that the right appearance was critical and 57 per cent as important, only 2 per cent of respondents felt it was not important. These figures can be compared to qualifications, with only one respondent seeing qualifications as critical, 19 per cent of employers felt it was important and 40 per cent suggested it was not important at all for selecting their customer facing staff.

In terms of the skills deemed necessary to do the required work, employers placed a far greater emphasis on 'soft' skills for customer facing staff. Ninety-nine per cent of respondents felt that social or interpersonal skills were felt to be of at least significant importance, and 98 per cent felt likewise about self-presentation, or aesthetic, skills. Conversely 48 per cent of employers felt that technical skills were important in their customer facing staff and 16 per cent stated they were not important at all. The skills that matter to employers in customer facing staff in tourism and hospitality are generally then 'soft', including aesthetic skills, rather than 'hard' technical skills, which will often be trained in when people join the organization (and see HRM in practice 5.2).

Of course we should recognize that the use of person specifications and competency frameworks may still involve a degree of subjectivity, especially in judging which potential employees have the 'right' kind of attitude or appearance. Evidence suggests that employers will often make judgements which penalize people for not having the 'right' appearance or attitude (Nickson et al., 2003). Clearly, then, there is the potential for overt and not so overt forms of discrimination in how person specifications and competency frameworks may be used by

HRM in practice 5.2   'Scotland with Style': aesthetic labour and employees who look good and sound right

Glasgow was once an industrial city. Now, over 85 per cent of the city's jobs are in services. Aiming for the city break tourist market, the city promotes its retail, cultural and hospitality attractions. Between 1994 and 2000, the number of major hotels in the city increased from 42 to 89, with 27 more planned. Glasgow has approximately 1000 bars and restaurants and is second only to London as Britain's culinary capital. Similarly, Experian acknowledges Glasgow as the second largest retail centre in the UK outside London. The city also now has a well-developed niche of designer retailers, boutique hotels and style bars, cafes and restaurants. Not surprisingly, the city was recently described by US magazine *Travel and Leisure* as 'The UK's hippest and most happening city'. Three million tourists visit the city each year, generating £670 m annually in the local economy. In recognition of this new economic success, the city re-branded itself as 'Scotland with Style' in 2004.

To take advantage of this booming tourist market and reflecting the city's new image, tourism and hospitality employers want staff with the right customer service skills. Job adverts specify that applicants be 'well spoken and of smart appearance' or 'very well presented'. One Scottish-based boutique hotel company, known pseudonymsly as Elba, has created a sophisticated recruitment, selection and training programme for its new staff. Elba has hotels in two Scottish cities and has expanded into England and France. Opening a new hotel in Glasgow, the company deliberately placed job advertisements in the *Sunday Times* rather than local evening newspapers. Opening a hotel in Newcastle, England, it placed TV adverts during programmes aimed at the youth market. As a consequence, its typical front of house employee is in his or her twenties, a graduate and well travelled. Recruitment literature featured a person description not a job description, asking applicants to assess themselves by the 13 words that characterized that company's image; 'stylish' and 'tasty' for example. After a telephone interview, application with CV and then a face-to-face interview, there was a 10-day induction at the Glasgow hotel in which extensive grooming and deportment training was given to the staff by external consultants. Sessions included individual 'make-overs' for staff, teaching them about hair cuts/styling, teaching female staff about make-up, male staff how to shave and, for all, the expected appearance standards. The sessions were intended to relay 'this is what we want you to actually look like ... you have to understand what "successful" looks like ... what "confident" looks like.' The hotel wanted staff that were confident, with a good attitude and appearance. 'There is an Elba look', said the hotel manager, 'neat and stylish…young, very friendly … people that fit in with the whole concept of the hotel' (Nickson et al., 2001: 180). The hotel wanted staff able to project the company's image and help it differentiate itself in a crowded and competitive market. It is a policy that seems to pay: the hotel claims above average occupancy rates for the city.

Derived from Nickson et al. (2001, 2005).

those making the final decision about who is to be employed by the organization, a point considered in further detail in Chapter 6.

Ultimately in considering the person specification or competency profile it would seem sensible for organizations to consider several points.

- Are all the items on your person specification/competency profile relevant to the job?
- Are you reasonably sure that none of your criteria would discriminate unfairly against a group of potential candidates?
- Would your person specification/competency profile enable a shortlisting and interviewing panel to distinguish clearly between candidates?

Having reviewed the importance of the job description and person specification/ competency requirements we can now move on to consider how organizations can attract the interest of appropriate potential employees. Initially, there may be a choice as to whether the organization looks to somebody within the organization or alternatively looks to the external labour market. For example, for a promotable position organizations which are seeking to sustain a strong internal labour market may have a policy to offer this position in-house first to existing staff. Equally, though, the organization may feel that offering such positions to the external labour market is important to bring in new ideas and new blood to the organization. In deciding their target group organizations may also wish to address issues such as under representation of a particular group, for example ethnic minority employees or women managers, a point that is further considered in the following chapter.

Generally speaking organizations have a number of methods which they can consider in seeking to engage with their target market for new employees. First, as we have already noted they may use existing employees. For example, this can be in relation to promotable positions or also in terms of word-of-mouth approaches, which are commonplace in tourism and hospitality, especially for front-line positions. Alternatively the organization may choose to use external contacts, such as job centres. Indeed, this may well be something that organizations see as important in their attempts to be good corporate citizens (and see HRM in practice 5.3).

HRM in practice 5.3   Jurys Inns: offering a helping hand to the unemployed

The Jurys Inn hotel is a three-star plus hotel chain targeting business travellers and leisure guests. It is the key brand of the Irish Jurys Doyle Hotel Group PLC that owns and operates three-, four- and five-star hotels in the UK, Ireland and the US, and has a workforce of 4000 employees. As any other companies in the highly competitive and unstable hospitality sector, the Jurys Inn hotel had to develop a successful strategy to stand out from the competition and weather the economic slowdown. Among the strategic initiatives was a recruitment and training strategy aimed at improving the quality of customer service. Every time Jurys Doyle Hotels opens a new Jurys Inn, they rely on key local employment providers, such as the Job Centre Plus, the local council and a local training provider, such as a college, to develop a gateway training programme for people willing to move into the hotel industry. Applicants who have passed the initial sifting process are then invited to an 8-week pre-employment training programme run in partnership between Jurys Doyle Hotels and the training provider. This programme has proved successful since it was first launched in 1993 and 20 people who are currently working in the company are estimated to have joined the pre-employment scheme. It is now estimated that there are, on average, 30 places available at each new Inn, representing 25 to 50 per cent of the staff base. After the pre-employment period, successful candidates and other new recruits alike join the Guest Service Staff (GSS) training 4 weeks before an opening. The main objective of this scheme is to develop a multi-skilled team able to operate within all areas of the hotel. Furthermore, the programme has no time limit and is available for every employee willing to advance their career. Finally, to make sure its employees are the most effective in the industry, Jurys Doyle Hotel strive to ensure that their staff gain external or professional qualifications such as National Vocational Qualifications (NVQ) or CIPD qualifications.

Jurys Inn's recruitment and training strategy has helped them expand in a recent context of economic slowdown. Aside from building Jurys Inn's skill base, the pre-employment scheme has contributed to creating jobs in cities often hit by unemployment, thereby improving employee loyalty to the hotel. In addition, it involves new recruits in the development of the building in which they are to work. This helps build the involvement of employees who might have had doubts about the scheme or working in a hotel. On the other hand, the GSS training aimed at developing multi-skilled staff, is beneficial both to the employer, who seek to maximize the use of its workforce, and to the employee who gains diverse levels of experience and benefit from more flexible working hours, as they are able to take on a number of different roles. As Edward Gallier, development and training manager for the UK and Ireland, puts it, 'Our employees can work anywhere in the Inn ... this means we have GSS who can deliver the services of a receptionist, room attendant or porter equally well, with the confidence good training gives them'.

Source: Gallier (2004).

A further key aspect of looking externally for new employees is the importance of advertising and media. An obvious starting point here is the printed media and specifically the press. The use of the print media to advertise jobs is one of the most popular formal methods of recruitment. When thinking about where adverts are best placed organizations need to be cognizant of the labour market on which they are hoping to draw for a particular job. In recognizing the most appropriate labour markets organizations could conceivably place adverts in either the local/national press or in trade and professional journals. For example, for a front-line position it is likely that the local press will be used, whilst for a managerial or specialist position the use of the national press or trade press may be more appropriate. In using the printed media it is important to consider the manner in which organizations can portray the desired image and here we will consider how this issue can be addressed.

When organizations advertise vacancies it is important that they convey the right message in order to attract suitable applicants and discourage those who do not have the necessary attributes. Equally important is that advertisements project a positive image of the company and in that sense adverts can be considered a selling document. Initially organizations have the choice to get it alone and contact the media directly or alternatively they can deal with an advertising agency, who can help in drafting and placing an advert. Advertising agencies can be thought of as experts who can offer advice on the choice of advertising copy and the choice of media. They may also have better contacts to ensure advertising space at short notice. The only drawback is that agencies may also be rather costly. Regardless of whether an agency is used or not there are certain key points which should be borne in mind in devising an advert and at the very least the following aspects should be apparent (Torrington et al., 2005: 128).

- Name and brief details of the employing organization.
- Job role and duties.
- Key points of the person specification or competency framework.
- Salary.
- Instructions about how to apply.

Moreover organizations should also consider the image they are portraying and the CIPD and the Institute of Professional Advertisers (IPA) outline the following criteria for judging excellence in recruitment advertising (CIPD, 2006):

- visual impact,
- typography and balance,
- clarity of message to the target audience,
- promotion of job vacancy,
- projection of a professional organizational image,
- focus on workplace diversity.

Review and reflect

Using the above criteria attempt to find a job advertisement for a tourism and hospitality organization which exemplifies at least some of these aspects and briefly describe why these aspects makes a job look attractive.

With regard to that last bullet point it is important to reiterate that adverts must not discriminate on grounds of sex, race, sexuality, religious orientation and disability.

In addition there are other areas which can potentially be used including TV, radio, cinema, careers exhibitions, conferences and open days and posters. Whilst TV, radio and cinema adverts have been utilized to recruit in areas like the military or teaching they are much less likely to be used by tourism and hospitality organizations. The other aspects though could all be conceivably used. For example,

HRM in practice 5.4   Who would you most like to be stuck in a lift with?

Hills (2004) reports on the recruitment process in Tiger Tiger, which is one of the UK's most popular nightclub groups. As part of their recruitment process they host open days to allow potential employees to sample the Tiger Tiger atmosphere. A general manager, Beverley Harley, is quoted as saying, 'the leisure sector is a particularly social and competitive one and we're on the hunt for hardworking team players'. As part of assessing whether applicants have these attributes, during the open day potential employees take part in various 'fun' activities, including being asked who they would most like to be stuck in a lift with and which type of animal they would choose to be.

TGI Fridays, the American restaurant chain, have successfully used open days to recruit staff in the UK. As a company with a very distinctive service style open days are felt to be useful to expose potential employees to the nature of the work they will be undertaking. As the company is looking for very outgoing individuals who can do things like juggle or sing whilst serving customers the open day is designed to assess such aspects. Team tasks and tricks and dances are just some of the things that potential employees will be expected to demonstrate in their 'audition' during the open day (Baker, 1999; and see HRM in practice 5.4).

Another source of recruitment is increasingly the Internet. IDS (2003) have recently noted how the use of the Internet in recruitment has tended to be complementary to existing methods, rather than replacing them. In this sense, although the Internet is playing a growing role in organizations recruitment strategies, its importance should not be exaggerated. For most companies the use of Internet tends to be in terms of sections on their websites that allow job seekers to check for current vacancies. Beyond this facility there may be more strategic approaches in using the web, particularly with regard to the ability to receive and process job applications online, something which is outlined in HRM in practice 5.5.

Smethurst (2004) notes other reasons for employers, including Whitbread, for using online recruitment, including:

- Reducing cost per hire.
- Increasing speed to hire.
- Strengthening the employer brand.

HRM in practice 5.5   Hilton International: spreading the web

Beal (2004) notes how Hilton International wanted to improve its fast-track Elevator programme – a selection tool introduced in 1998 and designed to recruit highly talented graduates as future hotel general managers. As new graduates had to learn the role of a manager in a short period of time, the tool had to be extremely reliable to pick up the right candidates. As such, the Elevator scheme, which involved hand-processing and scoring an application form, conducting a face-to-face meeting, psychometric testing and conducting a final 24-h assessment centre, proved costly and time-consuming, especially in terms of senior management involvement.

To streamline its selection tool, Hilton International commissioned the business-psychology consultancy Human Factor International to introduce a web-based screening system – a so-called 'virtual psychologist' – running in five European languages. This online tool would not have been possible without a technological breakthrough which allows for a time limit on the intellectual-reasoning part of the test. The system was successfully implemented in 15 working days, from Christmas 2003 to 20 January 2004. Since the running of the programme, Hilton has invited applicants through presentations at the main European hotel schools and universities to apply through the website http://www.hilton-university.com and complete the standard application form. Those who pass the initial sifting are then asked to fill in online 'personality' and 'workplace values' questionnaires. At this stage all candidates receive an electronic report analysing their results and providing tailored career advice. Successful candidates are then invited to complete three ability and skill tests of 15 min each before being selected to the assessment centre. At the end of the assessment centre unsuccessful candidates receive detailed e-mailed feedback outlining the reasons why they have not been chosen and inviting them to phone in if they want to have further explanations. As Christine Jones, Director of the Consultancy Human Factor International adds, 'Even unsuccessful candidates have told us they have been pleased with the feedback they have been given, and are comfortable with it' (p. 31).

By introducing the online system, Hilton has been able to reduce the number of assessment days without damaging the quality of its new recruits. Indeed, the 14 graduates who first joined Hilton through this tool had to pass only two final assessment centres rather than the five or six previously needed. As John Guthrie, Head of International Management at Hilton International comments, 'While unlikely to save significant costs in pure cash terms, getting rid of manual processes has freed up managers' time to concentrate on more value-adding work. Additionally, it helps to portray the organization as more contemporary and technologically oriented and strengthens our appeal in a competitive search for talent' (p. 31).

	Operative (%)	Management (%)
Job centre	87	13
Local press	80	30
Word of mouth	70	35
Employment agencies	32	57
Trade press	26	66
National press	8	24
Personnel consultants	2	42
Others*	22	22

*Others represented internal sources and in one chain an in-house recruitment centre.

Reprinted by permission from 'Personnel management in hotels – an update: a move to human resource management?', Kelliher, C. and Johnson, K. (1997). Copyright John Wiley and Sons Limited.

Figure 5.1 Sources of recruitment in the hospitality industry

- Greater flexibility and ease for candidates.
- Broaden the applicant pool.

Lastly, beyond individual company websites there are other commercial websites, such as http://www.traveljobz.net/, which aims to allow job seekers to access jobs in a wide variety of travel and hospitality jobs, including airlines, hotels, cruise lines, restaurants and other travel companies.

We recognized earlier in the chapter how a key aspect of recruitment and selection was cost effectiveness. As a result it is not necessarily sensible to use certain recruitment methods for certain jobs and in reality the aim should be to ensure the best method to hit the particular target group for a particular job and in a cost effective manner. The recognition of the need for a contingent approach to recruitment is apparent from the research outlined in Figure 5.1 (and see also HRM in practice 5.6).

At this juncture in the recruitment process the organization will hopefully have generated sufficient interest from suitable applicants. In that sense it is important for organizations to periodically review the recruitment process and evaluate its effectiveness against this kind of criterion. Additionally, the organization may also want to consider the issues of costs and equal opportunities issues.

HRM in practice 5.6   'Realistic' recruitment in the cruise industry

Raub and Streit (2006) recognise that, as within other tourism and hospitality settings, human resources are crucial to success in the cruise industry as guests are in constant contact with service staff and unlike conventional hotels cannot usually wander 'off site'. Regardless of the likely pressure that this is likely to create for front-line service staff many people might think that working in the cruise industry is likely to be exciting and fun. Life on board a cruise ship though can be difficult for staff, for example they are likely to face cramped and difficult living conditions. The unique work context in the cruise ship industry means that many organizations attempt to offer a 'realistic' and 'honest and objective' view of working life in the industry, which means that staff do not have an unrealistic view of working in the industry. Key to this approach is the use of several types of recruitment media such as interviews, company-specific videos, company presentations, written information (such as fact sheets) and web-based information. This realistic job preview is placed alongside the positive aspects of the job, for example the manner in which working on cruise ships can significantly broaden the professional and individual horizons of young employees. By balancing both positive and negative aspects of working in the industry in this realistic manner companies seem to be able to lessen high levels of labour turnover thus increasing retention and potentially enhancing job satisfaction.

Ultimately in evaluating the process of recruitment organizations can ask themselves several key questions:

- Do recruitment practices yield sufficient numbers of suitable candidates to enable the organization to select sufficient numbers of high-quality employees?
- Could a sufficient pool of suitable candidates be attracted using less expensive methods?
- Are recruitment methods fulfilling equal opportunities responsibilities?

Depending on the type of job, and presuming that there is more than one candidate, the final part of the recruitment procedure is the notion of shortlisting. The outcome of the recruitment process is to produce a shortlist of candidates whose background and potential are in accordance with the profile contained in the person specification/competency framework. Clearly this is a way of making good use of the information gathered to date about the candidate. We can also appreciate the need to ensure that things have gone smoothly so far. In this sense if there has been a problem, say with the advert, shortlisting can conceivably be a problem. If, for example, there are insufficient number of candidates who are appointable or indeed if there are too many candidates. Presuming that there are sufficient numbers of suitably qualified people for the position the conventional method is to shortlist by comparison with the person specification/competency framework. Torrington et al. (2005) though note that if there is a large number of people who have applied for a job there may be fairly arbitrary criteria, such as people being excluded because of their age or their handwriting style. As they recognize though such shortlisting techniques are wholly unsatisfactory, being potentially both unlawful and certainly unfair. A fairer approach is likely to be based on a rigorous and systematic view of each candidate via five stages (Torrington et al., 2005: 136):

1 Essential criteria for shortlisting.
2 Individual selectors produce their own list of a given number of candidates.
3 Selectors reveal list and try to reach consensus, if still not clear.
4 Discuss why certain candidates are preferred and others not.
5 Produce final shortlist after negotiation and compromise.

We have now reached the stage where the organization is ready to move on to selection.

Selection

To-date in this chapter we have essentially been examining the notion of recruitment and how organizations attempt to attract the interest of potential employees. We can now go on and examine the idea of how organizations match potential employees to jobs, via the processes of selection when organizations will decide who is the most appropriate person for the job. We will do this by contextualizing the process, and then go on and look at some of the techniques utilized by organizations in selecting new employees. We will then assess some of the possible problems within this process and finally examine the way most organizations approach the idea of selection.

As Heery and Noon (2001: 320) note selection is, 'the process of assessing job applicants using one of a variety of methods with the purpose of finding the most suitable person for the organization'. Increasingly many writers argue that the selection of staff may well be the most important aspect of HRM as staff are increasingly expected to become effective immediately. Allied to this point is the cost of various selection techniques which means organizations will want to get it right first time. However, despite this recognition there is no one best way which is universally recognized as the best method of selecting the right person for the job. Torrington et al. (2005: 141) argue that, 'the search for the perfect selection method continues, in its absence HR and line managers continue to use a variety of imperfect methods'. What this quote points to is that no one selection method can guarantee success in terms of choosing the right person for the job, especially given the level of human involvement in the process. As organizations recognize this conundrum they are adopting a variety of techniques to address questions of selection. Thus, the methods selected are influenced by the employer's view of what is required to provide a satisfactory basis for decision-making and awareness of the appropriateness of particular techniques to provide what is sought. Before we go on though and examine various selection techniques in detail it is important to recognize two points which complete the context of the selection process.

The first idea is that the selection process is a two-way process. Often the perception is that the organization has all of the power in the process of selection. However, this is not strictly true, even though it may seem that way when you are going through the process. Selection is in fact a two-way process, because people have the option to pull out of the process or turn down a job. For example, a major international hotel company may advertise a graduate trainee scheme and get an initially good response, such that over 300 application packs are sent out to potential employees. Of those only 127 are returned. Following the selection process 23 are offered jobs, 19 accept the offer and only 15 actually start with the company. What this example illustrates is that selection may also be occurring from the employees' point of view, especially when the labour market is buoyant or their particular skills are in demand. The second point is the selection criteria. Selection does not take place in a vacuum, there is also the context of whether the person will fit in with the job requirements, so the person/job interaction is important. As we have already noted there is also the question of whether the person will fit in with the group or work team or department and will they be able to work with colleagues. Finally there is the question of whether the person will fit in with the organizational culture and the way things are done in a particular organization. The ways organizations attempt to find this out are myriad, and we can examine some of the techniques that they utilize in the selection process. The first method, which is the most popular, is that of interviewing.

Although criticized, for example many argue interviewing is not very good in predicting actual performance in the job, the interview is usually the central element of the selection process in many tourism and hospitality organizations. Indeed, the interview is often characterized as being the third part of the 'classic trio' of application forms/CVs, references and interview. In that sense for many people their experience of the selection process will be filling in an application form, including supplying two references and then going along to an interview. As far as selection methods are concerned the interview is seen as the most straightforward and least expensive approach and what most candidates would expect. Employers in the UK often express concern about the fairness of psychometric testing and yet continue to use and seem relatively happy about interviews, despite the potential for bias and discrimination. The interview remains popular then despite poor evidence of validity and the fact that other methods have more predictive power in terms of job performance. Regardless of the latter points the interview remains enduringly popular as a selection tool, with 71 per cent of private service sector organizations using it as part of the selection process (CIPD, 2004). Although increasingly more sophisticated techniques are emerging, such as psychometric testing and assessment centres, they are in addition to rather than replacing the interview.

Review and reflect

Think about an employment interview that you have attended and whether you felt it was a 'good' or 'bad' interview and what influenced your judgement, either positive or negative.

Riley (1996) feels that the interview is sometimes unfairly criticized because too much is expected of it, and it is also done badly. Equally, he also makes the point that it is quick, convenient and when done well, an effective selection method. Riley (1996) describes the interview as 'A conversation with a purpose' and that purpose is to assess four objectives:

1 To decide if an applicant is suitable for a job.
2 To decide if the person will fit into the existing work group or organization as a whole.
3 To attract applicants to the job.
4 To communicate essential expectations and requirements of the job.

Essentially then the interview process is about gathering information which allows for an evaluation of the appropriateness of the individual for a particular job. Interviews can either be one to one, sequential or phone and again is it likely that for the majority of positions in tourism and hospitality the first type will predominate. To have a good interview regardless of which type it is, it is also suggested that certain conditions should be met (Torrington et al., 2005). These conditions are concerned with aspects such as attention being paid to noise levels, avoiding interruptions, lighting, dress and manner of the interviewer, positioning of furniture and attempts to create an informal atmosphere. These aspects are concerned with taking away as much of the anxiety of the situation as is possible to ensure interviewees perform to the best of their ability. Recognizing this point there are several things which should be recognized in interviewing (IRS, 2000, 2006; Torrington et al., 2005: 201–215):

- Interviewers should only talk around 20 per cent of the time, the remaining time should be filled by interviewees.
- Open questions are more useful, so questions starting with what, why, when, which and how can be very useful to elicit information from candidates. For example, instead of asking a question like 'Did you enjoy your last job?' the interviewer could ask 'What did you enjoy about your last job?'
- Interviewers recognize and like candidates from similar backgrounds to them, in terms of things like social class and educational background.
- It is estimated that interviewers often make their decision within the first 4–9 min of an interview.
- Interviewers are vulnerable to prejudices with regard to aspects such as sex, race and age.
- Interviewers are affected by physical cues, for example spectacles equals greater intelligence.
- Interviewers need to be aware of the 'halo' or 'horns' effect, when either in a positive or negative manner, some trait or personal characteristic influences or overwhelms all other thoughts.
- There is a need to recognize the importance of non-verbal communications, or what is commonly described as body language. For example, interviewers and interviewees should aim to be open in their stance and throughout the interview sustain animated, yet controlled body language.

Despite the many criticisms of the interview as a selection method it remains extremely popular. It is worth remembering as well that often many of the criticisms are largely about the interviewers themselves and not the process. As Watson (1994: 211) aphoristically notes, 'employment interviewing is like driving. Most people rate themselves highly; the consequences of mistakes can be serious and when something goes wrong there is a tendency to blame the other party'. Similarly, Taylor (1998: 130) has suggested that, 'individuals will not tolerate criticisms of their performance as lovers, drivers or interviewers, since all such criticisms strike deep into the core of the human ego'. As Riley (1996) argues although interviews are subjective and require judgement so do other management activities and the real problem is not the interview but the way it is carried out. To conclude it is worth noting the view of IRS (2000: 12) who suggest that, 'there are few more complex, intuitive, intelligent or sophisticated information processors than a competent and confident interviewer'. With the interview set to continue as an integral part of the selection process it is important for individual managers to recognize the need to develop their interviewing skills as an essential part of their managerial skillset.

Beyond interviewing there are a number of other techniques which organizations can conceivably utilize in selecting employees. An obvious aspect to this is the use of tests and psychometric testing. In general a test may refer to something like a dexterity test for a manually skilled employee or an attainment test, for example typing skills. More specifically, psychological or psychometric tests are tests which can be systematically scored and administered. These tests are used to measure individual difference in aptitude, ability, intelligence or personality. Organizations are increasingly using these types of tests, particularly for managerial positions (IRS, 2002). That said, psychometric tests are a source of great debate, particularly the use of personality tests. Much of this debate is concerned with whether tests of this nature can genuinely predict future workplace behaviour. Aptitude tests may test specific abilities in relation to verbal, numerical, spatial or mechanical skills to provide an indication of how well applicants will cope with the job. General ability or intelligence tests are used to test how well individuals think on their feet and will be about analytical reasoning and ability to think critically. The most controversial tests are personality tests, which are often described as Orwellian or biased, manipulative and intrusive as they attempt to assess how people will cope with demands, or how people will cope with stress, rigidity or attitudes to authority or creativity.

There are a number of issues which arise in the use of personality tests. For example, there are concerns about how comparable information is. Equally, there are major concerns expressed by bodies such as the Equal Opportunities Commission and Commission for Racial Equality about the gender and ethnic bias in tests (IRS, 2002; LRD, 2003). Lastly, a number of occupational psychologists have expressed concerns at so-called off the shelf models, which may be used in organizations in an inappropriate manner and may be, in the words of one personnel specialist, 'no more reliable than a *Cosmopolitan*-style questionnaire' (cited in Sappal, 2005: 40). In sum, rather like many of the other selection methods described above the proper use of psychometric testing can help organizations make objective and more reliable selection decisions as long as they are used in an appropriate manner and administered properly.

Other methods which could be used by tourism and hospitality organizations include things like presentations. For example, an applicant for a training manager's job is likely to be required to give numerous presentations and the organization may want to assess their presentation skills. Organizations may also use various group methods such as which often involve problem-solving. These activities may involve some element of role playing. By undertaking such problem-solving in small groups applicants will have the opportunity to demonstrate things like ability to work within a group, creativity, interpersonal skills and so on. One final method is the so-called in-tray exercise which will simulate an in-tray of a manager and the applicant has to go through the tray and make decisions on the problems that they find.

Finally we come to the last method of selection, the assessment centre, which ordinarily refers to a process rather than a physical centre. Assessment centres utilize a mix of all of the above techniques and due to the opportunity to use a variety of methods – all of which are potentially assessing different aspects of the candidates – they are often described as the 'Rolls Royce' of selection methods (IRS, 2005). In this sense they are widely considered the most objective and best predictive selection tool for future performance. Equally, though, we should also recognize that assessment centres are also complex to design, time consuming and costly meaning that they are often, though not exclusively, reserved for appointing managerial- or graduate-level staff (and see HRM in practice 5.7).

In order for the overall process of recruitment and selection to be considered successful it is important that it is considered fair by candidates, is cost effective, is user friendly, acceptable to both the organization and the candidates, and is reliable and valid. The reliability of a selection process refers to the extent to which

HRM in practice 5.7   The use of assessment centres by easyJet

IDS (2002) notes that as a major airline easyJet is concerned to get it right in recruiting staff, especially pilots, who are one of the company's most expensive resources in terms of salary, training and career development. The assessment centre for pilots was introduced in 1999 and has now been extended to the recruitment of cabin crew and call centre employees. The assessment centre for pilots is particularly demanding, covering 2 days. Potential pilots face a range of challenges which aim to assess aspects such as team-working, ability to cope under pressure, ability to adhere to standards and technical knowledge. Additionally, Captains who attend the assessment centre are also assessed against leadership and decision-making criteria. Day 1 of the assessment centre is largely concerned with a range of tests and activities such as group work, personality tests and interviews. If the applicants successfully get through day 1 they progress to day 2. The second day is a flight simulation exercise which assesses the candidate's basic handling skills, as well as broader aspects such as flight management and crew resource management skills.

Cabin crew undertake a 1 day assessment in which the company evaluates potential employees against a number of competencies, including conscientiousness, sense of urgency, initiative, empathy, self-confidence and enthusiasm. To assess these aspects candidates have an ice breaker and the 'easyJet test'. The test measures things like mathematical ability, knowledge of easyJet and other factors relevant to the job, for example knowledge of foreign currencies.

a selection technique achieves consistency in what it is measuring over repeated use. Validity can be seen in three different ways. First, face validity on refers to the issue of whether the selection procedure was seen to be valid to candidate and tester. Face validity can be particularly important in terms of organizations being able to attract good candidates in the future. Second, predictive validity is concerned with whether the outcome selection able to predict the ability to perform effectively when in post. Lastly, content validity is about ensuring that the test or exercise in assessing certain skills is actually relevant to the job in question.

Once the selection procedure is over there is also a need for organization to ensure that there is feedback to both the successful and unsuccessful candidates. Organizations should aim therefore to give feedback as soon as possible. It is also important to recognize that for the feedback to be meaningful it should be specific as opposed to being too vague to allow candidates to fully appreciate why they did not get the job. A benefit from giving constructive feedback is that at the end of the recruitment and selection process the organization is still maintaining a positive image. Rather like much of what we have previously discussed the provision of feedback is an essential part of how organizations can portray themselves in a positive manner throughout the recruitment and selection process.

Conclusion

Clearly tourism and hospitality organizations are faced with a mass of possible methods and techniques in which to approach the question of recruitment and selection. As we described in the introduction there is no one best way to recruit and select. Instead, organizations should be prepared to develop a contingent approach. On the one hand this may simply mean employing people on the basis of word of mouth or because they responded to an advert in the window of a restaurant, for example. On the other hand it may be the culmination of a lengthy and expensive selection process, particularly for managerial and graduate-level positions.

In answer to the question of whether there has been significant change in recruitment and selection in the tourism and hospitality industry in recent years the answer would be yes and no. Yes in terms of a shift to organizations looking for the 'right' people in terms of attitudes and behaviour and adoption of more sophisticated techniques, such as psychometric testing. Equally, though, we could also answer no in terms of the widespread use of traditional forms of recruitment and selection, such as interviewing. Moreover evidence continues to suggest that the recruitment and selection process in many tourism and hospitality organizations often remains ad-hoc and informal, especially for operative and front-line positions.

References and further reading

Armstrong, M. (1999) *A Handbook of Human Resource Management Practice*, Kogan Page, 7th edition.

Baker, J. (1999) 'Friday's people', *Caterer and Hotelkeeper*, 28 January, 30–31.

Beal, B. (2004) 'Psychological search for Hilton hotel managers', *Human Resource Management International Digest*, 12(1), 30–32.

Chan, B. and Coleman, M. (2004) 'Skills and competencies needed for the Hong Kong hotel industry: the perspective of the hotel human resources manager', *Journal of Human Resources in Hospitality and Tourism*, 3(1), 3–18.

Chartered Institute of Personnel and Development (2004) *Recruitment, Retention and Turnover: A Survey of the UK and Ireland*, CIPD.

Chartered Institute of Personnel and Development (2006) *The Guide To Recruitment Marketing*, CIPD.

Gallier, E. (2004) 'When the going gets tough', *Hospitality*, June, 35.

Heery, E. and Noon, M. (2001) *A Dictionary of Human Resource Management*, Oxford University Press.

Hills, R. (2004) 'Who would you most like to be stuck in a lift with?', *Sunday Herald*, 23 May, 12.

Income Data Services (2002) *Assessment Centres*, IDS Studies No. 735, September.

Industrial Relations Services (2000) 'The interview: its role in effective selection', *Employee Development Bulletin*, No. 122, February, 12–16.

Industrial Relations Services (2002) 'Psychometrics: the next generation', *IRS Employment Review*, No. 744, 28 January, 36–40.

Industrial Relations Services (2005) 'Centre of attention', *IRS Employment Review*, No. 816, 28 January, 42–48.

Industrial Relations Services (2006) 'In the hiring line: boosting managers' recruitment skills', *IRS Employment Review*, No. 846, 5 May, 42–48.

Jackson, M., Goldthorpe, J. and Mills, C. (2005) 'Education, employers' and class mobility', *Research in Social Stratification and Mobility*, 23, 1–30.

Jameson, S. (2000) 'Recruitment and training in small firms', *Journal of European Industrial Training*, 24(1), 43–49.

Kelliher, C. and Johnson, K. (1997) 'Personnel management in hotels – an update: a move to human resource management?', *Progress in Tourism and Hospitality Research*, 3(4), 321–331.

Labour Research Department (2003) 'Employers warned over bias in aptitude tests', *Labour Research*, December, 25.

Lockyer, C. and Scholarios, D. (2005) 'Selecting hotel staff: why best practice does not always work', *International Journal of Contemporary Hospitality Management*, 16(2), 121–135.

Marchington, M. and Wilkinson, A. (2005) *Human Resource Management at Work: People Management and Development*, CIPD, 3rd edition.

Nickson, D., Warhurst, C., Cullen, A.M. and Watt, A. (2003) 'Bringing in the excluded? Aesthetic labour, skills and training in the new economy', *Journal of Education and Work*, 16(2), 185–203.

Nickson, D., Warhurst, C. and Dutton, E. (2005) 'The importance of attitude and appearance in the service encounter in retail and hospitality', *Managing Service Quality*, 15(2), 195–208.

Nickson, D., Warhurst, C., Witz, A. and Cullen, A.M. (2001) 'The importance of being aesthetic: work, employment and service organization', in A. Sturdy, I. Grugulis and H. Wilmott (eds.) *Customer Service – Empowerment and Entrapment*, Palgrave, 170–190.

Price, L. (1994) 'Poor personnel practice in the hotel and catering industry – does it matter?', *Human Resource Management Journal*, 4(4), 44–62.

Raub, S. and Streit, E. (2006) 'Realistic recruitment: an empirical study of the cruise industry', *International Journal of Contemporary Hospitality Management*, 18(4), 278–289.

Sappal, S. (2005) 'Top scorers', *People Management*, 13 January, 38–40.

Smethurst, S. (2004) 'The allure of online', *People Management*, 29 July, 38–40.

Taylor, S. (1998) *Employee Resourcing*, IPM.

Torrington, D., Hall, L. and Taylor, S. (2005) *Human Resource Management*, Prentice Hall, 6th edition.

Warhurst, C. and Nickson, D. (2001) *Looking Good, Sounding Right*, Industrial Society.

Watson, T. (1994) 'Recruitment and selection', in K. Sisson (ed.) *Personnel Management: A Comprehensive Guide to Theory and Practice in Britain*, Blackwell, 185–220.

Websites

The Advisory, Conciliation and Arbitration Service (ACAS) has a useful publication on recruitment, which is available at http://www.acas.org.uk/index.aspx? articleid=526&detailid=584

The Chartered Institute of Personnel and Development (CIPD) has a very informative factsheet on recruitment which can be found at http://www.cipd.co.uk/subjects/recruitmen/general/recruitmt.htm?IsSrchRes=1

There are a variety of different links covering recruitment and selection at http://www.hrmguide.co.uk/hrm/chap8/ch8-links.html

Chapter 6
Equal opportunities and managing diversity

Chapter objectives

This chapter reviews the nature of equal opportunities and managing diversity in the tourism and hospitality industry. The main objectives of this chapter are to:

- Appreciate the differing aspects which drive approaches to equality and diversity.
- Consider the employment experience of socially defined minority groups.
- Discuss the role of legislation in attempting to create greater equality.
- Recognize the importance of managing diversity as a more business-oriented approach to equality.

Introduction

Increasingly when we look at adverts for positions in tourism and hospitality organizations we will see the statement that the employing organization is 'an equal opportunities employer'. Does this mean then that we are likely to find equality of opportunities within organizations? Have we managed to get rid of discrimination? Have we got a just society where sex, race/ethnicity, disability, age, religion and sexuality are no more important than eye colour? Is there equality in relation to issues such as recruitment and selection, training and development, remuneration, career development and promotion? It is these and other questions which we will consider in this chapter. Specifically we will recognize how certain social groups may experience disadvantage in the workplace, regardless of their qualities and abilities. The manner in which organizations are seeking to address the issue of equal opportunities may vary considerably and here it is helpful to recognize the useful distinction offered by Goss (1994) with regard to the issue of equal opportunities. Goss makes a distinction between what he terms a 'short'-term compliance agenda, and a much more proactive 'long'-term agenda. The former agenda is driven largely by the idea of complying with legislation to avoid penalties. For example, there is no upper limit on compensation awarded by an employment tribunal in discrimination cases and whether an employer unintentionally discriminates is no defence. Clearly, this type of agenda is driven by organizational self-interest. In contrast, the long-term agenda is premised on notions of efficient management of human resources, creating a good organizational image, managing diversity and social justice, though some of these aspects may, in reality, also be in the organization's self-interest. In many respects then we can think of equality and diversity in terms of:

- *Legal aspects*: failure to comply with legislation in this area can mean employers facing unwelcome publicity and potentially large payouts as a result of employment tribunal decisions.
- *Ethical aspects*: it is ethically and morally right for organizations to seek to offer equality of opportunity to all.
- *Business aspects*: it makes good business sense to encourage equality and diversity to ensure the organization draws on the widest possible labour market to make sure that they are maximizing the best use of all available resources. Equality also makes good business sense in terms of potentially widening the customer base and also portraying a positive company image.

Of course, in reality, the approach to equality and diversity adopted by organizations may well be informed by all of these aspects. Increasingly though within a more strategic HRM approach it is suggested that many organizations are recognizing the business case for equality and diversity.

Stredwick (2005) suggests that support for the business case is strengthened by recognizing three key issues. First, is the need to recognize demographic changes. With a declining birth rate traditional sources of labour (young, white, qualified and full-time) are in decline so organizations need to think about finding alternative sources of labour. Second, the changing nature of the workplace and specifically the shift from manufacturing to service employment means more and more women are entering the labour market. Consequently organizations have to respond to this change by ensuring they encourage the best applicants through enhanced career opportunities and a supportive environment for all. Lastly, with the shift to a service economy there is now a greater emphasis on customer relations, especially in an ever more competitive environment. By pursuing active approaches to equality and diversity management organizations not only offer opportunity to all segments of the labour market, but may also broaden their customer base by demonstrating such a commitment. That said, discrimination still remains a very real issue within society generally and workplaces specifically, so the chapter will now move on to consider steps which may be taken to eradicate discrimination in all its forms.

The employment experience of socially defined minority groups

A good starting point to further consider the issue of equal opportunities is to recognize some of the barriers that may effect the employment of certain groups of workers, initially considering women, black and minority ethnic people, people with disabilities and older people.

Women

Across the economy as a whole, women now make up 46 per cent of the workforce, though nearly half of all women working work part-time (EOC, 2005). Despite making up nearly half of the workforce women still remain under-represented in senior and middle management positions. For example, across the economy as a whole although there is now greater representation of women in the boardroom of Britain's leading companies, women still remain 'woefully under-represented' according to Cranfield University's annual survey of women in senior management positions (Cranfield University, 2004). There is also continuing disparity in women's pay, relative to men, with women earning around 82p for every £1 earned by men (EOC, 2005).

These disparities in the economy as a whole are also seen in the tourism and hospitality industry. Although women account for 70 per cent of employees, there are no female chief executives in the FTSE 350 travel, leisure and tourism companies (Rossiter, 2005). Indeed, more generally across Europe travel and leisure has the lowest level of boardroom representation with no representation at all compared to sectors like household goods and services where 18.9 per cent of boards are made up by women (EPWN, 2006). Moreover although the number of women managers in tourism and hospitality is significantly higher than many other industries, it still remains disproportionately low given the overall level of female representation within the workforce (Mayling, 2003). Women may also face particular barriers in the workplace in the tourism and hospitality industry, including (HCIMA, 1999):

- Lack of childcare provision.
- Difficulties of the dual role in maintaining a management career and caring for children and other dependents.
- Lack of flexible, part-time opportunities at higher levels in the industry.
- The macho atmosphere in certain workplaces, such as the kitchen.
- Sexism and sexist attitudes.
- Poor career planning.
- Shortage of positive female role models.

There are a number of ways in which organizations can begin to address some of these issues and HRM in practice 6.1 presents an example of a proactive response to encouraging women's employment.

Black and minority ethnic people

A recent report from the Cabinet Office (2003) noted that members of ethnic minorities are more than twice as likely to be unemployed even when age, sex and

HRM in practice 6.1   Opportunity Now: A proactive response to gender equality

Opportunity Now was originally set up as Opportunity 2000 in October 1991. Its aim was to increase the quality and quantity of women's participation in the workforce. Membership is open to any organization, large or small and by June 2005 over 350 organizations, including British Airways and Jurys Inn's, had signed up. Those organizations joining Opportunity Now commit themselves to overcoming the barriers to recruitment, retention and development of women. Opportunity Now provides advice to employers and shares information on best practice in areas such as developing flexible working arrangements, improving childcare, career break options and training and education to increase women's opportunity at work. To further help organizations Opportunity Now also runs a benchmarking exercise on gender equality, which helps employers to chart progress whilst at the same time providing a checklist for organizational change.

Derived from IDS (2003); Opportunity Now (2005).

level of qualifications are taken into account. Significantly the same report also notes how this disparity in employment has changed little over the last 18 years. This lack of economic activity is particularly pronounced in men from ethnic backgrounds aged 16–24 years. On the question of the progression of black and minority ethnic workers to middle and senior management positions a recent report by the Runnymede Trust (2000) found that only 1 per cent of senior managers and 3 per cent of junior managers were from an ethnic minority, despite the fact that ethnic minorities make up 8 per cent of the population as a whole. Similarly, a recent report from Cranfield University found that just 2.3 per cent of board members in the largest companies listed on the London Stock Exchange came from ethnic minority backgrounds (Smith, 2005). When ethnic minority employees are employed it is noteworthy that they tend to be concentrated in terms of occupational segregation, with a large number employed in the hospitality sub-sector in particular. For example, LRD (2005) notes that 52 per cent of Bangladeshi workers work in the restaurant industry compared with only 1 per cent of white males. In addition, LRD (2005) also notes a disparity in pay, with this 'black pay gap' meaning in some instances that workers from some communities earn an average of £7000 less than white workers.

As we have already noted the black and minority ethnic communities make up around 8 per cent of the UK's population and significantly will account for half the growth of the working age population in the decade 1999–2009 (LRD, 2005). Consequently, there is a need for organizations to be proactive in their attempts to promote racial equality. IDS (2001) suggest a number of practical steps which can be taken by organizations, including:

- Ensuring fair recruitment practices, such as recruitment schemes targeted at ethnic minority employees and targeted advertising to encourage more applicants from under-represented groups.
- Using images of ethnic minority employees in publicity and advertising material.
- Developing links with ethnic minority communities (often as a way of attracting new employees).
- Undertaking ethnic monitoring.
- Ensuring HR policies are in place to help foster and protect a diverse work environment (e.g. dignity at work and harassment policies).
- Accommodating different religious beliefs in the multicultural workforce.
- Introducing diversity awareness training (particularly for managers).
- Setting up internal networks for ethnic minority employees.
- Taking positive action on training and development.

There has also been a similar type of initiative for black minority ethnic employees as Opportunity Now. Launched in October 1995, Race for Opportunity (RfO) is a business-led initiative organized by Business in the Community and aims to put race and diversity issues higher up the business agenda, by investing in the UK's ethnic communities. RfO publishes an annual benchmarking report which assesses organizations in five key 'impact' areas, including leadership, community involvement and supplier diversity (IDS, 2006).

Disabled employees

Often our perception is that disability is likely to mean that a person is in a wheelchair or visibly impaired. However, of the 8.7 million adults who are registered disabled only 600,000 are in a wheelchair (Anon, 2004). Moreover 2.4 million are of working age and over 70 per cent of this figure are economically active or looking for work. In reality this means that a significant number of disabled people are thought to want to work. It is also instructive to note that 70 per cent of disabled people who are economically active or looking for work became disabled while in work (LRD, 2000). Thus there would seem a strong moral argument that employers should aim to help disabled people back into the labour market. In a similar vein to Opportunity Now and RfO there is also an attempt to be positive about disabled workers with the 'two-ticks' scheme. Under this scheme any employers using the two-ticks must (LRD, 2003):

- Interview all applicants with a disability that meets the minimum for a job vacancy.
- Ask disabled employees at least once a year what can be done to ensure they can develop and use their abilities at work.
- Make every effort when employees become disabled to ensure they stay in employment.
- Take action to ensure that key employees are aware of the needs of disabled people.
- Each year review achievements towards making the workplace welcoming and accessible for disabled people, plan ways to improve and let all employees and customers know about this progress and future plans.

Whilst the two-ticks campaign is important to changing workplaces practices, campaigners for the disabled are also attempting to shift perceptions about disability (and see HRM in practice 6.2).

HRM in practice 6.2   Perceptions of disability

A letter to *People Management* in 1997 from a representative of Capability Scotland noted how language used to describe disability often shapes attitudes and perceptions. The author of the letter notes how often people with disabilities are described as 'suffering' from the disability, which can lead to misconceptions such as the amount of time they are likely to take off work. The letter also suggests preferred terminology to ensure that people are aware of using pejorative terms like: the disabled, normal, mentally retarded and confined to a wheelchair. The preferred terms are people with disabilities, able-bodied, learning difficulties and wheelchair users.

Source: Bald (1997).

Older workers

Hope (2005) reports that the National Audit Office estimated that cost of stereotyping on the basis of age costs the UK economy £31 billion a year in lost contributions. For older workers it can be especially difficult to gain a new job, especially once they are over 45 years. Arkin (2005: 32) notes how some of the 'ridiculous comments' about older workers have the ring of comments which were often made 30 years ago with regard to sex and race discrimination. For example, he notes that prior to the introduction of the Race Relations Act (RRA) in the 1970s some people argued that employing someone from an ethnic minority in a shop would put customers off. Certainly such attitudes have been prevalent in the tourism and hospitality industry, with one well known restaurateur once famously suggesting that:

I fail to understand why employers ought not to be able to discriminate about potential employees on the basis of age, at least for those who are in contact with the public. We are in a business where image counts as much as content. Of course, it is unfair to turn down older people with the required technical skills to do the job, but so what? It is not a perfect world (Gottlieb, 1992: 20).

Review and reflect

To what extent do you agree with Gottlieb's sentiments and why?

Work by Qu and Cheng (1996) who surveyed 26 hotels in Hong Kong and Magd (2003) who interviewed 21 managing directors in small and medium sized hospitality enterprises in the UK is useful to appreciate how older workers tend to be perceived within tourism and hospitality. From a positive point of view the research suggests that employers tend to see older workers as having: low absenteeism, fewer accidents, low turnover rate, being motivated, hard working and diligent, having a sense of responsibility, good communication skills and credibility with customers. On the other hand, the research also revealed that older workers were perceived as inflexible and reluctant to change, have low productivity, find it hard to adapt to new technology and have difficulties in keeping up with the speed of work. Whilst most age-related discrimination is directed towards older workers, younger workers too can be affected. Smethurst (2004) reports research from the

CIPD which notes that the optimum age in the workplace to be judged as neither too old or too young is 35–40 years. For those under 35, 8 per cent of people had reported being discriminated against for being too young.

The legislative response

The above discussion gives us a sense of some of the issues affecting certain groups of employees. We can now move on to consider how these have been addressed, beginning with the emergence of equal opportunities legislation. There have been a number of laws introduced in the UK which have sought to address the problems of discrimination generally and specifically to reduce such discrimination in the labour market and the workplace.

Review and reflect

How successful is legislation likely to be in addressing equality issues?

Whilst legislation has now existed for over 30 years we should recognize that there is much debate about whether the legislation has been successful, and whether it has simply been embraced as rhetoric but without much success in implementation. For example, many believe that legislation cannot by itself eradicate a whole range of attitudes, which may encourage discriminating behaviour. On the other hand, whilst recognizing that the law cannot change attitudes overnight, it can, and does, effect change slowly. Some people would argue that it has in fact been too slow and its effects have been patchy. In that sense the law requires an end to discrimination; it does not actually require that employers do anything to promote equality. Related to this point there is also the distinction made by many commentators about the differences between the letter and spirit of the law. The former encourages a narrow interpretation of law, which may not be in the best interests of encouraging a more proactive approach to equality and diversity. The latter is potentially more flexible in offering the scope for decisions which encourage greater equality.

Having briefly contextualized the emergence of the legislative agenda we can now go on and examine the actual provisions and what they mean for organizations, starting with Table 6.1, which summarizes the range of anti-discriminatory legislation.

Table 6.1 Anti-discriminatory legislation

Act	Areas covered
Sex Discrimination Act 1975	Sex and marital status (the latter referring specifically to persons who are married)
Sex Discrimination (Gender Reassignment) Regulations 1999	Persons who intend to undertake a sex change, are currently in the process of doing so or have completed treatment
Employment Equality (Sex Discrimination) Regulations 2005	Introduced a new definition of indirect discrimination and added specific definitions covering discrimination on grounds of harassment
Race Relations Act 1976	Race, colour nationality, national or ethnic origin
Race Relations (Amendment) Act 2000	The duty of public authorities to take positive action to promote good race relations
Disability Discrimination Act 1995	Disabled persons
Disability Discrimination Act (Amendment) Regulations 2003	Removal of the exemption for employers of fewer than 15 people; shift in the burden of proof
Disability Discrimination Act 2005	Those with progressive conditions such as HIV and cancer will be treated as disabled from the point of diagnosis. Those with mental illness are no longer required to have their illness clinically recognized
Employment Equality (Sexual Orientation) Regulations 2003	Orientation towards persons of the same sex, of the opposite sex, of both the same sex and the opposite sex
Employment Equality (Religion or Belief) Regulations 2003	Religion or similar beliefs
Rehabilitation of Offenders Act 1974	Persons with 'spent' convictions
Human Rights Act 1998	Prohibition of forced labour and slavery; right to respect for private and family life (*inter alia*)

Derived from LRD (2006).

The Sex Discrimination Act (SDA) and RRA are particularly important in denoting the first systematic attempt to address discrimination. Both acts refer to the idea of direct and indirect discrimination. Direct discrimination is where employees of a particular sex, race or ethnic group are treated less favourably than other employees. For example, a policy to only recruit men to management posts. Indirect discrimination is where a particular requirement apparently treats everyone equally but has a disproportionate effect on a particular group and the requirement cannot be shown to be justified. For example, requiring a kitchen porter to speak fluent English, which is not a necessary requirement for the job. At present there are three government sponsored bodies which are responsible for promoting equality. With regard to sex and race the commissions are the Equal Opportunities Commission (EOC) and the Commission for Racial Equality (CRE), which were established in 1975 and 1976, respectively. The EOC and CRE are responsible for working towards eliminating discrimination, promoting equality of opportunity and reviewing how the law works. They also issues codes of practice, undertake formal investigations where there are allegations of discrimination and can, in certain circumstances, support individual legal claims. With regard to disability, as of April 2000 the Disability Rights Commission (DRC) has taken on the same role as the CRE and the EOC (and see the later discussion of the DDA).

Both the SDA and RRA are concerned with prohibiting discrimination in all areas of employment. For example, during the recruitment and selection process organizations should unsure that the right message is conveyed in recruitment advertisements, which as we noted in Chapter 5, should be carefully worded so that there is no indication that people of some backgrounds are preferred to others. Equally, in the selection procedure organizations should be wary of drawing up person specifications that are unjustifiably demanding. As we noted there is also a need to consider whether certain selection tests may discriminate against people from minority backgrounds. Only the EOC or the CRE can instigate proceedings in relation to advertising, but individuals can pursue claims via the employment tribunal system in all other aspects of employment. The legislative threat centres on possible adverse publicity to the organization as well as the direct and indirect costs of tribunal claims or commission investigation. Although in reality a relatively small number of cases actually end up being heard in an employment tribunal. For example, ACAS (2006) notes that it received 9942 cases with regard to either sex or race discrimination. Of these cases, 3283 were settled before the tribunal, 4267 were withdrawn, 1168 were either struck out by the tribunal or out of scope,

HRM in practice 6.3   Jobs for the girls

Legislation was introduced in Norway in 2002 to ensure at least 40 per cent of boardroom seats are reserved for women (Osborn, 2002). The decree initially affected state owned firms, but by 2005 all public companies had to enforce the quota. Whilst equality groups and trade unions were supportive of the move, employers feared that the initiative would make Norway uncompetitive and discourage foreign firms from investing in the country (Walsh, 2004). Indeed, Scandinavian countries generally are trail blazers in increasing the representation of women on boards. By 2006 Norway had the highest percentage of women at boardroom level at 28 per cent. Sweden had 22 per cent, Finland 20 per cent and Denmark 17.9 per cent (EPWN, 2006). These figures can be compared to other selected European countries such as the UK which had 11.4 per cent, Germany 7.2 per cent, Italy 1.9 per cent and Portugal where there are no women at boardroom level (EPWN, 2006).

leaving only 1224 cases ultimately reaching the tribunal to be heard. Nevertheless cases which are concerned with discrimination do not carry an upper limit for compensation, so organizations should aim to avoid such cases, which may prove to be very costly.

Two other points are also important to note with regard to the SDA and RRA. The first is positive action. Positive action may be confused with what is often termed positive or reverse discrimination, or what in the US is known as affirmative action. Positive discrimination seeks to redress previous inequality by giving priority to certain groups in the labour market. For example, an organization appointing a female candidate to a managerial position primarily because of her gender, rather than her managerial skills. Currently such an approach is illegal in the UK, but such approaches have been used in the US and other countries (and see HRM in practice 6.3).

Review and reflect

Outline arguments for and against positive discrimination.

Whilst positive discrimination is unlawful in the UK, positive action is not. Positive action may encompass a range of policy initiatives which aim to promote equality of opportunity through the provision of facilities, procedures or actions that redress disadvantage suffered by particular groups in the labour market or organization. For example, under positive action both the SDA and RRA make it lawful to encourage and provide training for members of one sex or racial group who have been under-represented in particular work in the previous 12 months. In addition advertisements can explicitly encourage applications from one sex or racial group if that group is under-represented within the organization, though there are no guarantees that they will get the job.

One final point when we are talking about sex or race discrimination is that of genuine occupational grounds, where discrimination is permitted due to sex or race being specified as a *Genuine Occupational Qualification (GOQ)*, which are outlined in sections 7(2) of the SDA and 5(2) of the RRA. A GOQ is likely to be based on things such as authenticity, decency, privacy and the delivery of personal welfare services. For example, a stylish Italian bistro may seek to retain its authenticity by employing only Italian staff. As we noted above the SDA and RRA are particularly important in being the first attempt to establish a legislative framework and also with regard to establishing many of the mechanisms which are now being incorporated in more recent legislative intervention, such as the DDA.

The DDA is similar to the SDA and RRA, though it offers protection only against direct discrimination. The DDA offers a broad definition of disability, with section 1 of the DDA talking of any, 'Physical or mental impairment which has a substantial and long-term adverse effect on his (or her) ability to carry out normal day-to-day activities'. Indeed, LRD (1999) in reviewing a number of employment tribunal decisions note that there is no definitive list of what amounts to psychical or mental impairment and employment tribunals are left to decide what may be considered a disability (and see HRM in practice 6.4).

The DDA initially made it unlawful for any company which had more than 15 employees to discriminate against employees, job applicants and contractors who are disabled. Recent changes though now mean that the provisions of the DDA now extend to all employers, regardless of size. Within tourism and hospitality there are many instances where managers may have to consider their response to potentially sensitive situations under the aegis of the DDA (and see HRM in practice 6.5).

To a large extent the approach to the scenarios outlined in HRM in practice 6.5 will be dictated by the notion of 'reasonable adjustments'. As we noted above although the DDA provides protection against direct discrimination with regard to indirect discrimination employers may set a requirement for use in recruitment

HRM in practice 6.4   Conditions amounting to physical or mental impairment

Employment tribunals have taken a wide view of disability and have ruled that all the conditions below *may* amount to a physical or mental impairment.

Asthma	Bipolar affective disorder
Migraines	Cerebral palsy
Photosensitive epilepsy	Chronic fatigue syndrome
Visual impairment	Colitis
Injuries affecting mobility	Congenital myotonic dystrophy
Abdominal pain	Deafness
Depression	Emphysema
Multiple sclerosis	Diabetes
Post-traumatic stress disorder	

Whilst these conditions have all been accepted as a disability in tribunal decisions they should still not be considered as a wholly definitive list. Other tribunals may not consider them as a disability due to differing circumstances with the individual bringing the case. More recently under the aegis of the DDA, HIV/AIDS, as well as mental illness and progressive conditions such as cancer have all been formally designated as being part of the act. Employees will be deemed disabled as soon as these latter conditions are diagnosed.

Derived from LRD (1999); LRD (2006).

HRM in practice 6.5   An appropriate response to disability?

As a manager think about how you might respond to the following scenarios.

An applicant for a waiting job, who otherwise impresses in the interview, is visually impaired. There may be some concerns about them tripping over furniture, reading blackboard menus to customers or dropping plates on laps and so on.

An applicant for a front line position in a travel agency is facially disfigured and you are concerned about whether their appearance may put off customers.

An applicant for a position as chef who is wheelchair bound.

or promotion processes which might be held to discriminate against people with disabilities. In such cases less favourable treatment can only be justified where it is relevant to the circumstances of the individual case and where the reason for the treatment is felt to be substantial. This is where the notion of reasonable adjustments becomes important. Employers have to consider whether the less favourable treatment can be overcome by reasonable adjustments to premises or the employment arrangements. For example, IRS (2003) notes some of the common adjustments made by employers in response to the DDA, including:

- Allowing absence for rehabilitation and treatment.
- Altering a person's working hours.
- Acquiring or modifying equipment.
- Adjusting premises.
- Transferring a person to another job.
- Assigning a person to other work.
- Providing a reader and interpreter.
- Providing support workers.
- Modifying instruction manuals.

With regard to the scenarios above, in the case of the chef health and safety considerations would mean that the use of a wheelchair within the kitchen would be impractical and it would be considered unreasonable to make significant adjustments to the premises. On the other hand, visual impairment is likely to require a much more proactive response from tourism and hospitality employers (and see HRM in practice 6.6).

A further facet of the DDA which is particularly apposite for tourism and hospitality organizations is the need to ensure that employees are aware of the needs of disabled customers. For example, organizations may develop disability awareness training in-house or use commercially available options such as IndividuALL's self-learning CD-Rom, Welcoming Disabled Guests. IndividuaALL is part of Tourism for All UK, a national registered charity which aims to provide advice and support to disabled people and tourism providers to enhance the accessibility of tourism provision to the disabled.

As can be seen in Table 6.1 it is only recently that discrimination based on sexual orientation and religion have become explicitly prohibited. There are approximately 1.3 to 1.9 gay and lesbian workers in the UK (LRD, 2003a) and the perception is

HRM in practice 6.6 Responding to the needs of visually impaired employees

Wendy Kerner is visually impaired being completely blind in one eye and having little vision in the other. She works as a purchase ledger clerk at the 37-bedroom Lauriston Hotel in Weston-super-Mare. Her main responsibilities are inputting petty cash, cheques and invoices into the hotel account's system and doing the weekly cheque run for the hotel's suppliers. Additionally, she also maintains the database of suppliers details and occasionally helps out in reception if the hotel is busy. In order to support her at work the hotel secured funding from the Government's Access to Work programme to purchase a range of equipment. The equipment included technology to enable her to print her work in Braille and software that enlarges print and speak while Kerner types. Working practices at reception were also altered slightly to move from a handwritten list of petty cash transactions to printing a Braille version which Kerner can read.

Source: Guild (2002).

that there is a higher proportion of gay and lesbian employees within hospitality and tourism. That said, there has been little research that has explicitly addressed the opportunities and experiences of gay men and lesbians within tourism and hospitality organizations. More generally, research has pointed to the discrimination faced by gay and lesbian employees. For example, LRD (2000a) reports a survey by the TUC which found that 44 per cent of gay or lesbian employees had suffered some form of discriminatory treatment, most commonly name calling and homophobic abuse, but in some cases dismissal. Even with the introduction of legislation in 2003 there still seems to be evidence of continuing discrimination. For example, recent research suggests that nearly half of gay men and lesbian women still fear discrimination if they 'come out' at work (Johnston, 2006). As with much of the other areas of legislation discussed in this chapter the key is for organizations to think about developing appropriate policies and procedures to ensure compliance with the legislation. With regard to sexual orientation Ward (2003) notes how research has highlighted the positive effects on motivation and job satisfaction for lesbian and gay employees who feel able to 'come out' in the workplace. To help gay and lesbian employees to 'come out' the same author outlines a series of appropriate policy responses.

- Understand the effects of the closet – being gay and lesbian and not feeling that the workplace is sufficiently supportive to allow them to come out will often have a negative impact on the individual and their standard of work.
- Recognize the benefits of 'coming out' – many gay and lesbian employees describe coming out as the most significant event of their working life, often leading to increased job satisfaction, motivation and enhanced commitment to the organization.
- Know your own people – action may be needed to ensure that the organization is one where staff feel safe to come out. This may require the organization to explore their employees' attitudes to sexual orientation to determine the appropriate policy responses.
- Raise awareness – as with other forms of discrimination, discriminatory behaviour can often be unwitting. There may be a need to raise awareness of the issues surrounding sexual orientation through things like discussion groups.
- Support a lesbian and gay network – 'invisibility' at work is often an issue for lesbians and gay men and an employee network can be useful to provide support and also raise the profile of sexual minorities with colleagues.
- Ensure support from top management – it is important to have a senior manager, who is not necessarily gay themselves, to act as a diversity champion for sexual minorities in the workplace.
- Create a culture where people can come out – much of the above suggests means by which this can be done. There is also a need to train managers to make the right decisions in support of such a culture.

Cooper (2003) reports evidence from 20 organizations in terms of their response to the new regulations on religious discrimination. Only seven of the organizations were conducting a thorough review of policies and making changes to practices, whilst the remaining 13 organizations were simply adding the word 'religion' to their discrimination policies. The same author cites several legal experts who suggest that there is a need for organizations to be proactive in their interpretation of the legislation. One legal expert is quoted in Cooper as suggesting that, 'religion is key to way some people identify themselves – it's more important than ethnicity or nationality – and they rightly expect companies to accommodate their religious needs and protect them from discrimination' (p. 27). Advice from the Department of Trade of Industry and Advisory Conciliation and Arbitration Service points to a number of areas that organizations should be considering with regard to religious

HRM in practice 6.7   British Airways responding to the legislation on religious discrimination

RfO (2004) reports how, in response to the new regulations prohibiting discrimination on religious grounds, British Airways consulted with their employees via a series of focus groups and meetings. The intent of the meetings was to ensure that the needs of different groups of employees were managed to conform to the legislation. In discussing the issues with employees some of the key issues raised were: availability of prayer rooms, uniform and dress code regulations, labelling of food and time off for praying and religious festivals. Consideration of these topics was then used to develop a frequently asked question section on the British Airways staff website.

discrimination. For example, they caution against word of mouth recruitment and also suggest employers should examine areas such as the provision of prayer room facilities and the possibility of flexible work to accommodate religious holidays (and see HRM in practice 6.7).

A further piece of legislation which is set to have a significant impact on human resource policies is that concerned with age. On its election in 1997 the Labour Government promised legislation to prohibit age discrimination, a situation that already existed in a number of other countries including large parts of Europe and the US. However, the Government eventually opted for a non-statutory code of conduct called *Age Diversity in Employment*. As a voluntary code, however, the code of conduct lacked teeth. Consequently, when in 2000 the UK decided to support the EU directive on equal treatment, the Government pledged to introduce legislation outlawing age discrimination by October 2006.

In common with the other areas covered by legislation the new legislation on age will aim to ensure that workers are not discriminated against in areas such as recruitment and selection, promotion and the provision of training. IRS (2004) note the unpreparedness of many employers for the age discrimination legislation noting, amongst other things, that one in three employers are unaware that the legislation will take effect in the near future. Indeed, in a more recent overview of the new legislation IRS (2006a, b, c) recognize that experience in other countries suggests that the introduction of the legislation is likely to see a significant number of claims for age discrimination. If organizations wish to avoid such a situation they should aim to develop a more proactive approach to the introduction of the legislation. For example they could become an Age Positive Employer Champion. Such employers are committed to tackling age discrimination in their own workplace and taking practical steps to change their employment practices. In addition, further steps to achieving an age-diverse workforce include (IRS, 2004: 48):

- Reviewing the employment cycle from recruitment to retirement in order to eradicate any age bias, encompassing areas such as recruitment advertising.
- Clearly communicate with suppliers expectations about creating an age-diverse workforce.
- Use the Age Positive logo on recruitment adverts.
- Remove any reference to date of birth from all application forms.
- Proactively appeal to older workers through recruitment advertising.
- Champion age diversity at a senior level within the business.
- Use external and internal PR to share good practice – feature employees as age-positive role modes.
- Adopt a flexible approach to recruitment.

Lastly, there is the Rehabilitation of Offenders Act 1974. The CIPD (2006) suggests that one fifth of the working population has a criminal record, with Drury (2001) recognizing that for men under 35 the figure is one in three. Although some employers may be wary of employing somebody with a criminal record it is important to recognize that the Act enables offenders who received less than a custodial sentence of up to two and a half years to be rehabilitated, and their convictions to be 'spent'. This means that after a certain amount of time potential employees are able to answer no to the question of whether they have got a criminal record or not. The length of time is dependent on the sentence received. It is important to recognize that it is illegal for an employer to discriminate on the basis of a spent conviction. Gledhill (2002) suggests that the hospitality industry, in particular, should look seriously to employing ex-offenders to address labour shortages and recruitment problems. He reports a Prison Service chef training scheme which aims to train inmates to National Vocational Qualification (NVQ) level 2 in food hygiene and food handling. Prisoners on the scheme cook for fellow inmates so get used to the pressure of working to deadlines and a number of ex-offenders were successful in gaining jobs on release.

One final point to note before the chapter moves on to consider managing diversity is the issue of a single equalities body. As we have previously recognized the EOC, CRE and DRC are responsible for the broad areas of sex, race/ethnicity and disability. Currently there are no bodies that are responsible for sexual orientation and religion. In response to this situation, and the emergence of age legislation in October 2006, the UK Government has now established a single equalities body. This new body will be known as The Commission for Equality and Human Rights (CEHR) and came into being with The Equality Act 2006. In October 2007 CEHR will merge the functions of the EOC and DRC, as well as taking responsibility for sexual orientation, religion and age. Surprisingly, the CRE will not immediately become part of the new organization, but at the time of writing it is envisaged that it will join by 2009.

Managing diversity

In reviewing the debate about equal opportunities, what we have been largely talking about to date is the meeting of statutory requirements to offer equal opportunities to all in the organization, or those who will potentially join the organization. In many respects this can be considered the short-term agenda as outlined by Goss (1994), where the emphasis is on meeting legal obligations to ensure separate groups are not discriminated against in the workplace. A longer-term agenda that aims to move away from such a narrow approach is suggested by the notion of managing diversity.

Managing diversity is also particularly important given that it would be remiss to imagine women or ethnic minorities or people with disabilities as a homogenous group. For example, women are divided by class, ethnicity, age and occupational status. Similarly, ethnic minorities are far from homogenous, for example there may be major differences in the opportunities and employment experience between Asian employees and black African employees. In that sense resistance to equal opportunities policies may not come simply from white, non-disadvantaged men. Opposition to equal opportunities may also be seen from particular groups in society due to the fear of backlash, or being seen to have achieved a position based on grounds other than merit. Of course, the legislative agenda does not necessarily seek to create such perceptions or stereotypes, for example it does not support positive discrimination. Nevertheless, the perception that equal opportunities is primarily driven by a defensive legislative agenda has led to the emergence of managing diversity as a potentially more strategic and business-oriented approach to engendering equality of opportunity. To consider this point we should consider three questions in relation to managing diversity, these being:

1 What is managing diversity?
2 How are equal opportunities moved on by managing diversity?
3 What action does managing diversity require?

In answer to the first question, Ellis and Sonnenfield (1994: 82) define managing diversity as, 'the challenge of meeting the needs of a culturally diverse workforce and of sensitizing workers and managers to differences associated with gender, race, age and nationality in an attempt to maximize the potential productivity of all employees'. In a similar vein, Kandola and Fullerton (1998: 8) suggest that:

> The basic concept of managing diversity accepts that the workforce consists of a diverse population of people. The diversity consists of visible and non-visible differences which include factors, such as sex, age, background, race, disability, personality and workstyle. It is founded on the premise that harnessing these differences will create a productive environment in which everybody feels valued, where their talents are being fully utilized and in which organizational goals are met.

With regard to the second question, Table 6.2 illustrates the manner in which the managing diversity and equal opportunities are suggested as being different.

So the question we can ask ourselves is to what extent are organizations moving to become diverse and multicultural and if not how can organizations address this issue. At one level many would argue that the tourism and hospitality industry is, in all respects, be it unit, locality, clientele or labour market, possibly the most international of industries. Baum (1996: A77), for example, notes how:

> Tourism … is almost unique in providing multicultural interface at a variety of levels and in many situations, simultaneously. It is an everyday experience for a Japanese visitor to London to be checked into a hotel by an Australian receptionist, supervised by an English front office manager of Afro-Caribbean origin, in a hotel owned by Middle Eastern financial interests, managed by an American hotel multinational who have appointed an Italian as general manager to the property.

Table 6.2 Differences between managing diversity and equal opportunities

Managing diversity	Equal opportunities
• Ensures all employees maximize their potential and their contribution to the organization	• Concentration on issues of discrimination
• Embraces a broad range of people; no one is excluded	• Perceived as an issue for certain groups in the labour market such as women, ethnic minorities and people with disabilities
• Concentration on issues of movement within an organization, the culture of the organization, and meeting business objectives	• Less of an emphasis on culture change and the meeting of business objectives, premised more on moral and ethical issues
• Is the concern of all employees, especially managers	• Seen as an issue to do with human resource practitioners
• Does not rely on positive action/affirmative action	• Relies on positive action

Source: This material is taken from *Diversity in Action: Managing the Mosaic* by Kandola, R. and Fullerton, J., 2nd edition (1998), with the permission of the publisher, the Chartered Institute of Personnel and Development, London.

However, whilst Baum's quote is useful in pointing to the multicultural nature of tourism and hospitality we should also recognize that multiculturalism of this nature does not axiomatically equate to genuine opportunity for all in tourism and hospitality organizations. For example, research that has been conducted in the US points to some limited success in diversity programmes. Wilborn and Weaver (2002) investigated diversity management training initiatives (DMTIs) by surveying 139 managers in a range of lodging properties. The managers were questioned about a variety of DMTIs including aspects such as diversity awareness training for managers, cross race/gender training teams, networking groups and minority internships. Nearly half the managers surveyed felt that their organization offered a good diversity management training programme. Significantly, managers who were exposed to DMTIs had more positive feelings towards such initiatives in terms of recognizing their importance towards organizational success. In a similar vein, Speizer (2004) notes the success of Denny's restaurant chain from being seen as one of the most racist companies in America to being number one on *Fortune* magazine's list of 50 best companies in America for minorities. To address the problem of racism, Speizer reports how Denny's appointed the first diversity officer to report directly to the CEO. With a budget of over $1 million dollars a year the diversity officer was able to develop a series of initiatives. For example, they hired over 100 diversity trainers and insisted that all employees – from senior executives to dishwashers – attend diversity awareness classes. Denny's also sought to encourage more customers from ethnic minority groups and also diversified their suppliers going from having no minority suppliers or contractors to spending over $616 million with minority suppliers between 1995–2000. On the other hand research undertaken by Groeschl and Doherty (1999) on a number of hotels in San Francisco points to a much more reactive approach, what they term a 'reactive diversification strategy'. Such an approach is largely concerned with complying with legislation in areas like affirmative action and training in equal opportunities areas such as the American Disability Act. As they note though, 'the hotels have not been able, so far, to make the next step from tolerating diversity to valuing it' (p. 266).

Clearly, then, managing diversity is something that organizations have to think about in a proactive manner. There are no easy prescriptions as to how this approach can be achieved, though Kandola and Fullerton (1998) offer what they consider to be an integrated and coherent model of the diversity-oriented organization. They also suggest this model can be used as a benchmark to drive organizational initiatives and strategy. The idea of such an organization is underpinned by the notion of the creation of a *mosaic* to encourage diversity in organizations:

Missions and values
Objectives and fair processes
Skilled workforce: aware and fair
Active flexibility
Individual focus
Culture that empowers

These aspects are now briefly discussed.

Diversity-oriented organizations will seek to develop a strong and positive mission and core values statement, which recognizes that managing diversity is an important long-term business objective for the organization. In support of the mission and vision all processes and systems in organizations (e.g. recruitment, selection, performance appraisals, promotion decisions and so on) need to be audited and re-audited to ensure that no one group predominates. With regard to the skilled workforce Kandola and Fullerton note the importance of ensuring that the entire workforce is aware of and guided by the principles of managing diversity. By understanding why diversity is important employees can act in a manner which ensures their biases and prejudices do not influence the way they make decisions and work with colleagues. Such an approach may also require a pro-active approach to equipping managers in particular with the right kind of skills to ensure managing diversity is supported by the requisite managerial capability. Active flexibility is important in ensuring that working patterns, policies, practices and procedures support the approach to diversity. For example, in recognizing the diverse needs of all employees Kandola and Fullerton note the importance of adopting a 'cafeteria' approach to issue surrounding work/life needs. In advocating an individual focus Kandola and Fullerton note how sometimes 'special events' that focus on a particular group can actually serve to reinforce stereotypes or increase hostility to particular groups. Resultantly, things such as cross-cultural training programmes should aim to foster respect for employees as individual actors, rather than treating employees as member of a particular group, with easily categories differences. Finally, underpinning much of the above is the need to sustain the right kind of organizational culture. We have already noted the importance of organizational culture in Chapter 2 and in terms of managing diversity there is a need to ensure the prevailing culture encourages participation and creativity from all organizational members.

Conclusion

At the outset of the chapter we asked whether we are likely to find equality of opportunities within organizations. The simple answer would be no. There was evidence within the chapter to suggest that certain groups in society still continue to face discrimination which has a deleterious effect on their employment experience. That said, the chapter also recognized the manner in which legislation aims to eradicate such discrimination and how managing diversity seeks to encourage organizations to adopt a more proactive response to ensuring opportunity for all. Although equal opportunities and managing diversity may be represented as being dichotomous in their approach, in reality many organizations will adopt an approach which has elements of both. Many would recognize that valuing and promoting diversity in the workforce probably relies on a delicate balance between legal requirements and a business-driven desire to be an employer of choice and to attract and retain the best employees, regardless of their backgrounds.

References and further reading

Advisory, Conciliation and Arbitration Service (2006) *Annual Report and Accounts 2005/06*, ACAS.

Anon (2004) 'Countdown to DDA day', *Caterer and Hotelkeeper*, 22 July, 34–36.

Arkin, A. (2005) 'Chip off the old block', *People Management*, 21 April, 32–34.

Bald, S. (1997) 'No excuse for patronising language', *People Management*, 3 April, 19.

Baum, T. (1996) *Managing Cultural Diversity in Tourism*, British Tourist Authority/English Tourist Board, Insights, A77–A84.

Cabinet Office (2003) *Ethnic Minorities and the Labour Market*, Cabinet Office.

Chartered Institute of Personnel and Development (2006) *Employing People with Criminal Records Factsheet*, CIPD.

Cooper, C. (2003) 'Minority support', *People Management*, 4 December, 24–27.

Department of Trade and Industry (2001) *Creating a Work-Life Balance: A Good Practice Guide for the Hospitality Industry*, DTI.

Drury, B. (2001) 'How to assess criminal convictions', *People Management*, 22 March, 52–53.

Ellis, C. and Sonnenfield, J. (1994) 'Diverse approaches to managing diversity', *Human Resource Management*, 33(1), 79–109.

Equality Opportunities Commission (2005) *Facts About Women and Men in Great Britain*, EOC.

European Professional Women's Network (EPWN) (2006) *Second Bi-annual EuropeanPWN BoardWomen Monitor 2006*, press release at http://www.europeanpwn.net/pdf/boardwomen_press_release120606.pdf (accessed 15 July 2006).

Gledhill, B. (2002) 'Releasing potential', *Caterer and Hotelkeeper*, 10 October, 32–34.

Goss, D. (1994) *Principles of Human Resource Management*, Routledge.

Gottlieb, M. (1992) Letter to the editor in *Caterer and Hotelkeeper*, 25 June 1992, 20.

Groeschl, S. and Doherty, L. (1999) 'Diversity management in practice', *International Journal of Contemporary Hospitality Management*, 11(6), 262–268.

Guild, S. (2002) 'Willing and able', *Caterer and Hotelkeeper*, 17 January, 29–29.

Hope, K. (2005) 'Holding back the years', *People Management*, 21 April, 24–30.

Hotel and Catering International Management Association (1999) *Managing Diversity: Women at Work*, Management Brief No. 3, HCIMA.

Income Data Services (2001) *Promoting Racial Equality*, IDS Studies No. 719, September.

Income Data Services (2003) *Opportunity Now*, IDS Studies No. 758, September.

Income Data Services (2006) *Promoting Race Equality*, IDS HR Studies, No. 825, July.

Industrial Relations Services (2003) 'Managing disability 2003: a progress report', *IRS Employment Review*, No. 785, 3 October, 11–17.

Industrial Relations Services (2004) 'Using age diversity policies to attract and retain older workers', *IRS Employment Review*, No. 808, 24 September, 42–48.

Industrial Relations Services (2006a) 'Age discrimination (1)', *IRS Employment Review*, No. 847, 19 May, 53–58.

Industrial Relations Services (2006b) 'Age discrimination (2)', *IRS Employment Review*, No. 848, 2 June, 51–57.

Industrial Relations Services (2006c) 'Age discrimination (3)', *IRS Employment Review*, No. 849, 23 June, 51–58.

Johnston, J. (2006) 'Half of gays believe they'll be discriminated against if they "come out" at work', *Sunday Herald*, 22 January, 14.

Kandola R. and Fullerton, J. (1998) *Diversity in Action: Managing the Mosaic*, CIPD, 2nd edition.

Labour Research Department (1999) 'How do tribunals define disability?', *Labour Research*, January, 32.

Labour Research Department (2000) *Tackling Disability Discrimination*, LRD.

Labour Research Department (2000a) 'UK soft on homophobia', *Labour Research*, July, 10–12.

Labour Research Department (2003) 'Making workplaces disability friendly', *Labour Research*, December, 15–16.

Labour Research Department (2003a) 'Two cheers for gay-bias rules', *Labour Research*, July, 11–13.

Labour Research Department (2005) *Black and Minority Ethnic Workers: Tackling Discrimination*, LRD.

Labour Research Department (2006) *Law at Work*, LRD.

Magd, H. (2003) 'Management attitudes and perceptions of older employees in hospitality management', *International Journal of Contemporary Hospitality Management*, 15, 7, 393–401.

Mayling, S. (2003) 'Can positive discrimination help women?', *Travel Trade Gazette*, 21 April, 8–9.

Opportunity Now (2005) *Review 05:06: All About Opportunity Now and Its Future Plans*, Opportunity Now.

Osborn, A. (2002) 'Norway sets 40% female quota for boardrooms', *The Guardian*, August 1, 13.

Qu, H. and Cheng, S. Y. (1996) 'Attitudes towards utilizing older workers in the Hong Kong hotel industry', *International Journal of Hospitality Management*, 15(3), 245–254.

Race for Opportunity (2004) *RFO Newsletter*, Summer, 16.

Rossiter, P. (2005) 'Women in Business', *Leisure Opportunities*, 23 March, 7.

Runnymede Trust (2000) *Moving on Up? Racial Equality and the Corporate Agenda: A Study of the FTSE 100 Companies*, Central Books.

Smethurst, S. (2004) 'Ageism rife in UK workplace', *People Management*, 15 January, 10.

Smith, L. (2005) 'Too few black and Asian faces at the top', *Guardian*, 17 November, 29.

Speizer, I. (2004) 'Diversity on the menu', *Workforce Management*, November, 41–45.

Stredwick, J. (2005) *An Introduction to Human Resource Management*, Elsevier, 2nd edition.

Walsh, C. (2004) 'A woman's place is on the board', *Observer Business*, 2 May, 5.

Ward, J. (2003) 'How to address sexual orientation', *People Management*, 23 October, 62–63.

Wilborn, L. and Weaver, P. (2002) 'Diversity management training initiatives: a profile of current practices within the lodging industry', *Journal of Human Resources in Hospitality and Tourism*, 1(4), 79–96.

Websites

The various equality commissions can be found at:

Commission for Racial Equality http://www.cre.gov.uk/
Disability Rights Commission http://www.drc.org.uk

Equal Opportunities Commission http://www.eoc.org.uk/

Although it does not come into official existence until October 2007 the CEHR already has a website, http://www.cehr.org.uk/

Stonewall is an organization that supports gay people's right to equality http:// www.stonewall.org.uk/ workplace

The Employers Forum on Age can be found at http://www.efa.org.uk

The Apex Trust is a voluntary organization that helps ex-offenders get back into employment http://www. apextrust.com/apextrust/exo_rehabact.shtm

For information on the various world religions see http://www.bbc.co.uk/religion/religions/index.shtml

Chapter **7**
Training and development

Chapter objectives

This chapter considers the key role of training and development in tourism and hospitality organizations. The chapter aims to:

- Distinguish the different levels of analysis to understand approaches to training and development.
- Appreciate the importance of government-level policy in establishing the context in which tourism and hospitality organizations develop their training policies.
- Recognize debates surrounding terms such as education, training and development.
- Consider the range of training methods available to tourism and hospitality organizations.

Introduction

It is increasingly recognized that human resource development (HRD) is crucial in ensuring effectiveness, quality and responsiveness in organizations to an ever changing and complex environment. Resultantly, training and development activities now seek to emphasize adaptability, flexibility and continuous development to ensure that organizations can survive and compete in an ever more competitive environment. However, the importance of training and development is not just apparent for organizations. As we increasingly are entreated to engage in lifelong learning, then training and development becomes important for individuals. Moreover, there is now also recognition of the importance of national competitiveness, especially in an ever more globalized world. Training and development, therefore, becomes important from an individual, organizational and national perspective. Therefore we see more and more talk of the importance of HRD which is likely to encompass notions of education, learning, training and development and the interchangeability or otherwise of these distinctions will also be something considered in this chapter. Before we begin to consider these issues in detail though it is useful to delineate different levels of analysis in understanding training and Table 7.1 outlines the ways in which we can think of training.

Throughout this chapter we will consider various aspects of these levels and begin initially by considering the importance of how national government policy impacts on training and development.

Understanding the context: national level responses to training

It is often argued that a nation's competitive advantage depends on the skills and inventiveness of its people. Often the manner in which organizations seek to respond to this issue will be determined to a large extent by the views of the government. Increasingly in the UK in the 1980s and 1990s there was an emerging consensus from government, policy makers and practitioners that training should be encouraged within organizations for the greater good of the economy. Despite the seeming acceptance by government and employers of the importance of training and the need to encourage it, there is a good deal of debate as to whether, in reality,

Table 7.1 Levels of analysis for understanding approaches to training and development

Level	Main organizations involved/activities undertaken
National/Governmental level	• Government policy, for example the UK Government seeking a more proactive approach to encourage training in organizations • Training initiatives, for example in the UK Investors in People (IiP) and Apprenticeships
Industry level	• National Training Organizations (NTOs), for example People 1st the Sector Skills Council (SSC) for hospitality, leisure, travel and tourism • Industry level initiatives, for example Excellence Through People and Welcome Host
Company level	• Creation of an overall view of company's approach to training, for example seeking IiP accreditation, being involved in Welcome Host and Excellence Through People • Ensuring 'fit' between what the company wants to achieve and how units can operationalize this
Unit level	• Ensuring on- and off-the-job training takes place • Monitoring individuals training and development plans • Performance development and monitoring, for example, seeking to enhance quality service through training
Team level	• Motivation and performance • Team building
Individual level	• Improvement in knowledge, skills and attitudes • Sustaining employability • Enhanced motivation and performance • Improving aspects of discipline and behaviour • Career progression

there has been the training revolution claimed. This point recognizes that over much of the preceding period the UK's record on training was poor compared to other nations such as Germany, Japan and Sweden who were felt to invest heavily in training and development. For example, Holden (2004: 314) notes how, 'Until

Table 7.2 VET policies and practices in selected countries

UK	Germany	Sweden	Japan	USA
Traditionally, voluntaristic with limited state intervention finance rather than industry oriented, class based.	Much more state direction, encouraging a dual system of concentrating on theory or practice.	State directed, aiming to create an active labour market approach to ensure employees remain employable. Employers are strongly encouraged to train.	Directed/voluntarist with the state setting and enforcing training standards. Large companies offering lifetime employment and significant training.	Voluntarist, uncoordinated, with emphasis on individual effort and individual payment.

Adapted from Holden (2004: 337) *Human Resource Management: A Contemporary Approach 4/ed*, Beardwell, Holden and Claydon, with permission from Pearson Education Limited.

the 1980s, training and development in British organizations were inadequate compared with other industrialized nations'. In this sense the UK has often been characterized as voluntaristic with regard to training and development, meaning that the state took a hands off view in terms of encouraging employers to train their employees. Instead, individual employers were largely left to their own devices with regard to how much, or indeed, how little training they would provide. Consequently there has been much debate about the levels of training expenditure both by Government and employers, with some expressing concerns that, if anything, real expenditure on vocational education and training (VET) have fallen in recent years. Hyman (1996: 306–307) exemplifies this scepticism in his recognition that 'what is more questionable … concerns the extent to which the majority of British employers have taken responsibility for strategically training and developing their employees', with much training simply being of the reactive 'fire-fighting' type. For many then there may be a gap between the perceived importance of training and the willingness to do something about it, with suspicions that in the UK too many organizations still see training as a cost and not an investment. Indeed, it could be argued that such a view may simply reflect the short-termism inherent in British business, where corporate objectives tend to be short-term and defined by short-term profit and financial criteria. Table 7.2 and HRM in practice 7.1 below

HRM in practice 7.1   National skill-creation systems and career paths in the tourism industry in the UK, Germany and the US

Studies of the UK, Germany and the US have found that patterns of career development and commitment to working in the tourism industry are strongly influenced by the national VET system. Germany, which has a more structured approach compared to the UK and US, encourages individuals to complete an apprenticeship prior to entering the tourism industry. Such an apprenticeship means that Germany's education and training system is geared to produce a much higher proportion of qualified staff for the tourism industry. As a result employees in Germany were able to secure relatively highly skilled and autonomous positions at an earlier age than their counterparts in the UK and the US. There is also evidence which points to the greater productivity of German tourism employees over their British and American counterparts. One report concluded that Germany's high productivity and service levels are due to the wider use of qualified manpower trained through the partnership arrangements for the dual system. This study notes that craft qualifications were held by 2.5 times as many employees in Germany compared to the UK. A conclusion to be drawn is that the dual system within which German employees for tourism are trained 'embeds' commitment to the sector to a much greater degree than elsewhere and this, combined with high levels of reward, contributes to a greater sense of professionalism and productivity. Finally, German employees were also more likely to advance more rapidly within the industry due to the training and education they receive.

Derived from STRU (1998); Finegold et al. (2000).

highlight the impact of the above discussion on the VET policies and practices in some selected countries.

Review and reflect

Outline arguments for and against government intervention in support of training and education.

Consequently there has been much support for the notion that Britain needs to invest in training and development to ensure that it does not become a low-tech, low-wage, low-skill, cheap labour economy wherein it seeks to compete on the basis of a low-skill, low-quality product market strategy relying on price-based competitiveness. What this has meant in practice is that in recent years the UK government has attempted to take a more active role by introducing a range of initiatives that aim to improve skill levels in the economy. Indeed, Keep (2005) considers the extent to which the UK may be entering a 'post-voluntarist' era, where the Government is seemingly increasingly prepared to take a more active role in encouraging learning and development. To an extent this change may be explicable by the sense that the UK is playing 'catch up' with a number of its international competitors. Resultantly, the Government has introduced a number of initiatives in recent year, such as National/Scottish Vocational Qualifications (N/SVQs), Investors in People (IiP) and Apprenticeships. All of these initiatives attempt to get employers to increase training and are now considered.

N/SVQs

The rationale for the introduction of N/SVQs in the late 1980s was to provide greater coherence in vocational qualifications and thus the existing vocational structure was rationalized into N/SVQs. N/SVQs are work-related, competence-based qualifications, which are appropriate to all industries and all levels of employment, from the shop floor to the board room. N/SVQs are statements confirming that the individual employee can perform to a specified standard and that they posses the skills, knowledge and understanding which makes possible such performance in the workplace. They provide a progressive route from Level 1, which is semi-skilled through to Level 5, which recognizes the skills needed to be an organizational leader. N/SVQs are important as they recognize achievements in the workplace and are based on assessing work experience and achievements. In terms of their broad equivalence to educational attainment then Level 2, for example, is broadly similar to GCSEs, Level 3 is broadly equivalent to A/AS Levels or Scottish Highers, Level 4 is higher national diploma/degree level and Level 5 is degree/postgraduate level (though within tourism and hospitality there are currently no options to seek Level 4 or 5 N/SVQs).

In the tourism and hospitality industry the largest number of registrations has tended to be at Levels 1 and 2, in areas such as food preparation and cooking and serving food and drink (QCA, 2003). Hales (1996; and see also IRS, 1999) suggests the case for developing and implementing N/SVQs is largely based on two reasons. First, their contribution in enhancing the competitiveness and performance of the UK economy by widening access to training and qualifications. Second, the benefits to participants (i.e. employees), in terms of increased recognition for workplace ability and competence, with the effect of increasing job satisfaction, motivation, a sense of achievement and standards of work. Hales reports on five case study organizations in the hotel sector. All of the case study organizations were small businesses employing between 22 and 44 employees, and four of them had adopted and continued to use N/SVQs, with one adopting and then subsequently dropping them. Hales research suggested that those hotels which had adopted and persevered with N/SVQs noted a pay-off in terms of better employee attitudes and behaviour, increased service quality and an overall improvement in business performance. However, he does remain sceptical about the extent to which N/SVQs may penetrate the small tourism and hospitality business sector generally, unless they are given active encouragement.

Others such as Lucas (1995) have been rather more critical of the qualification. Lucas suggests that Levels 1 and 2 arguably do not fit the criteria of training as systematically developing knowledge, skills and abilities. Consequently they represent 'qualifications without substance [and] lack any real sense of meaning or value' (Lucas, 1995: 60). Lucas' criticisms reflect more general critiques of N/SVQs with worries about their skill levels and whether they are too narrowly defined and task specific. There is also some disquiet about the overly bureaucratic nature of N/SVQs. The final criticism which rather reflects all of the above is the argument that there is little evidence that N/SVQs are able to cope with changing technologies, skill requirements and new methods of work (and for further discussion of the problematic aspects of N/SVQs or somewhat more cynically 'No Value or Quality', see Foote, 1999; Druce, 2004).

Investors in people

The second initiative is IiP, which is a national level initiative run by IiP UK and administered locally by Learning and Skills Councils (LSC) (Learning and Enterprise Councils in Scotland) under the supervision of IiP UK. IiP is designed to be applicable to all organizations whether large or small, public or private, manufacturing or service. IiP attempts to link training and development to business strategy and as a result improve business performance and secure competitive advantage for organizations. At its inception in 1991 organizations were expected to demonstrate their adherence to a number of general principles in order to qualify for the IiP Standard. The four general principles were:

1 *Commitment*: An IiP makes a public commitment from the top to develop all employees to achieve its business objectives.
2 *Planning*: An IiP regularly reviews the training and development needs of all employees.
3 *Action*: An IiP takes action to train and develop individuals on recruitment and throughout their employment.
4 *Evaluation*: An IiP evaluates the investment in training and development on performance of individuals, team and the organization to assess and improve effectiveness.

Organizations seeking IiP accreditation were tested against these four principles, which were measured using 23 indicators, later reduced to 12. More recently, following an extensive process of consultation with employers and organizations such as the Trade Union Congress, Confederation of British Industry and the Chartered Institute of Personnel and Development, the Standard was revised and re-launched in November 2004. The new Standard has three principles; plan, do and review and these are underpinned by 10 indicators of good practice, as indicated in Figure 7.1.

At the time of writing nearly 40 000 organizations across the economy as a whole had achieved the Standard (IiP, 2005). Generally, evidence from a range of studies suggests that the initiative has had a positive impact on those organizations gaining the accreditation (e.g. see Alberga et al., 1997). Hoque (2003: 565), whilst offering some caveats as to the success of the Standard, concludes that 'on average, training practice is better in IiP-accredited workplaces than in non-accredited workplaces'. Equally in relation to the tourism and hospitality industry a number of case studies point to the manner in which IiP can improve organizational performance (e.g. see Georgeson, 1999; HRM in practice 7.2).

Supporters of IiP would therefore argue that the standard thus improves business performance, with increases in aspects such as turnover, efficiency, profitability, enhanced customer service and improvements in company image; and

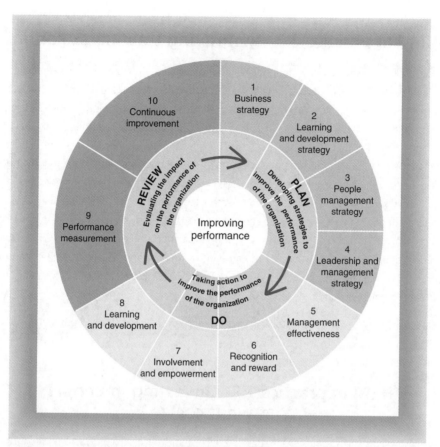

Figure 7.1 The principles of the IiP Standard, Source: IiP (2004: 5) reproduced with kind permission of Investors in People UK, © Investors in People, 2006

HRM outcomes, such as lower labour turnover, improved skills and competences, improved communications and increased motivation. At the same time there are also some criticisms, as outlined in HRM in practice 7.3.

Notwithstanding some of the criticisms IiP seems to have established itself as a positive and important attempt to encourage employers to adopt more systematic approaches to training and development to improve organizational performance and competitiveness. Indeed, it could be argued that the success of the standard can be gauged by the recognition on the IiP UK website, http://www.investorsinpeople.co.uk, that IiP has been adopted in over 30 countries as an example of attempting to encourage best practice HRD and improving the competitiveness of the country (e.g. see Kidger et al., 2004).

HRM in practice 7.2   Improving training at Pontins

Pontins is a British company that has a number of holiday centres which are catering primarily for families. The vast majority of Pontins employees are seasonal workers, many of whom will only work for the company for a short period of time. Despite the relatively high turnover of staff that this situation creates the company's commitment to the IiP Standard means that all employees have the opportunity to improve, no matter how short their stay is with the company. Drawing on the IiP guidelines the company now has a structure which means that every employee will have a personal development file with job description and aims, access to NVQs, access to funding for vocational training, assistance with professional qualifications and assessment of aims and goals and help achieving them. So even those employees who only stay a short period of time can gain a new qualification. As well as increasing the amount of training and delivering higher standards of service, the company has also seen improved employee retention, resulting in greater productivity and reduced costs.

Derived from http://www.investorsinpeople.co.uk/IIP/Web/Case+Studies/Pontin.htm

HRM in practice 7.3   Investing in people: at what cost?

Amanda Scott, then General Manager of the Copthorne Hotel in Glasgow, suggests that in many respects IiP embodied what any good manager should be doing – investing in their people. However, she also outlined a number of criticisms. Many companies that have attained the IiP Standard often already have good HR systems and procedures in place so gaining the award may simply be nothing more than a 'badging' process. Moreover it is a badging process that generates a lot of paperwork and bureaucracy, with the awarding body often using obscure and confusing jargon. She also suggests that the cost of IiP accreditation may well be prohibitive, 'As a management model it can deliver, but in my opinion £4000 for the privilege of a branding exercise … cannot be justified. It if was my personal money? I don't think so'. This latter point concerning the costly nature of IiP accreditation could be particularly important for smaller companies who predominate in tourism and hospitality. The CIPD has recently estimated that the total cost of seeking IiP is between £5000–£15 000 depending on the size of the organization and how much consultancy support the organization uses.

Derived from Scott (1999); CIPD (2006).

Apprenticeships

Government-subsidised apprenticeships were first introduced in 1995 as Modern Apprenticeships. Such apprenticeships aim to offer a career to those more motivated by workplace learning, rather than pure academic study. The aim was to take the best aspects from traditional apprenticeship schemes, update them and extend them to the service and public sectors (Gospel and Fuller, 1998). The scheme was recently re-launched in May 2004 as Apprenticeships, though in Scotland they remain Modern Apprenticeships. Apprenticeships are primarily aimed at 16–24-year olds (though at the time of writing there are also pilot programmes for those aged 25-plus) who want to obtain intermediate skills by combining a paid job with training. There are two levels, the Apprenticeship is for 2 years and at the end of this period the apprentice will achieve an NVQ Level 2 (National Vocational Qualification); there is also the Advanced Apprenticeship, which is for a period of 3 years and leads to NVQ Level 3. The Apprenticeship alternates between productive employment with on- and off-the-job training to provide a mixture of occupationally specific training as well as more generic key skills, such as communication, numeracy, literacy and teamworking.

Early accounts of the implementation of Modern Apprenticeships in tourism and hospitality offered guarded optimism with regard to their ability to attract young people to work in the industry. Mason (1997) recognizes how the scheme had attracted around 7000 young people by 1997, with the aim of having 10 000 apprentices by 2000. Mason reports on the success of the scheme within De Vere Hotels, which was aiming to have 100 apprentices across the UK by the end of 1997. The company reported that the scheme allowed them to embed and maintain a strong training culture within trainees. Trainees were also fully immersed in the company's organizational culture, the 'De Vere Way', which allowed the company to develop future managers. Similarly, Yates' Wine Lodge report a number of benefits from operating the scheme such as improved staff retention and loyalty, improved staff morale, enhanced skill sets for employees and more efficient and productive employees (Anon, 2003a). Whilst the examples of De Vere and Yates offers a positive view of Modern Apprenticeships other accounts are less encouraging. For example, Manson (2005) reports on a survey conducted for the LSC which found that only 920, or 4 per cent, of 23 000 hospitality employers were looking to offer apprenticeships in hospitality. Concerns have also been expressed at the high drop out rate, with around 80 per cent of hospitality apprentices leaving before completion (Anon, 2003a).

Industry level

The above discussion has considered the manner in which the VET infrastructure created by government will have a profound impact on training and development. Clearly with the creation of initiatives such as N/SVQs, IiP and Apprenticeships British Governments over the last 20 years or so have attempted to encourage employers to offer more training. Whilst all of these initiatives have had some impact in tourism and hospitality, they are not sector specific, unlike another governmental initiative, the creation of Sector Skills Councils (SSCs). IDS (2005: 14) notes how 'the overall aim to SSCs is to help employers within similar industries to improve their employees' skills base and to provide them with leverage, influence, support and expertise in this pursuit'. Although SSCs are funded by Government they are run by employers, who work in partnership with a range of stakeholders in each sector to (Marchington and Wilkinson, 2005):

- Produce intelligence and analysis of future sector skill needs.
- Reduce skill gaps and shortages by influencing the planning and funding education and training.
- Improve productivity.
- Develop occupational standards for skills in their sector.
- Increase opportunities for everyone in work to boost skills.

As noted in Chapter 1, the SSC for tourism and hospitality is People 1st, which came into existence in May 2004. People 1st's mission in the period 2004–2009 is to have an impact on completion rates for qualifications and learning programmes, investment in training, raising employee skill and productivity levels and reducing staff turnover through lifelong career development (People 1st, 2004). By the end of People 1st's first year of existence there was some disquiet as to its influence (Druce, 2005), though it is too early to offer any definitive comment on the impact of People 1st in improving skills and training within tourism and hospitality.

In addition to governmental initiatives, there are also non-governmental initiatives which have attempted to improve training within tourism and hospitality, such as Welcome Host, which is described in HRM in practice 7.4.

HRM in practice 7.4 Welcome Host: Professionalizing the tourism industry?

The Welcome Host scheme is based on Canadian hospitality programme called 'Superhost'. Introduced in British Columbia in 1986 to support the growth of tourism around the world expo in Vancouver. Other franchises include: 'Kiwi Host', 'Aussie Host', 'Alaska Host' and 'Super Host Japan'. Sweeney (1995: 8) describes Welcome Host as, 'an ongoing, comprehensive, community-based programme designed to upgrade the standards of service and hospitality provided within the tourism industry … By involving the whole community, the scheme provides access to more formal training for the smaller operator who may also come into contact with the visitor'. The basis of Welcome Host is people helping people and its objectives are about aiming to instil a sense of professionalism and pride in tourism. Importantly, Welcome Host is not just for tourism employees, such as travel agents and tour guides, but can also be taken by people like taxi drivers and traffic wardens and anybody else that tourists are likely to encounter in the destination. In addition to Welcome Host there are also a number of other programmes such as Welcome All, which is a course designed to help individuals acquire the knowledge and skills essential for providing facilities and services that meet the specific needs and expectations of people with disabilities and special needs; and Welcome International which is a training programme designed to give people working in the tourism or hospitality industry greater confidence when meeting and greeting international visitors in another language.

Training and development: no longer a dichotomy?

Having outlined the broad context in which organizations are developing their overall approach to training and the importance of Government policy within that process, we can now go on and look in greater detail at what exactly training and development are. Holden (2004: 313) recognizes how, 'it is difficult to arrive at a consensus definition of terms such as "development", "education" and "training" because of the varied ways in which they are translated into work and life situations'. Many would argue that training and development have traditionally been seen as separate and a reflection of an organization's hierarchy. This point can be appreciated in acknowledging the manner in which training and development have been traditionally conceptualized as being distinctive activities.

On the one hand, training is 'a planned process to modify attitude, knowledge or skill behaviour through learning experience to achieve effective performance in an activity or range of activities. Its purpose, in the work situation, is to develop the abilities of the individual and to satisfy the current and future manpower needs of the organization' (MSC 1981, cited in Armstrong, 1999: 507). On the other hand, development has often been seen as being much more about the growth or realization of a person's ability through conscious or unconscious learning. Development programmes also usually include elements of planned study and experience, and are frequently supported by a coaching or counselling facility. In that sense training was often perceived as being for non-managerial staff, whilst development was the preserve of managers, and this reflected the more nebulous concepts of reasoning, abstraction and personal growth (see Baum, 2006: 204–214 for further discussion of this issue). Now though it is increasingly recognized that within a HRM/HRD approach organizations will see the two aspects as being very much interconnected so training should be seen as part of and a precondition of development.

Review and reflect

If you are currently undertaking a tourism or hospitality degree to what extent do you consider it to be training, education or development? What are some of the influences in making your decision?

Training and development then can be seen as a key instrument in the implementation of HRM practices and policies and there may be a number of benefits from undertaking training. For example, McKenna and Beech (2002) suggest a number of benefits generally stemming from training, including:

- Helps employees learn jobs more quickly and effectively.
- Improves work performance of existing employees and keeps them up to date in specialist skills.
- Leads to a greater volume of work resulting from fewer mistakes and greater rapidity.
- Frees management time, less of which is spent rectifying errors, also reduces wastage.
- Can help to reduce turnover among new and established staff.

HRM in practice 7.5   Training and TQM in the restaurant industry in Canada

Salameh and Barrows (2001) recognize how a critical element of TQM is creating an organizational culture which is supportive of quality and customer satisfaction. TQM also requires that all members of an organization are involved in the process of quality improvement. Training therefore becomes crucial to the implementation of TQM. Research conducted by Salameh and Barrows in a coffee house restaurant and a casual dining restaurant in Canada demonstrated a number of similarities in the respective restaurants. Training programmes differed from job to job depending on the complexity of the job and associated tasks, and the length of time also varied. Both companies also used a range of training methods, such as on-the-job training, videos, seminars and extensive induction programmes. The case study organizations also recognized the challenges of training, including the time factor, keeping programmes simple, being proactive rather than re-active, and, in a mirror of the intent of TQM, seeing training as a process of continuous improvement. Managers suggested that there were a number of positive outcomes from training in support of TQM, including decreased labour turnover, greater employee commitment, increases in sales, greater customer responsiveness and enhanced quality service. In sum, the research suggested that training did result in a continuous performance improvement, a key goal in TQM.

- Incorporating safety training can help reduce accidents.
- Can help to attract good workers.
- Is a precondition for flexible working.
- Creates an attitude more receptive to coping with change.
- Operationalizing certain management techniques, for example Total Quality Management (TQM) and empowerment (see HRM in practice 7.5).

Whether organizations accept the arguments for the benefits of training might reflect whether they are one of two types of organizations, who are characterized as having extreme training positions – the road to failure or the road to success.

- The road to failure
  - A failure to recognize or implement management practices designed to meet, not only existing, but future skills needs.

– An unrealistic reliance by managers upon national and local labour markets to satisfy company skills at whatever level.
– A willingness to regard the practice of poaching the skilled labour of others as the chief response to skill pressures, regardless of the consequences at company level and in pay in inflation terms.
- The road to success
  – Progress through the sharing of a common vision, from top management through every level of the organization.
  – High status being accorded training and development practices based upon results and their relevance to the needs of the organization.
  – Company structures which allow for the development of individuals and encourages the acquisition of skills to meet business goals.
  – Business systems flexible enough to accommodate investment in people, with agreed budgets and clear targets subject to regular evaluation.

If we consider which one of these archetypes tends to describe tourism and hospitality industry as a whole then it may well be that the balance of evidence suggests the road to failure best describes the industry. Lucas (2004), for example, argues that the industry remains relatively unqualified and access to training tends to be restricted to those in large multi-establishment organizations. That said, there are, of course, examples of sophisticated and systematic training and development programmes in some companies (see HRM in practice 7.6).

HRM in practice 7.6   The training Oscars

Set up in 1987 by the then Department for Education and Science the National Training Awards are the UK's number one accolade for businesses, organizations and individuals who achieved lasting excellence and success through training and learning. In recent years there has been some success for the tourism and hospitality industry. For example, in 2003 five companies triumphed in a multi-sector field of 1000 entries. For the competition that year entries for the national competition increased by 25 per cent, but for the hospitality sector there was a 70 per cent rise in applicants. In the most recent awards in 2005 Nando's, the Chicken restaurant chain, won awards for its outdoor management development programme and its staff training programme.

Derived from Anon (2003b); Hope (2005).

There is also the further point that the structure of the industry in terms of firm size. With the predominance of small firms there is greater likelihood of informal proprietor and on-the-job training (OJT). Moreover, training incidence is at its lowest in non-standard forms of employment, for example workers who are numerically flexible are likely to get little or no training. There may be an important role though to be played by the SSC, People 1st. The success model views training as an integral part of core organizational strategy, rather than an ad hoc operational issue. Moreover, this notion would seem to be a precondition for any claims to be an HRM organization which is practicing soft HRM. Ultimately, then there may be those organizations who see training as an investment and those who pay lip service to the idea of training and in the good times spend money on training and in the bad times spend less or hardly anything on training. Consequently, a lot of organizations will, in times of skill or labour shortages, recruit from other organizations rather than invest in their existing employees, something that has certainly been apparent in tourism and hospitality.

Conducting training

We have examined in some detail the wider picture of training and in this section of the chapter we can now move on to consider the manner in which training may be conducted and training methods used by organization. To contextualize this discussion it is worth noting the three broad categories in which training is likely to be located, these are (Marchington and Wilkinson, 1996):

- *Socialization initiative*: Particularly in terms of induction and becoming familiar with the prevailing organizational culture.
- *Development initiative*: This is more concerned with developing individuals, for example, preparing for promotion, coping with new technology or organizational change, such as attempting to become a more customer focused organization.
- *Disciplinary initiative*: Where some sort of training is offered to individuals who have fallen below the organizations acceptable level of quality, output or customer standards, and this could be about rectifying deficiencies in technical skills or attitudinal training.

In terms of developing the training there is the potential for huge variations in how organizations go about devising and delivering training. Additionally, Marchington and Wilkinson (2005) note that trainees themselves will bring significant 'baggage' to the learning event, for example the mix of prior knowledge, skills, attitudes, motivations and expectations. Furthermore trainees may also have very diverse reasons for being involved in the training, for example, some trainees may be there under duress. Consequently, we should be cautious in terms of being too prescriptive in describing how organizations should approach training. Nevertheless, there would seem a need to have some sort of systematic approach to developing training. For example, Go et al. (1996) advocate the need for a systematic approach as outlined in their nine-step approach to developing training within the organization.

Step 1: Assessing training needs

Analysing training needs is a crucial part of HRD as the identification of needed skills and active management of employee learning is integral to developing corporate and business strategies. Many would argue that for training to be effective it is necessary to discern not only the training needs of the individual and the group, but also how their needs fit the overall organizational objectives. Essentially then training needs analysis allow for an appreciation of the need to ensure that there is a fit between training and the company culture, strategy and objectives. Equally, the training needs of the individual needs to be reconciled with those of the organization. In terms of developing a training needs analysis aspects such as job descriptions, job analysis, person specifications or whether performance objectives agreed at appraisals have been met may all potentially be useful indicators.

Step 2: Preparing the training plan

The training plan is concerned with outlining what needs to be done based on the training needs of individuals, departments and the organization as a whole. In effect the training plan provides an outline sketch of what the training should address, as well as considering practical aspects such as the method, time and location of the training.

Step 3: Specifying the training objectives

A key question to be asked before the training is operationalized is: what are the training objectives? It is important when employees are undertaking training that they understand what they should be able to accomplish when the training programme has been completed.

Step 4: Designing the training programme

Go et al. (1996) suggest a number of issues need to be considered in designing the training programme, including:

- Programme duration.
- Programme structure.
- Instructional methods.
- Support resources (e.g. a training facility) and the selection of training materials (e.g. videos).
- Training location or environment, which may also be determined by the task, for example, whether it involves practical skills.
- Instructor and instructors experience.
- Origin of the training programme.
- Criteria and methods for assessing participants learning and achievement.
- Criteria and methods for evaluating the programme.

Step 5: Selecting the instruction methods

There are a multitude of methods that organizations can use to train and develop staff. All of these various methods will have both strengths and weaknesses and in that sense there is no one 'best' training method. Rather, there is a need for organizations to adopt a contingent approach to training in developing training methods. Although there are a great variety of training methods, generally most writers broadly categorize them into three different types of training, in-company on-the-job, in-company off-the job and external off-the-job, all of which are now briefly considered.

In-company, on-the-job

This type of training is enduringly popular and accounts for about half of all the training delivered across all industries and sectors in the UK (CIPD, 2005). Often known colloquially as 'sitting next to Nellie', OJT training involves learning through watching and observing somebody with greater experience perform a task. OJT is a very popular method of training where new skills and methods are taught to employees. The advantages of OJT is that it is cheap, the trainees get the opportunity to practice immediately, trainees get immediate feedback and it can also help in integrating trainees into existing teams. Equally, there may be some drawbacks from this type of training. 'Nellie' may not be trained herself in skills and methods of training, which will often lead to training being rather piecemeal or not properly planned. Equally, Nellie may also pass on bad habits, although increasingly organizations may use the idea of training the trainer to ensure a more professional approach.

Another variant of OJT is mentoring, wherein a senior experienced member of staff takes responsibility for the development and progression of selected individuals. Ordinarily this process of mentoring would be for managerial staff and the selected individual will often be somebody who has aspirations to reach senior management levels. This type of relationship is more like father–son or mother–daughter than that of traditional master–apprentice. The trainee, or mentoree, will observe the skills displayed by the mentor and learn from their experience. Mentoring can also be a useful two-way process in terms of the mentor becoming more reflective about their own job and being forced to think about ways of improving their own performance. In a similar vein, shadowing allows employees the chance to see different part of the organization in other departments. Finally, under the broader heading of OJT is the idea of job rotation. In this approach those undergoing the training are placed into a job without any prior training, when they have learnt that job they move on to another job and so on, this may also eventually lead to multi-skilling or functional flexibility, as discussed in Chapter 4.

In-company, off-the-job

In contrast to OJT, off-the-job training takes place outside of the employee's normal place of work. Off-the job training will often involve a training intervention run by a specialized training department. This type of training could be relatively straightforward (see HRM in practice 7.7) or be concerned with achieving proficiency in more advanced skills.

HRM in practice 7.7   Heading off the induction crisis

Induction is often misunderstood as simply being about inducting people into the organization during the first day in a new job. However, induction will often extend beyond the first day and may involve events up to 12 months after the initial appointment. The need for a period of induction is increasingly seen as being important in socializing employees, especially in strong culture organizations, an issue considered in Chapter 3. In addition it may also be crucial to address the problem of the so-called 'induction crisis', where a new work environment can be perplexing and even frightening for new employees. As a result employees may leave the organization during this period. Induction will not axiomatically always avert an induction crisis, but a well-designed induction programme can go some way to addressing this issue. Typically in inducting new employees' tourism and hospitality organizations are likely to consider the following aspects:

- History of the organization
- Consideration of the mission statement and organizational objectives
- Outline of company ethics
- The structure of the organization
- Appearance standards
- Uniforms and dress codes
- Pay systems and benefits
- Holiday and sickness arrangements
- Rules and regulations of the organization
- Discipline and grievance procedures
- Details of any trade unions or staff associations
- Welfare policies and social facilities available in the organization
- Health and safety measures
- Introduction to immediate supervisor/line manager
- Introduction to fellow workers

There is a wide array of other methods that come under the broad heading of off-the-job training. In a relatively passive sense lectures can be good for the transmission of information to a relatively large number of trainees. Indeed, it is likely that most of us in our student, organizational or professional life will have sat

HRM in practice 7.8   A flying start

Trapp (2003) notes how British Airways first introduced e-learning in 2000 initially to a large degree of scepticism from their employees. Since then though the take-up of e-learning opportunities has increased significantly amongst their staff. The technology has been used in several ways, for example in helping with the introduction of a new check-in system. British Airways staff are particularly drawn by the flexibility of e-learning, which allows them to learn when they want to learn. Employees can also do as much or as little as they wish. Elements which are covered by e-learning may be job specific, such as allowing cabin crew staff to brush up on specialist safety training or improving knowledge of wines; to more generic training such as learning how to make PowerPoint presentations.

through a lecture. Often the quality of a lecture will be dependent on the individual who is delivering it. Notwithstanding this point it is generally recognized that the maximum concentration span of most individuals is typically less than 20 minutes. In a rather more active vein there are a number of other methods which will involve greater interactivity. For example, case studies, role plays and simulations may all be usefully used by tourism and hospitality organizations, particularly in developing customer service skills. Lastly, there may also be opportunities for employees to learn via interactive computer learning packages, or what is often termed e-learning, something which British Airways has developed with some success, as outlined in HRM in practice 7.8.

Review and reflect

Think of any on-the-job or off-the-job training which you have undertaken in the workplace. Which was most useful and satisfying and why?

External, off-the-job

The final aspect of training is that which again is undertaken off-the-job, though in this instance it is external to the organization. In an era of continuing professional development employees may be encouraged to undertake formal study to enhance their careers, for example taking courses such as the Chartered Institute of Personnel and Development's courses for personnel/HRM managers or in a more general sense a Master in Business Administration (MBA). A further aspect of external off-the-job training is what is termed outward bound courses. Outdoor training ordinarily consists of a series of exercises which act as an opportunity for team building, problem solving or leadership skills to be developed outside of an employee's or manager's 'comfort zone' (Trotter, 2005). In recent years such courses have grown enormously in popularity and there have been a number of hospitality and tourism organizations who have offered this kind of training, including Hilton and Thomas Cook. Some castigate this type of training as a fad or fashion with limited application to commercial situations or more seriously unsafe or downright dangerous, especially if there is too much emphasis on physical challenges or exercises. Some argue though that is this type of training is done properly and managed by experienced and qualified trainers outdoor-based development can offer a highly effective tool for improving managerial performance in particular.

Step 6: Completing the training plan

With the establishment of the main design features and the methods which are to be used, the training plan can now be completed. Go et al. note that a complete training plan will have details about the target group (e.g. all service staff), the topic to be considered (e.g. customer handling), method(s) to be adopted (e.g. role play), time (e.g. two hours) and location (e.g. conference centre).

Step 7: Conducting the training

Go et al. suggest that if other aspects of the nine-step approach are adhered to the training activity/programme should be effectively delivered. Though rather like Marchington and Wilkinson they do also recognize a number of factors that might impact on the training, such as participant selection, ensuring the group feels comfortable physiologically and psychologically and ensuring the person delivering the training is properly prepared and has the right skills.

Step 8: Evaluating the training

The penultimate stage of the nine-step approach is to evaluate the training in order to glean feedback from the trainees. There are a number of methods of evaluating training, as identified by Holden (2004: 328):

- Questionnaires or so-called 'happiness sheets' are a useful way to elicit trainees' responses to courses and programmes.
- Tests or examinations are common in more formal training courses and are useful for checking the progress of trainees.
- Projects can be useful in providing useful information for instructors.
- Structured exercises and case studies allow for trainees to apply their learned skills and techniques under observation.
- Tutor reports allow for instructors to offer an assessment of the utility of the training.
- Interviews of trainees can be formal or informal, individual or group, or by telephone.
- Observation of courses by those responsible for devising training strategies can be very useful in the development of future training.
- Participation and discussion during the training, though this requires a highly skilled facilitator.
- Appraisal allows for the line manager and trainee to consider the success or otherwise of training that has been undertaken during performance reviews.

Of course a combination of these methods can be used in evaluating training and it is likely to be important to incorporate both trainee and trainer feedback in assessing the success or otherwise of training interventions.

Step 9: Planning further training

After the training and its evaluation, training has, in effect, come full circle and the planning process can begin again.

Conclusion

Training and development can be understood at a number of levels and it is particularly important to recognize the likely impact of government policy, in particular, in creating the VET infrastructure in which organizations will develop their policy and practice. Governments may either be relatively proactive in attempting to create an environment where training and development is seen as crucial or much more voluntaristic in leaving such decisions to organizations. For a long time the UK Government adopted a voluntaristic approach to training but it has become increasingly involved in developing training initiatives in recent years to address a perceived gap in training. In addition to the national level infrastructure we also recognized that the sectoral level is equally important and notwithstanding the emergence of initiatives such as Excellence in People and Welcome Host, tourism and hospitality has often been perceived as a sector with an indifferent training record. Notwithstanding debates about the provision or otherwise of training in tourism and hospitality when organizations do train they can draw upon a variety of differing methods, which are likely to differ in relation to differing occupations and skills. In that sense there is no one best training method, but rather different methods and techniques will be appropriate given the nature of the task and skills demands and importantly what is most cost effective for organizations.

References and further reading

Alberga, T., Tyson, S. and Parsons, D. (1997) 'An evaluation of the Investors in People standard', *Human Resource Management Journal*, 7(2), 47–60.

Anon (2003a) 'Staying the course', *Hospitality*, March, 16–17.

Anon (2003b) 'Hospitality companies fare well in training awards', *Caterer and Hotelkeeper*, 18 December, 10.

Armstrong, M. (1999) *A Handbook of Human Resource Management Practice*, Kogan Page, 7th edition.

Baum, T. (2006) *Human Resource Management for Tourism, Hospitality and Leisure: An International Perspective*, Thomson Learning.

Chartered Institute of Personnel and Development (2005) *On-the-Job Training Factsheet*, CIPD.

Chartered Institute of Personnel and Development (2006) *Investors in People Factsheet*, CIPD.

Druce, C. (2004) 'NVQs fail to meet the industry needs, agree colleges and employers', *Caterer and Hotelkeeper*, 21 October, 9.

Druce, C. (2005) 'Hospitality waits for People 1st to deliver results on skills crisis', *Caterer and Hotelkeeper*, 12 May, 6.

Finegold, D., Wagner, K. and Mason, G. (2000) 'National skill-creation systems and career paths for service workers: hotels in the United States, Germany and the United Kingdom', *International Journal of International Human Resource Management*, 11(3), 497–516.

Foote, R. (1999) 'NVQs: tension from both sides', *Hospitality Review*, October, 12–16.

Georgeson, R. (1999) 'Case studies: Investors in People: Ruffles Country House Hotel, St Andrews and The Willow Tea Rooms', *The Hospitality Review*, January, 21–25.

Go, F., Monachello, M. and Baum, T. (1996) *Human Resource Management for the Hospitality Industry*, Wiley.

Gospel, H. and Fuller, A. (1998) The Modern Apprenticeship: new wine in old bottles? *Human Resource Management Journal*, 8(1), 5–22.

Hales, C (1996) 'Factors influencing the adoption of NVQs in small hospitality businesses', *International Journal of Contemporary Hospitality Management*, 8(5), 5–9.

Holden, L. (2004) 'Human resource development: the organization and the national framework', in I. Beardwell, L. Holden and T. Claydon (eds.) *Human Resource Management: A Contemporary Approach*, Prentice Hall, 4th edition, 313–360.

Hope, K. (2005) 'Class act', *People Management*, 15 September, 16–17.

Hoque, K. (2003) 'All in all, it's just another plaque on the wall: the incidence and impact of the Investors in People standard', *Journal of Management Studies*, 40(2), 543–571.

Hyman, J. (1996) 'Training and development: the employer's responsibility?' in B. Towers (ed.) *The Handbook of Human Resource Management*, Blackwell, 2nd edition, 306–328.

Income Data Services (2005) *Understanding Sector Skills Councils*, HR Studies Update, No. 791, February.

Industrial Relations Services (1999) 'NVQs and SVQs mean business', *Employee Development Bulletin*, No. 109, January, 6–14.

Investors in People (2004) *Moving Your Organization Forward: The Investors in People Standard*, IiP UK.

Investors in People (2005) *Company Report 2004–2005: Stepping in the Right Direction*, IiP UK.

Keep, E. (2005) 'Skills, training and the quest for the holy grail of influence', in S. Bach (ed.) *Managing Human Resources: Personnel Management in Transition*, Blackwell, 4th edition, 211–236.

Kidger, P., Jackson-van Veen, M. and Redfearn, D. (2004) 'Transferring the Investors in People concept from the UK to The Netherlands', *Journal of European Industrial Training*, 28(6), 499–518.

Lucas, R. (1995) *Managing Employee Relations in the Hotel and Catering Industry*, Cassell.

Lucas, R. (2004) *Employment Relations in the Hospitality and Tourism Industries*, Routledge.

Manson, E. (2005) 'Hospitality lags behind other industries over apprenticeship scheme', *Caterer and Hotelkeeper*, 7 April, 8.

Marchington, M. and Wilkinson, A. (1996) *Core Personnel and Development*, CIPD.

Marchington, M. and Wilkinson, A. (2005) *Human Resource Management at Work: People Management and Development*, CIPD, 3rd edition.

Mason, A. (1997) 'Apprenticeships – do they work?' *Hospitality*, September/October, 26–27.

McKenna, E. and Beech, N. (2002) *Human Resource Management: A Concise Analysis*, Pearson Education Limited.

People 1st (2004) 'Permanent CEO for new skills body', *People 1st Press Release*, 7 October 2004.

Qualifications and Curriculum Authority (2003) *Establishing Qualification Requirements: Hospitality and Catering Industry*, QCA.

Salameh, M. and Barrows, C. (2001) 'The role of training in achieving TQM in restaurants', *Journal of Quality Assurance in Hospitality and Tourism*, 1(4), 73–95.

Scott, A. (1999) 'Investing in people?' *The Hospitality Review*, January, 25–30.

Scottish Tourism Research Unit (1998) *International Benchmarking and Best Practice Study of Training and Education for Tourism*, STRU.

Sweeney, A. (1995) 'Improving interpersonal relationships between staff and visitors with the "Welcome Host" scheme', *Proceedings of the Fourth Annual Council for Hospitality Management Education (CHME) Research Conference*, University of Brighton, 101–119.

Trapp, R. (2003) 'A flying start', *People Management*, 6 February, 36–38.

Trotter, A. (2005) 'Smells like team spirit', *Guardian Office Hours*, 21 March, 2–3.

Websites

Details of the various programmes run by Welcome Host can be found at http://www.welcometoexcellence. co.uk/WIIndex.htm

Details of the British Hospitality Association's Excellence Through People scheme can be found at http:// www.etp.org.uk/Home/Default.aspx

Investors in People has a number of case studies, including several from the tourism and hospitality sector at http://www.iipuk.co.uk/IIP/Web/Case+Studies/default.htm

For details of the UK training and education framework visit the QCA website at http://www.qca.org.uk/

The American Society for Training and Development has some useful resources on workplace training and learning at http://www.astd.org/astd

Chapter **8**

Performance management and performance appraisal

Chapter objectives

This chapter discusses performance management and performance appraisal. Specifically, the aims of the chapter are:

- To appreciate the difference between performance management and performance appraisal.
- To consider challenges facing tourism and hospitality managers in operationalizing performance appraisal schemes.
- To explore the differences between evaluative and developmental aspects of performance appraisal.
- To recognize the range of skills required by tourism and hospitality managers to successfully conduct performance appraisals.

Introduction

In considering the nature of performance management and performance appraisal we firstly need to appreciate how these two aspects are related but equally should not be seen synonymously. In fairly simple terms performance management can be seen as a holistic process which aims to bring together a number of aspects, including appraisal. Thus, performance management may be thought of as being more strategic in its intent to achieve high levels of organizational performance. By contrast, performance appraisal is best seen as being more operationally focused, with a focus on individual employees short- to medium-term performance and development (CIPD, 2005a). Consequently, to fully contextualize the notion of performance appraisal it is important to locate it within wider issues concerned with performance management systems (PMS) which may have an organizational, team or individual focus. Armstrong (2001: 469) suggests that performance management has a number of aims:

> Performance management is about getting better results from the organization, teams and individuals by understanding and managing performance within an agreed framework of planned goals, standards and competing requirements. It is a process for establishing shared understanding about what is to be achieved, and an approach to managing and developing people in a way which increases the probability that it will be achieved in the short and long term. It is owned and driven by management.

Clearly, then, organizations are always seeking improvements in their performance and these can be sustained by either development-type initiatives or more evaluative or even punitive measures, potentially encompassing aspects of discipline. In that sense performance management and performance appraisal can arguably be seen to again reflect to some degree the notions of 'hard' and 'soft' HRM. For example, the harder approaches would point to the need for organizations and managers to seek control over their employees; on the other hand softer approaches would point to the role of PMS in establishing greater commitment and developing careers. Recognizing the above discussion this chapter will aim to consider the question of what options are open to an organization seeking to improve the performance of its employees.

The nature of performance management and performance appraisal

Recent research undertaken by the CIPD provides a snapshot of a number of features of performance management, as outlined in Table 8.1.

Clearly one of the most important aspects of enhancing performance is performance appraisal, which is a critical element of performance management and a key feature of organizational life. As Bach (2005: 289) notes, 'performance appraisals have become far more than just an annual ritual and are viewed as a key lever to enhance organizational performance'. Performance appraisal is defined by Heery and Noon (2001: 7) as, '... the process of evaluating the performance and assessing

Table 8.1 Features of performance management

Feature	Percentage
Individual annual appraisal	65
Objective setting and review	62
Personal development plans	62
Career management and/or succession planning	37
Coaching and/or mentoring	36
Competence assessment	31
Performance related pay	31
Self-appraisal	30
Twice yearly/biannual appraisal	27
Continuous assessment	14
360-degree appraisal	14
Subordinate feedback	11
Rolling appraisal	10
Peer appraisal	8
Competence related pay	7
Team appraisal	6
Contribution related pay	4
Team pay	3

Source: This material is taken from *Managing Performance: Performance Management in Action* by Armstrong, M. and Baron, A., 2nd edition (2005), with the permission of the publisher, the Chartered Institute of Personnel and Development, London.

the development/training needs of an employee'. LRD (1997: 3) similarly note how performance appraisal is, 'A process of reviewing individual performances against pre-determined criteria or objectives, involving the gathering of information, one or more meetings and some form of report which may include a performance rating'. In sum, then, appraisal is a process that allows for an individual employee's overall capabilities and potential to be assessed for the purposes of improving their performance.

A recent survey by IRS (2005a) suggests that over 90 per cent of workplaces have some form of performance appraisal, usually a conventional top-down appraisal system. Moreover there has been a shift in recent years which have seen more and more organizational members subject to such appraisal, which had traditionally been geared more to managerial staff. Clearly given the skills mix which was discussed in Chapter 4, which points to a predominance of semi and unskilled workers in tourism and hospitality, there may well be a questioning of whether it is worthwhile appraising such workers, especially unskilled workers, as these jobs are likely to involve little technical expertise. For example, notwithstanding the earlier point about more organizational members being appraised, IRS (1999) suggested that less than a quarter of organizations across the economy as a whole surveyed semi or unskilled workers. If these employees are to be appraised some difficulties may be encountered in attempting to establish readily observable standards and criteria by which performance can be measured. There may also be the additional issue in tourism and hospitality of the predominance of small- and medium-sized enterprises. Goldsmith et al. (1997) note that appraisal is unlikely to be something that is realistic for a small family-concern type business or a single person operation. Consequently they advocate that appraisal has certain minimum requisites or parameters, including (p. 165):

- the equivalent of at least 20 full-time non-managerial employees;
- a minimum of one layer of professional management between the organization's proprietor and operative staff;
- some evidence of departmentalization where individual departments have their own heads or supervisors.

Given the above discussion it might seem reasonable to imagine that appraisal is less likely to be a part of a systematic approach to HRM in tourism and hospitality. However, the evidence seems to suggest that the opposite may in fact be true. For example, Lucas (2004) in her interrogation of the Workplace Employee Relations Survey data, found that 85 per cent of managers in the hospitality and tourism industry had responsibility for performance appraisal. Interestingly, Lucas also found that performance appraisal is more likely to be used in the hospitality industry compared to all private sector service organizations. Similarly, Hoque (1999) found that 89 per cent of the 232 hotels he surveyed regularly used appraisal, compared to 62 per cent of similar sized establishments in manufacturing. Woods et al. (1998) also found a high incidence of appraisal within the US. In a survey of 1000 hotels covering all geographic areas, all types of market segment, ownership type, size and number of employees Woods et al. found that two-thirds of his sample had an annual appraisal. Clearly appraisal then is a significant part of broader HRM concerns in hospitality and tourism and we can now go on to consider some of the challenges facing managers in operationalizing appraisal schemes.

Appraisal in practice

To begin to assess the impact of performance appraisal we should start with a simple question: Why should organizations appraise people at work? A range of writers (see e.g. Bach, 2005; IRS, 2005a, b) suggest a number of reasons, including:

- Appraisal can be an integral part of ensuring that organizational members are aware of what is expected of them and can thus play an important part in socializing organizational members to 'buy in' to the organizational culture. For example, Groeschl and Doherty (2002: 58) note how, 'Its value as an organizational socialization process is closely associated with organizational attempts to manage "culture", another essential element of the HRM approach to the employment relationship'. Indeed, Bach (2005) notes that increasingly organizations are now using performance management as a means to introduce cultural changes in organizations.
- Improve current performance.
- *Provide feedback*: We all seek approval and conformation that we are doing the right thing, and we also like to advise or direct others on how they should do things.
- Increase motivation.
- Identify training and development needs.

- Identify potential.
- Let individuals know what is expected of them.
- Focus on career development and succession planning.
- Award salary increases/performance related pay.
- Evaluate the effectiveness of the selection process.
- Solve job problems.
- *Set objectives*: Using the *SMART* mnemonic, *s*pecific or *s*tretching (define precisely what is required in clear language), *m*easurable (both quantitatively and qualitatively), *a*ccepted (objectives agreed and not imposed), *r*ealistic (achievable and fairly allocated) and *t*ime-bound (clear target dates). For example, in a tourism and hospitality context it might be things like servers trying got increase their sales per shift, chambermaids cleaning more rooms, receptionists attempting to become more skilled in information technology, improving communication skills or learning to speak a foreign language.

In reality, in most workplaces staff are being continually monitored and assessed by management in an informal manner. Indeed, ACAS (2005: 2) suggest that, 'regular dialogue between managers and their staff about work performance should, of course, be encouraged'. That said, the danger with such informality is that it is very much dependent on individual managers and whether they are giving regular feedback. Consequently, ACAS further note that an appraisal system can develop a greater degree of consistency by ensuring that managers and employees meet formally and regularly to discuss performance and potential. What we are concerned to examine in this chapter is the formalized manner by which staff are assessed during performance appraisals. That is, the process of reviewing individual performance against pre-determined criteria or objectives, involving the gathering of information and one or more meetings on a quarterly, 6 monthly or annual basis, and producing some form of report which is likely to include a performance rating. As described above performance appraisal can be seen in a fairly positive vein and useful in terms of things like raising morale, clarifying expectations, improving upward and downward communication and so on (and see HRM in practice 8.1).

Review and reflect

What are some of the likely difficulties in appraising employees in tourism and hospitality?

HRM in practice 8.1 Appraisal: Some good news

Research conducted by Armstrong and Baron (2005) on behalf of the Institute of Personnel and Development in the late 1990s found that employees and managers offered favourable rather than unfavourable views on appraisal. Some of the comments from the research included:

'You need appraisal to get the best out of people and develop them.'

'In a one-to-one meeting, people can bring things out to their supervisors who say "I've never been aware of that: why didn't you tell us before?" That's definitely an advantage.'

'For me, the real strength of the process lies in the continuing dialogue and negotiation as the year goes on.'

'You're one-to-one with your boss. You've chatted, and it wasn't as if it was your boss. It was more relaxed. He would listen and then you'd chat about it. I enjoyed it.'

Despite the above discussion, which points to why performance appraisal might be thought of as a 'good' thing, in reality there is much debate and concern surrounding the notion of appraisal. For example, W. Edwards Deming, a leading advocate of TQM, has suggested that appraisal is wrong in principle and an ineffective management philosophy, describing it as a 'deadly disease' (cited in Bach, 2005). Similarly, Stephen Covey, the well-known management guru, has described appraisal as a 'disgusting habit', outmoded and more suited for an industrial age that no longer exists (cited in IRS, 2005a). Indeed, as long ago as 1957 the famous management theorist Douglas McGregor, of Theory X and Y fame, was suggesting that appraisal is the most contentious and least popular part of a manager's job. Managers dislike the process as they do not like 'playing God', which leads to a judgemental and ultimately de-motivating approach:

The respect we hold for the inherent value of the individual leaves us distressed when we must take responsibility for judging the personal worth of a fellow man. Yet the conventional approach to performance appraisal forces us, not only to make such judgements and to see them acted upon, but also to communicate them to those we have judged. Small wonder we resist! (McGregor, 1957: 90).

HRM in practice 8.2   Appraisal: Some common negative managerial thoughts about appraisal

'Well, here we go again, I'm sure you don't like this business any more than I do, so let's get on with it.'

'Now, there's nothing to worry about. It's quite painless and could be useful. So just relax and let me put a few questions to you.'

'I wonder if I will end up conning you more than you will succeed in conning me.'

'Right. Let battle commence!'

Managers may also regard appraisal as a waste of time and overly bureaucratic and may also see it as a process that involves relatively high costs in setting up the scheme and training employees in using the scheme (and see HRM in practice 8.2).

In part, some of these negative views of appraisal could potentially be addressed by training for managers to ensure that they are clear of the importance of appraisal. For example, IRS (2005a: 9) note that, 'if managers are not properly trained and committed to the appraisal system, the performance review can become just a paperwork exercise, at best, or – at worst – a harmful one'. This view points to the issue of whether appraisals per se are problematic or whether much of the problem lies in carrying out the appraisal, specifically whether appraisals are performed poorly by uninterested or badly trained managers. Training, then, may help managers to appreciate the importance of appraisal within a broader performance management approach and also the need to develop coaching skills to facilitate a more developmental approach.

Such training may be appropriate in attempting to address some of the problems which may plague appraisal such as (Bach, 2005; Torrington et al., 2005; IRS, 2005a):

- Prejudice, for example, sex or race discrimination.
- Subjectivity and bias, especially with regard to rater bias.
- Insufficient knowledge of the appraisee – so appraiser position is based on position in hierarchy, rather than any real knowledge of person's job.
- The 'halo' and 'horns' effect where managers rate employees on the basis of their personal relationships rather than by objective measure of their competencies and abilities.

- The problem of context – the difficulty of distinguishing the work of appraisees from the context in which they work, especially when there is a degree of comparison with other appraisees.
- What might be termed the 'paradox of roles' in terms of the conflation of judge and counsellor (mentor) role which can lead to confusion. For example, in the shift from an evaluative to a developmental approach managers have to manage such tensions.
- The paperwork – overly bureaucratic and simply about form filling.
- The formality – for both appraiser and appraisee it can be an uncomfortable experience.
- Outcomes are ignored.
- Everyone is 'average or just above average', for example, managers may find it difficult to give an employee a bad rating as they would not want to justify the criticisms in the performance review interview.
- Appraising the wrong features – too much stress on easily identifiable things like timekeeping, looking busy, being pleasant and so on.
- 'Recency bias' leading to a tendency to base appraisals on the recent past, regardless of how representative it is of performance over the course of the previous year.

In many respects the above issues reflect what Bach (2005) calls the 'orthodox critique', wherein many of the problems above could potentially be addressed by seeking to remedy the imperfections in the design and implementation of the appraisal system or by improving managerial training in conducting appraisals. For some though there may well be much more fundamental criticisms to be made about the process of appraisal.

Bach (2005) notes the emergence of more critical accounts of appraisal, in particular recognizing how, 'unitary assumptions about the benevolent purposes of appraisal are replaced by a more radical ideology concerned to examine managerial objectives, especially tighter control over behaviour and performance, the potential to individualize the employment relationship and the scope for managers to use appraisal as a veneer to legitimate informal management' (p. 305). For example, many of the criticisms, drawing on the work of Foucault, see appraisal as inherently sinister and about aiming to control all aspects of employee behaviour and eliminating scope for employee resistance, so appraisal is simply about bolstering managerial power and control; a point that is similar to some of the criticisms of organizational culture outlined in Chapter 3. In sum, Bach suggests that critical perspectives seek to highlight that it should not be assumed that clearer objectives and training of appraisers will necessarily yield satisfactory results. Consequently it is important to recognize how, 'the contested nature of appraisal, the specific managerial objectives sought, and the nature of the context in which it is applied, all have an important bearing on the impact of the appraisal process' (p. 306).

Thus, we can appreciate that appraisal is very much a contested issue, both conceptually and practically. Equally, though, as Holdsworth (1991: 65) rightly suggests, 'appraisal is a compulsively fascinating subject, full of paradoxes and love–hate relationships. And appraisal schemes are really controversial … Some schemes are popular, with overtones of evangelical fervour, while others are at least equally detested and derided as the "annual rain dance", "the end of term report", etc.' (and see HRM in practice 8.3 for how a number of the issues discussed above were played out within ANO, a French hotel chain, which introduced a new appraisal system).

Ultimately, despite the debates surrounding its utility, appraisal is a fact of organizational life, and as Bratton and Gold (2003: 252) note, 'making judgements about an employee's contribution, value/worth, capability and potential has to be considered as a vital relationship with employees'. Moreover, as we noted above there may be an argument, rather like employment interviewing, to say that the process in itself is not necessarily flawed, but the individuals operationalizing it are insufficiently skilled.

Review and reflect

What are some of the skills likely to be required by managers in order to conduct a good appraisal?

Given the reality of performance appraisal being an inevitable part of a manager's life we can now look at the practicalities in appraising employees. In appraising employees a number of writers have outlined two main perspectives the evaluative and the developmental. In the former approach the main aim is to make a judgement about an appraisees performance, with such a judgement being made against aspects such as the job description and established objectives, which may be linked to extrinsic rewards. Often this will also involve managers making rating or ranking decisions that differentiate between staff on the basis of their relative

HRM in practice 8.3   The rhetoric and reality of appraisal in ANO Hotels

Groeschl and Doherty (2002) report on the introduction of a new appraisal system in ANO, which is part of a French multinational travel and tourism group and operates at the three star level. In 1998 a standardized appraisal system was developed for the company as a whole in order that it could be implemented in all their brands, including ANO. This attempt at standardizing appraisal was to ensure that all employees across the company's various brands would be appraised against the same criteria to ensure a consistent evaluation of employee performance. The new appraisal system was developed at the corporate headquarters and the working group which developed the system initially evaluated the old system to identify weaknesses. Once this was done they then developed suggestions and proposals for the new system, which were then sent to regional management teams for their comments and feedback. These exchanges continued for 6 months before finally there was agreement on the standardized criteria and a number of aims and objectives. A key aim of the new system was to ensure a basis for planning for action, particularly with regard to career progress. The new appraisal system was an example of a development-oriented appraisal system and the appraisal format was considered a formal and sophisticated document. Employees were assessed with ratings ranging from 'very good' to 'insufficient' on 13 standardized competencies, including aptitudes and skills. Although the process of introducing a new appraisal system seemed well planned and thought out there was still some issues that emerged. For example, some managers seemed unable to sufficiently differentiate from day-to-day feedback with the formal appraisal process. Appraisers would also often be inconsistent in their preparation for appraisal, failing to notify appraisees sufficiently in advance or not filling in the appraisal form correctly. Appraisers would also often run appraisals in public spaces, such as bars and restaurants, which runs counter to the advice often offered in textbooks. Lastly, there was also significant variance in the appraisers style. Some appraisers recognized the developmental nature of the new system and developed an advisory/supportive role in the appraisal; whilst others were much more judgemental and authoritarian. In sum, although ANO had clear objectives, documentation and guidelines, all of which reflected good practice HRM, the implementation proved rather trickier. Closer monitoring of the process by the HR managers, or line managers with a strong interest/involvement in HRM could have improved the situation. Equally, the case seems to point to the need to provide managers with the appropriate skills which allows them to take on more of a facilitator or coaching role in the appraisal process.

HRM in practice 8.4   Appraisal talking points: Evaluating or developing?

As we have already noted there may be some debate as to whether performance reviews of appraisals should be evaluative or developmental. Consider how you would respond to the talking points below in assessing this conundrum.

Talking point 1

As part of an appraisal process you want to tell a member of staff in your travel agency that you feel as though they lack initiative and that this is severely hindering their performance in their front-line job. How do you approach this issue?

Talking point 2

Should appraisal be linked to pay?

Talking point 3

Should appraisal look forwards or backwards?

performance. On other hand, developmental approaches are likely to have a different premise, where the appraiser and appraisee aim to discuss the progress, hopes and fears of the appraisee in a mutually supportive atmosphere and where the ultimate aim is on developing performance by building on employees strengths (and see HRM in practice 8.4).

In reality, within any given organizational setting there may not be such an absolute and clear cut distinction and their may be elements of both evaluative and developmental approaches, such that the purpose of performance appraisal has tended to oscillate between concerns about short-term performance to a more developmental orientation. Appraisal has also been used as a disciplinary tool by some organizations, with poor performance being something that appraisals systems have sought to address, a point to which we will return later. As we have already noted above though the character and emphasis of appraisal has increasingly changed in recent years. For example, Bach (2005: 291) notes how:

> During the 1990s there was a shift from almost exclusive emphasis on reward driven systems, based on individual performance related pay and quantifiable objectives, towards more rounded systems of performance management with a stronger developmental focus.

HRM in practice 8.5   The use of BARS in the American hotel industry

BARS aims to evaluate managers' actions. Umbreit et al. (1986) developed a BARS format to evaluate what hotel managers do in their jobs using seven rating scales for a number of key aspects of job performance. The aspects of job performance were: communication skills, handling guest complaints and promoting guest relations, developing marketing strategies and monitoring sales programmes, motivating and modifying employee behaviour, implementing policy, making decisions, and delegating responsibilities, monitoring operations and maintaining product quality and handling personnel responsibilities. For example, with regard to communication skills, at the top of the scale at 7 is a manager who communicates effectively by for example calling a meeting to explain why the hotel will be cutting staff. In the middle is a manager who communicates satisfactorily between 4 and 5, for example, a manager who meets with several employees once a week for an informal talk about the hotel's activities. Lastly, at the bottom is a manager who experiences difficulties in communicating with staff at 1–2, for example, during an executive meeting a manager who dismisses a subordinates comments as stupid.

Source: Woods et al. (1998).

We will consider this point in due course. However, it is important to recognize that many appraisal systems will still retain attempts to measure performance, often using a variety of techniques. For example, Woods et al. (1998) found that hotels in their survey used one or more of four approaches, these being management by objective (MBO) (48 per cent), behaviourally anchored rating scales (BARS) (41 per cent), narrative essay (37 per cent) and graphic rating scale (28 per cent). Other methods which organizations may use include performance standards and matching performance against job descriptions, rating an employee based on a scale, which may for example range from 'outstanding' to 'unacceptable' and critical incidents (and see also HRM in practice 8.5).

HRM in practice 8.5 gives an indication of the types of activities which may be assessed in judging the performance for managers in the tourism and hospitality industry. Clearly, in addition to these aspects there may be a range of other attributes that can be used to measure the individual performance of an employee. For example, CIPD (2005b) reporting on a survey of over 500 organizations across the

Table 8.2 Criteria used to measure individual performance

	Respondents (%)			
	Very important	Important	Not very important	Not used as a measure
Customer care	45	40	7	5
Quality	47	44	3	4
Flexibility	22	56	13	4
Competence	53	40	3	2
Skills/learning targets	18	57	16	4
Business awareness	17	52	21	6
Working relationships	35	53	7	3
Contribution to team	34	57	4	2
Financial awareness	11	47	28	10
Productivity	34	49	9	6
Aligning personal objectives with organizational goals	29	48	16	4
Achievement of objectives	52	42	3	1

Source: This material is taken from *Performance Management Survey Report* by CIPD (2005), with the permission of the publisher, the Chartered Institute of Personnel and Development, London.

economy outline a number of criteria and their relative importance to how organizations measure individual performance, and these are considered in Table 8.2.

Similarly, IDS (1989, cited in McKenna and Beech, 2002) suggest a number of performance factors which are likely to be appraised, the most important being:

- Knowledge, ability and skill on the job.
- Attitude to work, expressed as enthusiasm, commitment and motivation.
- Quality of work on a consistent basis and attention to detail.
- Volume of productive output.
- Interaction, as exemplified in communication skills and ability to relate to others in teams.

As we noted above though the focus of appraisal is increasingly argued to be shifting to one of a more developmental focus. Given that much of the discussion above has outlined an approach to appraisal which is predominately top-down, there may be other approaches, which may be seen as less biased and potentially offering greater scope for development. Some of these other approaches are now briefly discussed.

Self-appraisal: Bach (2005) notes the manner in which the appraisal process in a number of organizations increasingly expects employees to take greater owner-ship, 'with employees assigned greater responsibility for establishing their own performance goals and for obtaining feedback on their performance' (p. 293). With self-appraisal, then, instead of employees' being passive recipients of their line manager's appraisal they are increasingly involved via some form of self-assessment, often being more critical than if the manager conducted the appraisal (McKenna and Beech, 2002). In such an approach employees are increasingly expected to take the lead in the discussions – it should not just be a case of downwards feedback from the line manager. Indeed, in some instances employees may draft their own performance reviews, which then forms the basis for the discussion with their line manager (IDS, 2005).

Peer appraisal: Fellow team members, departmental colleagues or selected indi-viduals with whom an individual has been working provide the assessment of performance.

Upward appraisal: Managers are appraised by their staff (and see the discussion of attitude surveys in Chapter 10).

Customer appraisal: Redman (2006) notes the increasing importance of customers in the appraisal process, which in part reflects the emergence and development of TQM and customer care programmes. As he recognizes, 'one impact of these initia-tives is that organizations are now increasingly setting employee performance stand-ards based upon customer care indicators and appraising staff against these' (p. 163). For example, Redman notes how these can be both in terms of 'hard' quantifiable measures, such as whether a drink is delivered in a certain amount of time in a restaurant; to 'soft' measures, which are more qualitative, such as whether a warm and friendly greeting is given by staff in giving the customer the drink. Moreover, Redman notes the use of service guarantees, 'which involve the payment of com-pensatory moneys to customers if the organizations do not reach the standards' (p. 163), which again also means a greater use of customer data in appraisal ratings.

In terms of the use of customer service data and how it may be used to appraise employees, Redman notes how it can be gathered by a variety of means.

- *Customer surveys*: Organizations are now becoming increasingly sophisticated in the manner in which they gather customer feedback, which is gathered via a number of means such as the use of customer care cards, telephone surveys, interviews with customers and postal surveys.

- *Range of surveillance techniques*: Managers may 'sample' the service encounter. For example, if a travel company had a call centre managers could listen to some of the calls between customers and the call centre operatives.
- *'Mystery' or 'phantom' shopper*: Mystery shoppers observe and record their experience of the service encounter and report these findings back to the organization. Although this method may be seen as rather controversial – employees may view the mystery shoppers as 'spies' or 'snoopers' and indulge in 'shopper spotting' – it is widely used in the tourism and hospitality industry. Redman argues that the controversy surrounding mystery shoppers may be dissipated to an extent if they are used primarily for encouraging and rewarding good performance, rather than punishing staff for performing poorly.

Review and reflect

If you have been subject to any of the above aspects in your working life in tourism and hospitality how did you feel about being assessed by these means? Did you feel that it gave a fair representation of your performance?

Customer feedback may be used as a stand-alone aspect of performance management, or may be an integral part of 360-degree feedback.

Multi-rater or 360-degree feedback: CIPD (2006) notes how 360-degree feedback has been increasingly talked about, if not necessarily widely used. Performance data is generated from a variety of sources, which can include the person to whom the individual being assessed reports, people who report to them, peers (team colleagues or others in the organization), and internal and external customers. It may also include self-assessment and will often be part of a self-development or management development programme. 360-degree feedback is felt to provide a more rounded view of people, with less bias than if an assessment is conducted by one individual.

The practicalities: the appraisal form and interview

Most PMS are likely to have a formal final performance review, where an individual employee is assessed against their objectives (inputs and outputs). This review is also likely to allow for a review of training and development needs. With regard to the practicalities of conducting the review, it is likely that most companies will use the appraisal form to structure the discussion. ACAS (2005) notes how most performance appraisal forms should contain provision for:

- basic personal details, such as name, department, post, length of time in the job;
- job title;
- job description;
- a detailed review of the individual's performance against a set of job related criteria;
- an overall performance rating;
- general comments by a more senior manager;
- comments by the employee;
- a plan for development and action.

In approaching the appraisal interview the discussion to date gives a sense of some of the potential pitfalls that might befall a manager in conducting an appraisal interview. To an extent as well the nature and tone of the appraisal interview will be dictated by whether a scheme is seeking a broadly evaluative or developmental approach. That said, Torrington et al. (2005) in their review of appraisal interviewing advocate the need to seek an approach which is concerned with seeking joint approaches to enhance performance. Underpinning such an approach is a problem-solving style, which is summarized in the following manner:

> The appraiser starts the interview by encouraging the employee to identify and discuss problem areas and then consider solutions. The employee therefore plays an active part in analysing problems and suggesting solutions, and the evaluation of performance emerges from the discussion at the appraisal interview, instead of being imposed by the appraiser upon the employee (Anderson, 1993: 102, cited in Torrington et al., 2005: 341).

Much of the above discussion points to the need for managers to have the right skillset that allows them to appraise well; as well as understanding how appraisal fits in to the wider issue of performance management and organizational strategy generally. In terms of practical skills though there may be aspects such as asking the right questions, the ability to be a good listener and giving useful feedback. In sum, CIPD (2005a: 4) offers a view on what 'good' and 'bad' appraisals look like:

On the one hand a 'good' and constructive appraisal meeting is one in which:

- Appraisees do most the talking.
- Appraisers listen actively to what they say.
- There is scope for reflection and analysis.
- Performance is analysed and not personality.
- The whole period is reviewed and not just recent or isolated events.
- Achievement is recognized and reinforced.
- Ends positively with agreed action plans.

On the other hand a 'bad' appraisal meeting:

- Focuses on a catalogue of failures and omissions.
- Is controlled by the appraiser.
- Ends with disagreement between appraiser and appraisee.

Managing poor performance

Of course there is always the potential issue of how to manage poor performers and a clear rationale for the introduction of PMS is to seek to identify and address any instances of poor performance. If a PMS is underpinned by regular meetings, feedback and coaching then these issues should be picked up relatively quickly. Organizations can then attempt to address poor performance through some form of improvement development programme, which will often involve employees being given extensive help in the form of training and coaching. Armstrong (2001: 484–485) suggests that there are five basic steps in handling performance problems:

1 Identify and agree the problem through analysing feedback and getting agreement from the employee what the shortfall has been.
2 Establish the reason(s) for the shortfall and avoid crudely attaching blame for problems in the job.
3 Decide and agree on the action required, whether it be things like a change in attitude, behaviour or improvements in certain skills or abilities.

4 Resource the action by providing coaching, training and guidance to ensure that changes can be made.

5 Monitor and provide feedback, which may also include an element of self-management in the learning process.

Thus, as IDS (2005: 9) notes, 'in this way, most poor performers will either improve to a satisfactory level within a given timescale or as a last resort would be liable for dismissal under capability procedures', an issue that is further discussed in Chapter 12.

Conclusion

Despite concerns performance appraisal remains a key part of organizational life. Often an integral part of a broader PMS performance appraisals are a crucial, if rather unloved, part of a manager's job. We recognized in the chapter how debates about performance appraisal may not just reflect fundamental criticisms but also more prosaic issues, such as managers not having the necessary skillset to conduct appraisals which are more developmentally oriented in particular. Many of these issues are particularly pronounced in the tourism and hospitality sector where the predominance of SMEs, the nature of the skills mix in the industry and difficulties in judging 'softer' and less quantifiable aspects of performance may all mean that the development of a systematic approach to appraisal remains problematic. Nevertheless evidence suggests that the majority of tourism and hospitality organizations are seeking to appraise their employees. Given this reality it is important for organizations and managers to recognize the challenges in conducting positive appraisals. Recognition of these challenges and the skills needed to address them means that 'playing God' may not be quite so painful for managers as has often been the case in the past.

References and further reading

Advisory, Conciliation and Arbitration Service (2005) *Employee Appraisal*, ACAS.

Armstrong, M. (2001) *A Handbook of Human Resource Management Practice*, Kogan Page, 8th edition.

Armstrong, M. and Baron, A. (2005) *Managing Performance: Performance Management in Action*, CIPD.

Bach, S. (2005) 'New directions in performance management', in S. Bach (ed.) *Managing Human Resources: Personnel Management in Transition*, Blackwell, 4th edition, 289–316.

Bratton, J. and Gold, J. (2003) *Human Resource Management – Theory and Practice*, Palgrave, 3rd edition.

Chartered Institute of Personnel and Development (2005a) *Performance Appraisal Factsheet*, CIPD.

Chartered Institute of Personnel and Development (2005b) *Performance Management Survey Report*, CIPD.

Chartered Institute of Personnel and Development (2006) *Performance Management Factsheet*, CIPD.

Goldsmith, A., Nickson, D., Sloan, D. and Wood, R. (1997) *Human Resources Management for Hospitality Services*, International Thomson Business Press.

Groeschl, S. and Doherty, L. (2002) 'The appraisal process: beneath the surface', *Journal of Human Resources in Hospitality and Tourism*, 1(3), 57–76.

Heery, E. and Noon, M. (2001) *A Dictionary of Human Resource Management*, Oxford University Press.

Holdsworth, R. (1991) 'Appraisal' in F. Neale (ed.) *The Handbook of Performance Management*, IPM, 64–81.

Hoque, K. (1999) 'New approaches to HRM in the UK hotel industry', *Human Resource Management Journal*, 9(2), 64–76.

Income Data Services (2005) *Performance Management*, IDS Studies, No. 796, April.

Industrial Relations Services (1999) 'New ways to perform appraisals', *IRS Employment Review*, No. 676, March, 7–16.

Industrial Relations Services (2005a) 'Appraisals (1): not living up to expectations', *IRS Employment Review*, No. 828, 29 July, 9–15.

Industrial Relations Services (2005b) 'Appraisals (2): learning from practice and experience', *IRS Employment Review*, No. 829, 12 August, 13–17.

Labour Research Department (1997) *Performance Appraisal*, LRD.

Lucas, R. (2004) *Employment Relations in the Hospitality and Tourism Industries*, Routledge.

McGregor, D. (1957) 'An uneasy look at performance appraisal', *Harvard Business Review*, 35(3), 89–94.

McKenna, E. and Beech, N. (2002) *Human Resource Management: A Concise Analysis*, Pearson Education Limited.

Redman, T. (2006) 'Performance appraisal', in T. Redman and A. Wilkinson (eds.) *Contemporary Human Resource Management: Texts and Cases*, Prentice Hall, 2nd edition, 153–187.

Torrington, D., Hall, L. and Taylor, S. (2005) *Human Resource Management*, Prentice-Hall, 6th edition.

Umbreit, T., Eder, R. and McConnell, J. (1986) 'Performance appraisals: making them fair and making them work', *Cornell Hotel and Restaurant Administration Quarterly*, 26, 4, 59–69.

Woods, R., Sciarini, M. and Breiter, D. (1998) 'Performance appraisal in hotels', *Cornell Hotel and Restaurant Administration Quarterly*, 39(2), 25–29.

Websites

Workforce Management has a description of a 360-degree appraisal process in Yum Brands Inc (*Workforce Management*, April 2005, pp. 59–60). This article can be found at http://www.workforce.com/index.html at the main site use the free registration facility then find the article via the search facility.

The CIPD Performance Management survey can be found at http://www. cipd.co.uk/surveys

There are a number of helpful tips and tools to improve appraisal at http://www.businessballs.com/performanceappraisals.htm

Chapter 9

Reward strategies in the tourism and hospitality industry

Chapter objectives

This chapter considers reward strategies in the tourism and hospitality industry. Specifically this chapter will:

- Review differing employer and employee objectives with regard to pay.
- Consider debates about minimum and maximum wages and comparability of pay across tourism and hospitality sub-sectors and occupations.
- Recognize the importance of tipping as part of the reward package in tourism and hospitality.
- Discuss the variety of additional non-monetary rewards available to tourism and hospitality employers.

Introduction

The first problem we face when thinking about the notion of reward strategies is a terminological one. When we talk about rewards we are likely to hear a variety of terms. For example, Foot and Hook (2005) note a number of commonly used terms used to describe payment systems, including 'compensation', 'remuneration', 'reward', 'payment', 'wages' and 'salaries'. Increasingly in a prescriptive HRM sense there is much talk of 'total remuneration planning', 'reward management' or 'reward strategy' as denoting a more strategic and holistic approach to the rewarding of employees. Therefore in this more prescriptive view it is argued that employees seek a range of monetary and non-monetary rewards – the so-called 'cafeteria approach' – from employment of which money is only one aspect, even if it is often the primary consideration for employees. Thus, employees may seek both extrinsic and intrinsic and financial and non-financial rewards at work. That said, a more realistic assessment is that in reality the provision of extrinsic rewards is certainly the most substantive issue in the effort–reward bargain and often the most problematic aspect of employment. Therefore this chapter will focus on the notion of extrinsic rewards and in particular pay as it will often be the main reason why people work. In considering pay and other aspects of remuneration, this chapter will also recognize how the nature of tourism and hospitality as an employing sector will significantly impact on the development of reward strategies. For example, the existence of a relatively large number of unskilled and semi-skilled employees means low pay is endemic in many parts of the tourism and hospitality sector, particularly the sub-sector of hotel and catering.

Employee and employer views of pay

Torrington et al. (2005) recognize how, 'the contract for payment will be satisfactory in so far as it meets the objectives of the parties' (p. 569). In recognizing this point we can now consider how these objectives are likely to differ depending on whether it is employees or employers.

Employee objectives for the contract for payment

Purchasing power
The absolute level of weekly or monthly earnings will determine the standard of living of individual employees, so they will aim to maximize their purchasing

power. In simple terms, employees will ask themselves how much they can buy with their earnings. Torrington et al. suggest that employees will rarely be truly satisfied about their purchasing power. Indeed, it could be argued that purchasing power has become ever more resonant in an era of conspicuous consumption in which marketing and advertizing portray a wide array of goods or services which people should be aspiring to consume.

Felt to be fair

In many respects the notion of felt to be fair is captured in the idiom of 'a fair's day pay for a fair day's work'. In this sense employees tend to have a strong sense of what they feel is an appropriate level of payment which is fair to the job they are doing. As Torrington et al. note the employees who feel underpaid are likely to withdraw from the job and are more likely to be absent or late, for example. This situation can be exacerbated if an employee has no real choice in terms of potentially moving elsewhere. Of course employees may not simply feel underpaid, there may be some instances were employees actually feel they are overpaid. In such instances employees may feel guilty or attempt to look busy, which from an organizational point of view may not necessarily be particularly productive.

Rights

Here Torrington et al. recognize the fundamental issue of the rights of employees to a particular share of a company's profit or the nation's wealth. Clearly, the manner in which wealth is currently shared out is one which engenders much debate and many employees might feel that they are not getting a reasonable or fair share of the wealth that is created. This general sense of unease will often be expressed by trade unions in particular, who will seek to create a more fair division of wealth based often on notions of social and economic justice.

Relativities

Torrington et al. note that a question often asked by employees is 'how much do I (or we) get relative to ... group X?' (p. 597). In that sense the notion of relativities is similar to the issues considered in the discussion of felt to be fair. Here though the employee will not ask whether remuneration is fair to the job done, but instead whether it is reasonable compared to jobs done by other people. Comparison may take place at a number of levels from the immediacy of the person sitting at the next desk to other companies or other professional or occupational groups. Much of this comparison may not be based on an entirely objective view. For example, in comparing one job with another there may be significantly more responsibility in a job that perhaps shares a similar title or job description.

Notions of felt fair, rights and relativities are particularly important and will often lie at the heart of much of the debate and controversy which is generated about pay and especially whether people are being 'fairly' paid (see HRM in practice 9.1).

Review and reflect

Are the chief executives described in HRM in practice 9.1 'greedy bastards', as John Edmonds suggests, or fairly remunerated?

Recognition

Torrington et al. note how most employees want to see their personal contribution recognized either to be reassured of their worth or to facilitate career progression. Part of this recognition may well be financial recognition, though in reality there may be other aspects as well as the financial in recognizing and improving performance.

Composition

Composition refers to the issue of how a pay package is made up and how this may vary between individual employees, depending on things like age or sex. For example, younger employees may be much more concerned with high direct earnings at the expense of indirect benefits such as pensions, which are likely to be of more interest to older employees. Other issues surrounding the composition of pay packages include aspects such as overtime and incentive or performance-related pay.

Employer objectives for the contract of payment

Prestige

As Torrington et al. note, 'there is a comfortable and understandable conviction among managers that it is "a good thing" to be a good payer' (p. 598). Clearly part of the reason for being a good payer is to attract the best labour which is available to an organization. Torrington et al. warn that being a good payer does not axiomatically bestow a reputation as a good employer. That said, they also suggest

HRM in practice 9.1   The disparities between those who have and those who do not have in tourism and hospitality

Much of the debate about disparities in pay focuses on notions of fairness and equity and the difference between those at the top and bottom of the earnings ladder. Indeed, the issue of pay inequality has often been at the forefront of trade union campaigns to increase wages for those lower down the organizational hierarchy. For example, John Edmonds, then general secretary of the GMB union, once famously railed against private sector bosses who awarded themselves inflated pay increases describing them as 'greedy bastards' (Milne and White, 1998) who were indulging in the 'politics of the pig trough' (Milne, 1998). Certainly this debate has some resonance for tourism and hospitality and over the years there has been plenty of evidence to suggest that there is a significant pay gap between those who have and those who do not have in tourism and hospitality.

Travel and Leisure Industry Salary Survey 1997 found that the highest paid directors at the UK's top 12 tourism and hospitality companies earned an average of £478 500, compared to a staff average of £11 360. Some of the so-called 'fat cats' were:

Peter George – Ladbroke chief executive £1 280 000

Gerry Robinson – Granada chairman £728 000 (though in December 1999 by cashing in share options he made a pre-tax profit of £5.26 million)

Sir Ian Prosser – Bass chairman £678 000

Caterer and Hotelkeeper (23 December 1999) reported that chief executives in the hospitality industry received an average pay increase of 20.8 per cent, compared to 3.5 per cent for employees.

Caterer and Hotelkeeper (18 May 2000) reported how David Thomas, Chief Executive of Whitbread, saw his total salary raised by 25.8 per cent, while group profits dropped by 14.8 per cent. His overall earnings were £593 103. The same article also reports how the average basic salary of 20 selected chief executives in the hospitality and leisure sectors was £330 835, which with bonuses and benefits rose to £370 293.

Leisure and Hospitality Business (25 July 2002) reported the highest paid chief executives packages for 2001/2002. The highest earner was Tom Oliver, Director of Six Continents Hotels and Resorts, who had a basic salary of £527 000, bonuses of £533 000 and benefits of £207 000, giving him an overall package of £1 267 000. The lowest paid director was Paul Dermody of the De Vere Group. His basic salary was £231 000, his bonus was £50 000 and his benefits £13 000, giving him a total salary of £294 000.

IRS Employment Review (19 May 2006) report a survey of salaries in the leisure industry. Amongst other things it notes that the average employee in the industry earns £18 602 a year, just 4.4 per cent of the average £501 613 paid to chief executives.

HRM in practice 9.2   The NMW in the leisure industry

IDS (2004) note that in the past many companies in the leisure sector have preferred to keep their rates well ahead of the NMW. However, more recently the level at which the NMW has been uprated has meant that some leisure employers have found it more difficult to be a higher paying employer. In the past by paying above the NMW some leisure employers were seen as 'good' employers, especially given the large number of unskilled jobs in the sector. As one company is quoted as saying, 'Now when we are asked what we pay, we have to say "minimum wage" which puts a real stigma on both the job and the staff who do these jobs'.

that being seen as a low-paying employer will mean an organization has a reputation as being a poor employer.

Competition

Here a key issue is the need to pay rates that are sufficiently competitive to sustain the employment of the right number of appropriately qualified and skilled employees for the organization's needs. Unlike prestige the key aspect in considering competition is the need for a good fit to ensure for example that employers are not over paying employees.

Clearly an important part of prestige and competition is the manner in which the organization is interacting with the external labour market and ensuring that they are getting the right kind of labour at the right kind of price (see HRM in practice 9.2 and 9.3).

Control

Torrington et al. note the manner in which organizations have to consider controlling pay and particularly the extent to which money may be saved, though changes with regard to legislation in areas such as redundancy mean that such measures are less apparent in organizations.

Motivation and performance

At one level there is a simple issue facing organizations in terms of their ability to use payment to motivate employees to perform well. In reality though there may be a number of means to achieve this. For example, the use of performance-related pay.

HRM in practice 9.3   Challenging perceptions of 'McJob'

McDonald's has often been at the forefront of arguments that suggest that work in tourism and hospitality is inherently low paid and with little meaning. For example, Douglas Coupland, the author of *Generation X: Tales for an Accelerated Generation*, coined the term McJob to describe a low-paying, low-prestige, low-dignity, low-benefit job, no-future job in the service sector. Recently the company has sought to address these issues head-on with a sustained campaign to change perceptions about the McJob descriptor. A key part of this re-branding has been attempts to draw attention to fairness with regard to career opportunities and remuneration. For example, the company has suggested that the pro-portion of employees who regard their pay as 'fair' is 30 per cent higher than comparable companies. Part of the reason for this finding may be the manner in which McDonald's pay well above the lowest rate of the NMW for 16–17-year olds. The company has a lowest rate of £4 per hour for this group of employees, a full pound above the state's 16–17-year-old development rate. Of course, McDonald's have a relatively large number of employees who will be in the 16–17 age bracket and so arguably could be seen to be a 'good' employer to that particular segment of the labour market. Interestingly this is in contrast to the rate for 18–21-year olds and those aged 22 years, where the lowest rate is at the level of the NMW, although with increments staff can eventually earn a top hourly rate of £8.70.

Derived from Anon (2006); Overell (2006).

Cost

Torrington et al. note how just as employees are concerned with their purchasing power, so employers are interested in the absolute cost of payment. In particular, organizations will be concerned of the impact on labour costs on profitability or cost effectiveness. This issue has a particular resonance in tourism and hospitality due to its labour intensive nature, meaning that the proportion of labour costs is higher than most other industries.

Change management

Pay may be used as part of a broader change management process. For example, there may be additional bonuses available for employees willing to develop new behaviour, attitudes or skills, which are required as part of a cultural change process.

In sum, employers will be seeking an approach to reward management which is likely to have several principal objectives, including:

- Attract and retain suitable employees.
- Maintain or improve levels of employee performance.
- Comply with employment legislation.

Clearly, the approach that an organization develops towards reward strategies does not exist in isolation and there will be a number of other influences on pay determination that will affect such considerations, including:

- *Beliefs about the worth of the job* – for example, the size, responsibility, skill requirements and 'objectionableness' of duties.
- *Individual characteristics* – for example, age, experience, seniority, general qualifications, special skills, contribution, performance and potential.
- *Labour market* – the level and composition of any given reward package will be influenced by labour supply and demand at either national or local labour market level, and whether an organization is seeking to create a strong internal labour market.
- *Strength of bargaining groups* – for example, the potential for trade unions to influence pay determination. At any given time the relative strength of trade unions will be influenced by other external economic factors, such as the level of unemployment and feelings of job security.
- *Government intervention and regulatory pressures* – for example public sector policy and other policy initiatives. Most obviously, the statutory national minimum wage (NMW), but also in terms of public policy towards aspects such as trade unions and collective bargaining.

There are a wide range of things then which can conceivably influence and shape the rewards that employees may get and the 'market rate' for a particular sector or occupation. Let us now begin to develop this framework within the context of tourism and hospitality.

Remuneration in tourism and hospitality

Generally when we are talking about remuneration in the tourism and hospitality industry, we can start with the fairly negative observation that relative to other industries the majority of jobs and occupations within the sector are poorly remunerated (Lucas, 2004; Baum, 2006). When we recognize that often there is low status ascribed to the industry the perception held by a number of people is that for many tourism and hospitality is an employer of last resort, with mundane, degrading employment. The prevalence of low pay and perceptions about low status can be seen as being two key issues which continue to sustain the negative view held by many of tourism and hospitality work (Lindsay and McQuaid, 2004). To begin to examine remuneration in tourism and hospitality in detail we should begin by recognizing the work of Mars and Mitchell (1976) and their notion of the 'total rewards system'. The 'total rewards system' has several aspects, which are: basic pay and subsidized food and lodging, which can be considered as the 'formalized' aspect of the wage–effort bargain; and other aspects which can be considered as more informal rewards, these being tips, which are semi-formalized, and 'fiddles and knock offs', which are non-formalized. In reality, it is apparent that the notion of a 'total rewards system' is in fact a misnomer and there are a variety of other aspects in terms of a range of benefits that may be used by tourism and hospitality organizations to make up a reward package, a point which we will further consider later in this chapter. Nevertheless, at least initially the notion of the total rewards system provides a useful starting point to consider some fundamental issues and concerns in understanding reward practices in the tourism and hospitality industry, particularly with regard to basic pay and tipping.

Basic or base pay

In a general sense Torrington et al. (2005) note that there are a number of approaches to the setting of base pay rates. Here, of course as we noted earlier in this chapter managerial actions may be constrained by the manner in which the state influences pay determination, most obviously with the provision of minimum wage legislation. In addition to this aspect though Torrington et al. also note the importance of external market comparisons and for example whether employers will pay at or above 'the going rate' for a particular job. There are also internal labour market mechanisms in which the skills and experience of employees will have a bearing on their pay. A further mechanism to determine pay is job evaluation, which is a systematic attempt to aid the establishment of differentials across jobs within a single employer. As a consequence the organization's wage budget is divided among employees on the basis of assessing the nature and size of the job they do. The last mechanism identified by Torrington et al. is that of collective bargaining, where pay rates are determined through collective negotiations with trade unions or other employee representatives. As will be discussed in the following chapter though, trade union representation has always been very low in the tourism and hospitality sector and collective bargaining has tended to play little influence in pay determination in the sector. Instead, determination of pay in tourism and hospitality has traditionally been a matter of managerial prerogative (Lucas, 2004).

In considering pay in tourism and hospitality the first point which is worth noting is the enduring and prevailing existence of low pay in the sector. For example, Wood (1997a: 69) notes how, 'the majority of academic evidence concurs in suggesting both that basic rates of pay in hotels and catering are inadequate and employers are frequently ruthless in pursuing low-pay strategies'. Thus tourism and hospitality, and particularly the hotel and catering sub-sector, is low paid, both in absolute terms (i.e. purchasing power) and relative terms (compared to most other workers) (see also HRM in practice 9.4).

Whilst the hotel and catering sub-sector is clearly low paid, the picture in other areas of the tourism sector may be more mixed. On the one hand, Baum (2006) notes how other sub-sectors such as travel agencies, airlines and tour operators, who are often staffed by young and female employees, also offer relatively poor remuneration. Often this will mean that for a number of front-line positions, such as travel advisors, the pay rate will be at or near the NMW. For example, MyTravel, a major provider of package holidays and other leisure travel services, offers a salary range for a travel advisor of £9000–£11 500 (http://www.mytravel-careers.co.uk/retail/accessed 15 May 2006). On the other hand, a recent survey conducted by Croner in conjunction with the Association of British Travel Agents (ABTA) suggests that the median basic salary for workers in the travel industry was £21 753, which rose to £23 135 when other aspects such as commission and bonuses were added (IRS, 2006b). These figures are clearly significantly higher than the figures for the hotel and catering industry noted in HRM in practice 9.4. Moreover, whilst relatively low pay may be true for a number of front-line positions in tourism and hospitality it is a different picture for other occupational

HRM in practice 9.4   Condemned to low pay? A history of low pay in the hospitality industry

1975 – The Hotel and Catering Economic Committee suggested on the basis of low pay of 60 pence an hour for men and 55 pence an hour for women, 49 per cent of full-time men and 88 per cent of full-time women in hotels and catering were low paid, compared to 11 per cent and 53 per cent in 'all industries' across the economy.

1986 – Byrne estimated that between 57 and 64 per cent of full-time workers in hotel and catering employment were low paid (i.e. defined as earning less than two-thirds of male median earnings).

1989 – A British Hotels, Restaurants and Caterers Association survey revealed catering managers earned 27 per cent less than average non-manual workers and non-manual employees earned 28 per cent less than the average for manual workers.

1999 – The Office of National Statistics *New Earnings Survey 1999* found that waiters/ waitresses (average gross annual salary £8879), along with kitchen porters and kitchen hands (average weekly wage £180.50) were the lowest paid of all UK employees (the average yearly pay across all occupations was £20 919).

2003 – The Office of National Statistics *New Earnings Survey 2003* found that hotel and restaurant employees were the lowest paid in the country. Average gross annual pay for full time restaurant and hotel employees was just £16 533, compared to a UK average of £25 170.

2005 – The Office of National Statistics *Annual Survey of Hours and Earnings 2005* found that hotels and restaurants had the lowest median gross annual earnings at £14 653. The highest paying sector was financial intermediation at £29 962. The median for all industries and services was £22 903.

Derived from Wood (1997a); Bozec (1999); Anon (2003); IRS (2006a).

groups. For example, IRS (2006c) note that in First Choice Airways' a first officer can expect to start work with the company at a basic salary of £31 011, with a captain's salary ranging from £67 576 to £94 113. Generally though, as with the hospitality sub-sector, the bulk of employees within tourism-related occupations are likely to be relatively low paid (Baum, 2006). To an extent though Baum also recognizes that within a number of tourism jobs aspects such as travel opportunities, uniforms

HRM in practice 9.5   Work as leisure

Guerrier and Adib (2004) conducted research by interviewing and observing 14 overseas tour reps in Mallorca. They found that for this group of employees there will often be a blurring between work and leisure, which may allow the worker to enjoy some of the benefits of leisure at work. As an example overseas tour reps may not distinguish between their work and non-work lives. Customers may be their friends, their workplace is where they would 'hang out' anyway and their work does not demand a subordination of self but only a presentation of their authentic, fun loving and sociable self.

and a generally pleasant working environment may encourage something of a trade-off between a desire for higher levels of pay and less acceptable conditions or other benefits (see HRM in practice 9.5).

Wage regulation in tourism and hospitality

Although we noted above that pay determination has largely been dictated by the managerial prerogative in more recent times the introduction of the NMW has introduced greater regulation by statutory means. The NMW marks a significant change in the British employment landscape and will be discussed in due course. To place the emergence of the NMW in context though it is worth briefly mentioning wages councils, which had previously played a role in setting a *de-facto* minimum wage. For a large number of those working in tourism and hospitality, and particularly hotel and catering, the wages councils provided a minimum safety net with regard to wages for nearly 50 years. First introduced in 1909 as trade boards, and first covering the hospitality sector from the mid-1940s, wages councils peaked in the 1950s covering over 3.5 million workers, providing surrogate collective bargaining for the low paid (Metcalfe, 1999). At the time of their abolition in 1993 there were three wages councils that covered different sub-sectors of the commercial hospitality industry and the mean hourly rate they set was £2.97 per hour which was £115.96 for a 39-hour week or £6029.92 per annum (Goldsmith et al., 1997). From 1993 to the introduction of the NMW in 1999 there was no real protection for employees and evidence suggests that a number of employers took advantage of this omission in an attempt to drive down wages (Lucas and Radiven, 1998; Lucas, 2004).

The NMW now seems a well established aspect of the employment landscape but prior to its introduction there was vociferous debate about whether it should even be introduced. For example, the British Hospitality Association (BHA) was implacably opposed to the NMW. Much of the debate was centred on whether the argument was best understood from a moral or economic point of view (see Wood, 1997b for an overview of the debate). For example, in the interests of social justice proponents of the NMW suggested that all employees should be 'decently' paid. On the other hand, opponents pointed to the likely rise in unemployment created by rising payroll costs stemming from the NMW. It was in this context that the NMW was introduced by the Labour Government. Once the minimum wage was accepted as a key policy plank of New Labour's notion of 'fairness at work', the main issues became practical ones, such as the level the wage was set at and the way it was implemented and enforced. To a large extent these issues were determined by the Low Pay Commission (LPC), which was established in July 1997 as a statutory body and has continued to play a key role even after the enactment of the minimum wage legislation. The LPC consists of nine members who represent the interests of employers, unions and employees, and 'objective' independent expert academics (Thornley and Coffey, 1999). Indeed, the LPC was able to largely agree on the terms of the implementation of the NMW and is suggested as providing an exemplar of a positive social partnership between employers and employees in particular (Metcalfe, 1999; though see Thornley and Coffey 1999 for a more critical account).

The LPC reported in 1998 with the *National Minimum Wage Act* coming into being in the same year and the NMW actually starting on 1 April 1999. There was much discussion and horse trading in relation to issues such as the level of the NMW and whether things like tips would be included. For example, with regard to the rate the Confederation of British Industry suggested £3.20, the Trades Union Congress had suggested £4.00 and many trade unions and pressure groups, such as the Low Pay Unit (LPU), using the formula of applying half male median earnings to the New Earnings Survey, suggested £4.61. George Bain, then chair of the LPC, had gone on record to suggest that £3.75 was not outrageous (Barnett, 1997) and it was calculated that if Wages Councils had still been in existence the rate in April 1999 would have been £3.90 (Metcalfe, 1999). Ultimately though the main rate was set by the LPC at £3.60 (see HRM in practice 9.6).

The reaction to the NMW was mixed. On the one hand employers views were generally favourable about what they felt was an acceptable rate. For example, the

HRM in practice 9.6   The LPC: Shaping the NMW in tourism and hospitality

Main recommendations:

- NMW to be £3.60 with an upgraded rate of £3.70 in June 2000.
- Development rate for 18–21-year olds £3.20 per hour rising to £3.30 by June 2000.
- NMW not expected to be subject to regular annual revision and not index-linked in any fashion.
- 16–17-year olds exempt.

The Government response:

- Acceptance of the £3.60 figure, which came into force on 1 April 1999.
- Development rate to be £3.00 per hour.
- No guarantees that the upgraded rate would apply to either the development or full rate in June 2000.
- Exemption of young workers.
- Tips and service charges distributed centrally via payroll to count against NMW, but cash tips paid by customers directly to staff not included.
- A maximum figure of £20 to be deducted for the cost of employees' accommodation.

Derived from Walsh (1998); Metcalfe (1999).

BHA applauded what they considered to be a 'realistic' wage, supported the 'sensible' level for 18–21-year olds, but expressed regret that there were no regional variations (Clavey, 1998). There were also some concerns from some tourism employers that the accommodation offset would count towards payment of the NMW but only at the rate of £20 per week (Fox, 1998; at the time of writing this offset now stands at £27.30).

On the other hand, trade unions and the LPU were less sanguine at what they felt to be an overly prudent and overcautious rate. As Bill Morris, then General Secretary of the Transport and General Workers Union, pithily put it, 'Thank you for the principle, shame about the rate' (cited in Metcalfe, 1999: 193). Similarly, Rodney Bickerstaffe, then General Secretary of Unison, applauded the implementation of the NMW whilst also suggesting that, '£3.60 for an hour of anyone's life at the end of the 20th century in one of the richest countries on earth is not something to be proud of' (cited in Clavey, 1998: 10; and see HRM in practice 9.7).

HRM in practice 9.7   A 'Living Wage'?

The GLA (2006) note that since the inception of the NMW, at what many trade unions felt to be an unnecessarily low level, there has been much discussion of what is an 'acceptable' level for the NMW. More recently, a campaign has emerged in support of a 'living wage'. Originating in America, the living wage campaign aims to address what it considers to be 'poverty wages'. Currently it is suggested that the 'living wage' for London should be £7.05 (similar campaigns have been started in other parts of the UK) and campaigners are seeking to target industries such as tourism and hospitality to ensure that companies are paying this wage. With mayoral support in London and a commitment from the London 2012 Olympic project team to the living wage, the campaign has enjoyed some success in raising the issue of low pay.

Despite the disappointment on the part of trade unions and other lobbying bodies at the rate at which the NMW was set, approximately two million workers did receive a wage increase as a result of the legislation, with many of these workers being women, part-timers, youths, non-whites and single parents (Metcalfe, 1999). Of course many of these workers were to be found in tourism and hospitality with the LPC estimating that around 800 000, or 42 per cent, being in the retail and hospitality sectors (LRD, 1998).

Although the tourism and hospitality industry was disproportionately affected in terms of the number of employees who benefited from the NMW, due to its low rate it has been suggested that in reality there has been 'minimum impact' and 'much ado about nothing', even in smaller businesses (Rowson, 2000; Turnbull, 2000; Adam-Smith et al., 2003). Indeed, a survey undertaken of low-paying sectors by Income Data Services (IDS) prior to the introduction of the NMW found that a number of larger tourism and hospitality companies, such as Centre Parcs and Marriott, where already paying at, or over the rate at the point of implementation (IDS, 1999, though see also HRM in practice 9.8).

Employer concerns about issues such as loss of competitiveness and job losses have also proved to be wide of the mark (LRD, 2001). For example, Lucas (2004) notes how employment has increased in the hospitality sub-sector by over 200 000 since 1999.

As was noted earlier in this chapter the LPC having initially recommended the rate for the NMW has had the responsibility of reviewing its operation and in the

HRM in practice 9.8   Pizza Hut and Pizza Express: Taking away from their employees

Pizza giants, Pizza Hut and Pizza Express, found themselves at the centre of controversy when the NMW was implemented. Both companies responded to the implementation of the NMW by seeking to reign in costs. Pizza Hut removed paid taxi fairs home for their staff, claiming that they could no longer afford this benefit with the introduction of the NMW. Pizza Express initially retained a basic rate of pay of £3.10, with the expectation that tips would make up the shortfall, despite the law saying that tips could only be included if they were paid through the bill. As a result of this decision the company was ultimately forced to pay out £250 000 in back pay to waiting staff.

Derived from Anon (1999a, b).

period from 1999 has recommended regular annual uprating, though this has reflected prevailing economic circumstances rather than any particular uprating formula. Interestingly though in the period 2002–2006 the adult minimum wage has increased by 27.4 per cent, while average earnings increased by just 17 per cent (LPC, 2006). Though in its most recent report the LPC does acknowledge that the phase in which they are committed to increasing the NMW above average earnings is now complete and in future will have no presumptions that increases above average earnings are required. Importantly, the LPC also recommended that 16–17-year olds be brought under the umbrella of the NMW from October 2004 (see Table 9.1). Bringing 16–17-year olds under the aegis of the NMW again disproportionately impacted on tourism and related industries with retail and hospitality respectively accounting for 45 per cent and 21 per cent of the overall total brought under minimum wage protection (LPC, 2006).

Although the NMW is a relatively recent phenomenon in the UK nearly all OECD countries have minimum wage setting arrangements (Metcalfe, 1999). A number of Scandinavian countries and countries such as Germany and Italy rely on collective bargaining mechanisms to set minimum wages, ordinarily at a sectoral level. In a large number of countries though there are statutory requirements and it is interesting to compare the UK with a number of other countries (see Table 9.2).

Table 9.1 How the UK NMW has evolved since 1999

Adult rate (for workers aged 22+)		Development rate (for workers aged 18–21)		16–17-year olds rate	
1 April 1999	£3.60	1 April 1999	£3.00	–	–
1 October 2000	£3.70	1 October 2000	£3.20	–	–
1 October 2001	£4.10	1 October 2001	£3.50	–	–
1 October 2002	£4.20	1 October 2002	£3.60	–	–
1 October 2003	£4.50	1 October 2003	£3.80	–	–
1 October 2004	£4.85	1 October 2004	£4.10	1 October 2004	£3.00
1 October 2005	£5.05	1 October 2005	£4.25	1 October 2005	£3.00
1 October 2006	£5.35	1 October 2006	£4.45	1 October 2006	£3.30

Source: http://www.lowpay.gov.uk/ Reproduced with permission from the LPC.

Review and reflect

In considering debates about the NMW and the pay disparities outlined in HRM in practice 9.1, is there an argument for a *maximum* wage?

In addition to basic pay there are a number of other aspects which can be considered in reviewing payment issues in tourism and hospitality. IDS (2005a, b) in their annual review of hotels, pubs and restaurants note a number of additional areas where employees could enhance basic pay. Just over half of the 20 hotels they surveyed offered a premium for night work. This payment could either be a flat rate, for example night porters in one hotel could earn £1800 more than day porters. Alternatively some of the surveyed hotels paid a premium for those hours worked at night with IDS citing the example of food and beverage staff receiving an additional 30 pence an hour for every hour worked past midnight. With regard to the broader issue of bonus and incentive schemes, all but two of the surveyed hotels offered a bonus or incentive scheme. Many of these schemes attempt to incentivize front-line staff to offer good quality service in showing appropriate behaviours and attitudes and may use some of the customer appraisal techniques discussed in the previous chapter, such as mystery guests. In over half of the schemes payments are related to sales, with profit- and performance-related payments being the next most

Table 9.2 Comparison of the level of the adult minimum wage across selected countries, end 2004

Country (and year first introduced)	In UK £[a]	Age at which full rate usually applies	Adult rate as a percentage of full-time median earning
Australia (1996, some form since 1907)	5.37	21	58.5/55.1[b]
Belgium (1975)	4.92	21	48.5
Canada (women 1918–1930, men 1930–1959)	3.66	16	39.5
France (1950, 1970 in current form)	5.20	18	56.6
Ireland (2000)	4.15	20	51.7
Japan (1959, 1968 in current form)	2.71	–	33.7
Netherlands (1968)	5.04	23	46.4 (50.1)
Portugal (1974)	1.99	16	38.0 (44.4)
Spain (1963, 1976 in current form)	2.34	16	30.0 (35.0)
United Kingdom (1999)	4.85	22	43.2
United States (1938)	3.37	20	32.2

[a] Adjusted for purchasing power parities (August 2004).

[b] Depends on the earnings survey used.

Figures in brackets include annual supplements.

Derived from Metcalfe (1999); LPC (2005).

common measure. The criteria differed across the hotels. IDS cite the example of Hilton where heads of division receive a bonus based on profit, service and people management, whereas staff received a bonus based on sales. In one of the surveyed hotels food and beverage staff received a bonus based on service charge. Only one of the surveyed hotels had a share option scheme and one also operated payments for guest mentions. A further issue is that of pay progression and IDS note how a number of the fast food companies that they surveyed linked pay to progression. For example, McDonald's links pay increases to performance appraisals, which are based on four fixed levels, 0 per cent for 'needs improvement', 3 per cent for 'good', 4.5 per cent for 'excellent', 6 per cent for 'outstanding', with most employees receiving a 3 per cent rise. Pay progression may also be linked to the completion of training in Prêt A Manger, where employees have to pass three assessments and written tests to progress. Similarly, within the travel industry a recent survey of salaries reported in IRS (2006b) found that bonus payments were common at all levels of the industry. For example, half of the companies in the survey paid commission to employees, based on their sales.

The practice of tipping

The notion of tipping is important in a number of ways, not least in its economic importance. For example, Lynn (2003) suggests that consumers tip over $16 billion a year in the US. Tipping may allow some tourism and hospitality workers to significantly augment their income, though the potential impact with regards to issues such as job satisfaction and emotional well-being equally need to be considered. Ogbonna and Harris (2002) also note the possibility of tipping being used as a managerial mechanism to encourage individualization and subjugation of employees. Tipping in this latter view becomes an important managerial tool for the indirect control of employees in the employee–customer interaction, as well as potentially suppressing interest in more collective power, for example through trade union organization. Ogbonna and Harris (2002) note how employees in the UK restaurant they studied resisted managerial attempts to resort to a system in which tips would be kept by the company in return for a 10 per cent increase in pay; in addition in the same case study management threatened to abolish tipping if the employees became unionized.

Review and reflect

What are likely to be some of the financial and emotional hazards for tourism and hospitality employees who are reliant on tips to sustain a reasonable wage?

It is important to note that tipping is very much culturally bound and as Ogbonna and Harris (2002: 726) recognize, 'although tipping is an internationally recognizable behaviour, the actual practice is heavily influenced by societal cultural considerations'. For example, tipping is widely practiced within the US, but is not as widespread in the UK and elsewhere (see HRM in practice 9.9).

HRM in practice 9.9   Tipping in different countries

The US is generally recognized as having the most highly developed approach to tipping. For example, it is not unusual for hotel guests to have to tip five people before they get to their room. In the US for many tipped positions the general expectation is that customer should tip at least 15 per cent. Tipping is less prevalent in other countries such as Australia, New Zealand and Sweden. For example, in New Zealand tipping is not considered a normal cultural practice and moves to a US-type approach appear unlikely. Managers and employees in New Zealand saw the institutionalization of tipping in the US as distasteful and were particularly unanimous in their denunciation of the US practice of using tips to boost poor wages. It was felt that employers should fairly remunerate employees and that this should not be left to customers. In many south-east Asian countries it is not customary to tip and tipping can be a sensitive topic, especially if social conventions are breached and people lose 'face'. In contrast, research in France – where tipping is unusual – found that if a waitress touched customers she got more and better tips. This 'touch effect' is found in other countries, such as the US, but seems particularly pronounced in France due to the tactile nature of social relations.

Derived from Callen and Tyson (2000); Casey (2001); Dewald (2001); Gueguen and Jacob (2005).

Tipping is then largely driven by socio-cultural norms and/or individual conscience. In relation to tourism and hospitality we should recognize that some workers are in a position to enhance basic wages from tips, but this is only true for those in tipped positions. Even for those in tipped positions it should also be acknowledged that tips are notoriously unpredictable. Lynn (2001; and see also Lynn, 2003) conducted a meta-analysis of a number of studies which had examined the relationship between restaurant tipping and service quality and found a weak relationship. Consequently, for many front-line staff tipping may be more influenced by external factors such as the race and gender of the customer, prevailing weather conditions or even the result of football or rugby matches that are played near the restaurant (Ogbonna and Harris, 2002).

The point is often made as well that tipping means losing sight of the fact that the vast majority of people in tipping positions are generally in low-wage, low-status occupations. Despite this point there is an argument, usually from employers, that tipping is a good motivator and that abolishing tips and paying higher wages is not the answer, while alternatively others argue that tips are an unwelcome part of the tourism and hospitality industry and a 'fair' fixed living wage would be more desirable (Wood, 1997a). Critics of tipping would also argue that the practice weakens social relationships as a number of interactions in tourism and hospitality become overtly economic exchanges. It is also argued that tipping increases power differences as in menial low-status jobs tipping reinforces and makes salient the inferior status of workers. For example, Ogbonna and Harris (2002) found that a number of waiters and waitresses they interviewed felt that they were often abused physically and mentally and had to accept subtle forms of sexual exploitation. Engaging in sexualized flirting with customers may be part of a process that degrades and debases front-line workers, often for comparatively little financial reward (a point further considered in Chapter 11). There is also the final related point that tipping tends to encourage a very individualistic view of the workplace and does little to sustain a harmonious workplace relationships and that tipping tends to weaken organizational commitment.

Clearly there is much debate about the efficacy and morality of tipping, though given the reality of this practice still being prevalent in a number of tourism and hospitality environments it is worthwhile briefly considering the underlying motives for tipping and how servers may maximize their tips. With regard to motives underlying tipping Lynn et al. (1993) suggest the following:

- Desire for good service in the future.
- Desire for social approval.
- To compensate servers equitably for their work (i.e. reward their effort).
- Desire for status and power.

Furthermore, Lynn (1996 and 2003) reports on research which suggests a number of ways in which servers' are likely to increase their tips:

- Server introduction in a genuine and professional manner.
- Squatting next to table, though this is more likely to work in a casual dining environment, compared to fine-dining where it may be considered inappropriate.
- Smiling at customers.
- Touching customers.
- Credit card insignia on tip trays.

- Writing 'Thank You' on checks.
- Drawing a 'happy face' on checks.
- Wearing a flower in hair and other means of personalizing the server's appearance.
- Entertaining customers by for example telling a joke.
- Forecasting good weather.
- Calling customer by name.

Of course, there are several obvious caveats to the above discussion. First, the research is based in the US and as we noted earlier in this chapter tipping is a culturally bound phenomenon. Second, not all of these tip-enhancing techniques will be appropriate for every type of restaurant or service setting, or indeed every server. Consequently some of these aspects may work better than others and should be used advisedly, both by individual employees and managers who encourage servers to use such techniques.

Fiddles and knock-offs

Whilst basic pay, accommodation and tipping represent the more formalized aspects of the reward package in tourism and hospitality it is also briefly worth considering fiddles and knock-offs. Mars and Nicod (1984) found a large range of fiddles in their work and note how 'they are acts of dishonesty which the people involved do not consider dishonest' (p. 116). Fiddles generally involve pilferage from organizations, usually in a monetary sense. Knock-offs can also be considered a form of fiddle involving the purloining of (usually) small items such as soap, linen and towels. Generally, these practices are institutionalized within the organization and may be dependent on a degree of management and supervisory collusion, although certain boundaries and parameters will be set to delineate what is 'acceptable'. Indeed, with regard to this notion of acceptability organizations may tighten up on a 'blind eye' approach to fiddles and knock-offs when business slackens and the organization is looking to reduce labour costs (Lucas, 2004). A further important point noted by Wood (1997a) concerns the notion of individualism and the extent to which this is exacerbated by these practices. Thus, 'Whatever arrangements exist for the allocation of fiddles and knock-offs there are some grounds for believing that, as with tipping, these aspects of informal rewards militate against the development of a collective workplace or occupational ethic, fostering individualism and competitiveness' (p. 88).

Other benefits

Although Mars and Mitchell characterized their model as a 'Total Rewards System', many critiques have suggested that the use of total in this instance is clearly a misnomer, and neglects a variety of other rewards which may be made available by the organization. For example, in their survey of 20 hotel companies IDS (2005b) found that three quarters provided free meals and staff discounts on rooms, restaurants and shops within the hotel. Twenty per cent offered free use of leisure facilities, including spas, beauty therapists, chiropodists and gyms.

HRM in practice 9.10 Total rewards fly in at First Choice Airways'

First Choice Airways' is a UK leisure airline and part of First Choice Holidays plc. The company employs over 14 000 staff, including nearly 400 pilots. The rigorous entry requirements and on-going training and competency testing at least twice a year are indicative of the high level of responsibility associated with being a pilot. Resultantly the company has recently reviewed the total reward package offered to pilots and as a consequence developed a 'Pilot Change Agenda'. A key part of the change agenda was to ensure the pilots felt valued. Amongst other things this has led to the company to review the pay and other rewards offered to pilots and to develop a new 'total reward' perspective. Traditionally pilots already had a very good rewards package including: competitive base pay; two final-salary pension schemes; a money purchase pension scheme; free medical checks; private medical insurance; concessions of £1000 per year to spend on First Choice holidays, and the option to buy further holidays on a tax efficient basis; free uniforms; duty and subsistence allowances; share plans; voluntary benefits, for example childcare vouchers and other insurance and generous annual leave entitlement. Under the new change agenda additional aspects of the total reward system include a new bonus plan that links payments to adherence to corporate values and desired behaviour or performance, a new share plan scheme, flexible working options and a new long service award scheme. Of course, the nature of this package is very much driven by the highly competitive environment in which the company is operating and the unique nature of pilots as a group of employees in terms of their skills and qualities.

Source: IRS (2006c).

Around a sixth of hotels offered a pension scheme. Only one hotel provided life assurance, dental, optical and private medical care. A minority of respondents paid maternity pay above the statutory minimum, with 70 per cent paying sick pay above the statutory minimum. A similar survey conducted in the travel industry and reported in IRS (2006b) also noted a range of benefits. Over 70 per cent of the 34 companies surveyed offered a company pension scheme, though only 11 per cent of companies offered a final salary pension scheme. Over half of the companies offered private health insurance, with 39 per cent offering life insurance and see HRM in practice 9.10.

Although HRM in practice 9.10, in particular, illustrates the possible range of additional benefits that could be made available, in reality research suggests that most tourism and hospitality workers are less likely to enjoy such benefits. For example, Lucas (2004) cites figures from the Workplace Employee Relations Survey which compares the tourism and hospitality industry with all private sector services in terms of non-pay terms and conditions. With regard to employer pension scheme, company car/allowance, private health insurance and sick pay in excess of statutory requirements tourism and hospitality employers were significantly lagging behind other employers in both private service sector and all industrial sectors.

Conclusion

We have examined a range of issues which cover rewards and payment which demonstrate that arguably a fair and effective deal is still some way off for the bulk of the tourism and hospitality workforce, and especially those in the hotel and catering sub-sector. In an ideal world the effort–reward bargain would satisfy all parties but the reality is different so for employers the strategy that is pursued seems to coincide with the controlling operations and cost aspects of Torrington et al.'s framework and for the employees there is little choice and no real sense of aspiring to any of the loftier principles embodied in the Torrington et al. framework. Furthermore prescriptive accounts of 'total reward' schemes that support the notion of employees picking and choosing from a range of options to tailor a pay and benefits package that meets their particular needs, need to be treated with a good deal of caution in tourism and hospitality where the cafeteria approach remains rare. Of course, as we acknowledged, there are exceptions to low pay both sub-sectorally and occupationally, though for the majority of employees in tourism and hospitality notions of 'fair' remuneration remain somewhat elusive. Indeed, this may seem rather paradoxical as often those entrusted with delivering high-quality service may be the lowliest paid in the organization.

References and further reading

Adam-Smith, D., Norris, G. and Williams, S. (2003) 'Continuity or change? The implications of the National Minimum Wage for work and employment in the hospitality industry', *Work, Employment and Society*, 17(1), 29–47.

Anon (1999a) 'Restaurant chains make staff pay for the minimum wage', *Caterer and Hotelkeeper*, 22 April, 4.

Anon (1999b) 'Pizza Express hits out at MP's slur on pay', *Caterer and Hotelkeeper*, 15 July, 10.

Anon (2003) 'Hospitality is lowest-paying industry', *Caterer and Hotelkeeper*, 23 October, 6.

Anon (2006) 'Is McJob still bad for you?' *Guardian Work*, 10 June, 2.

Barnett, A. (1997) 'No gain without Bain for the minimum wage', *Observer Business Section*, 8 June, 16.

Baum, T. (2006) *Human Resource Management for Tourism, Hospitality and Leisure: An International Perspective*, Thomson Learning.

Bozec, L. (1999) 'Government report says hospitality is one of worst payers', *Caterer and Hotelkeeper*, 28 October, 4.

Callen, R. and Tyson, K. (2000) 'Tipping behaviour in hospitality embodying a comparative prolegomenon of English and Italian customers', *Tourism and Hospitality Research*, 2(3), 242–261.

Casey, B. (2001) 'Tipping in New Zealand's restaurants', *Cornell Hotel and Restaurant Administration Quarterly*, 42(1), 21–25.

Clavey, J. (1998) 'Unions slam level of minimum wage', *Caterer and Hotelkeeper*, 4 June, 10.

Dewald, B. (2001) 'Restaurant tipping by tourists in Hong Kong', *Anatolia: An International Journal of Tourism and Hospitality Research*, 12(2), 139–151.

Foot, M. and Hook, C. (2005) *Introducing Human Resource Management*, Prentice Hall, 4th edition.

Fox, L. (1998) 'ABTA shows concern over minimum wage', *Travel, Trade Gazette*, 2 December, 6.

Goldsmith, A., Nickson, D., Sloan, D. and Wood, R. (1997) *Human Resources Management for Hospitality Services*, International Thomson Business Press.

Greater London Authority (2006) *A Fairer London: The Living Wage in London*, GLA.

Gueguen, N. and Jacob, C. (2005) 'The effect of touch in tipping: an evaluation in a French bar', *International Journal of Hospitality Management*, 24(2), 295–299.

Guerrier, Y. and Adib, A. (2004) 'Gendered identities in the work of overseas tour reps', *Gender, Work and Organizations*, 11(3), 334–350.

Income Data Services (1999) 'Implementing the National Minimum Wage', *IDS Report*, No. 783, April, 8–13.

Income Data Services (2004) 'The impact of recent NMW increases in the UK leisure industry', *IDS Pay Report*, No. 906, June, 16–17.

Income Data Services (2005a) 'Pay in hotels', *IDS Pay Report*, No. 943, December, 11–15.

Income Data Services (2005b) 'Pay in pubs and restaurants 2004/5', *IDS Pay Report*, No. 931, June, 11–15.

Industrial Relations Services (2006a) 'ASHE 2005: earnings growth fails to keep pace with inflation', *IRS Employment Review*, No. 840, 3 February, 31–35.

Industrial Relations Services (2006b) '£21 753 a year for travel industry employees', *IRS Employment Review*, No. 843, 24 March, 28.

Industrial Relations Services (2006c) 'Smooth take-off for First Choice Airways' new reward strategy', *IRS Employment Review*, No. 843, 24 March, 29–32.

Labour Research Department (1998) 'Short changing young workers', *Labour Research*, December, 11–13.

Labour Research Department (2001) 'Is the minimum wage debate over?' *Labour Research*, May, 11–13.

Lindsay, C. and McQuaid, R.W. (2004) 'Avoiding the "McJobs": unemployed job seekers and attitudes to service work', *Work, Employment and Society*, 18:2, 297–319.

Low Pay Commission (2005) *National Minimum Wage Low Pay Commission Report 2005*, The Stationery Office.

Low Pay Commission (2006) *National Minimum Wage Low Pay Commission Report 2006*, The Stationery Office.

Lucas, R. (2004) *Employment Relations in the Hospitality and Tourism Industries*, Routledge.

Lucas, R. and Radiven, N. (1998) 'After wages councils: minimum pay and practice', *Human Resource Management Journal*, 8(4), 5–19.

Lynn, M. (1996) 'Seven ways to increase servers tips', *Cornell Hotel and Restaurant Administration Quarterly*, 37(3), 24–29.

Lynn, M. (2001) 'Restaurant tipping and service quality', *Cornell Hotel and Restaurant Administration Quarterly*, 42(1), 14–20.

Lynn, M. (2003) 'Tip levels and service: an update, extension, and reconciliation', *Cornell Hotel and Restaurant Administration Quarterly*, 44(5/6), 139–148.

Lynn, M., Zinkhan, G. and Harris, J. (1993) 'Consumer tipping: a cross-country study', *Journal of Consumer Research*, 20, December, 478–488.

Mars, G. and Mitchell, P. (1976) *Room for Reform? A Case Study of Industrial Relations in the Hotel Industry*, Open University Press.

Mars, G. and Nicod, M. (1984) *The World of Waiters*, George Allen and Unwin.

Metcalfe, D. (1999) 'The British National Minimum Wage', *British Journal of Industrial Relations*, 37(2), 171–201.

Milne, S. (1998) 'Politics of the pig trough', *Guardian*, 15 September, 10.

Milne, S. and White, M. (1998) 'Read my lips "you greedy bastards"', *Guardian*, 15 September, 7.

Ogbonna, E. and Harris, L. (2002) 'Institutionalization of tipping as a source of managerial control', *British Journal of Industrial Relations*, 40(4), 725–752.

Overell, S. (2006) 'Fast forward', *People Management*, 9 February, 26–31.

Rowson, B. (2000) 'Much ado about nothing: the impact on small hotels of the national minimum wage', *The Hospitality Review*, January, 15–17.

Thornley, C. and Coffey, D. (1999) 'The Low Pay Commission in context', *Work, Employment and Society*, 13(3), 525–538.

Torrington, D., Hall, L. and Taylor, S. (2005) *Human Resource Management*, 5th edition, Prentice Hall.

Turnbull, D. (2000) 'Minimum impact', *The Hospitality Review*, January 12–14.

Walsh, J. (1998) 'Pay commissioner denies fudge on development rate', *People Management*, 25 June, 9.

Wood, R. C. (1997a) *Working in Hotels and Catering*, International Thomson Press, 2nd edition.

Wood, R. C (1997b) 'Rhetoric, reason and rationality: the national minimum wage debate and the UK hospitality industry', *International Journal of Hospitality Management*, 16(4), 329–344.

Websites

For an interesting discussion of the campaign towards a 'living wage', see http:// www.livingwage.org.uk/
The US version of the campaign also has a website at http://www.letjusticeroll.org/index.html
The Low Pay Commission has lots of useful material on their site at http:// www.lowpay.gov.uk/
There is lots of interesting material on tipping at http://www.tipping.org/index.shtml and http://www.bbc.co.uk/dna/h2g2/alabaster/A640018

Chapter **10**

Employee relations, involvement and participation

Chapter objectives

This chapter considers the notions of employee relations, employee involvement and employee participation to review the extent to which employees may influence managerial decision-making. In particular, the chapter aims to:

- Recognize debates about employee/industrial relations.
- Assess the differing ways in which conflict may be conceptualized and resolved in the tourism and hospitality workplace.
- Consider the role, or lack of it, for trade unions in the tourism and hospitality industry.
- Appreciate how employee involvement and employee participation mechanisms can be used by tourism and hospitality organizations.

Introduction

The idea of some kind of employee influence in organizational decision-making is one that seems to attract much support amongst all the parties who are involved in the employment relationship; that is, employers, employees, trade unions and the state. Indeed, as Blyton and Turnbull (2004) note recent years have seen renewed interest in employee involvement and participation. This renewed interest is partly explicable by the Labour Government's attempts to promote 'partnership' at work as well as the influence of the European social agenda, which has encouraged greater employee participation through a number of European Union (EU) Directives. However, although there may be universal support in principle for the need for employee influence in decision-making, in reality there are likely to be sharply differing views on the degree (the extent to which employees are able to meaningfully influence managerial decisions), level (task, departmental, establishment or corporate), range (the range of subject matters likely to be discussed, from what might be trivial issues such as food in the staff canteen to fundamental strategic decisions) and form (either direct of indirect through representation) of such influence (Marchington and Wilkinson, 2005).

Recognizing the above discussion Blyton and Turnbull (2004) suggest a continuum from no involvement through to employee control, although in reality most organizations are likely to fit somewhere in between in the categories of receiving information, joint consultation and joint decision-making, which in a generic sense are likely to be characterized as being either employee involvement, participation or industrial democracy. Underpinning much of this discussion is a need to understand the nature of employee relations and the manner in which many argue that this notion marks a major shift from a more collective view of the employment relationship as embodied in the notion of industrial relations. Initially then the chapter will consider this debate about how best to conceptualize the contemporary employment landscape. Following this discussion we will then move on and examine how these debates can be understand with regard to the 'frames of reference' (Fox, 1966) adopted by management in terms of dealing with potential conflict in the workplace. Conflict can be considered at a number of levels, one of which is the potential conflict of interests between trade unions and employers. However, the tourism and hospitality industry is often suggested as being one where trade unions have little or no influence. The veracity or otherwise of this view will be discussed, including why tourism and hospitality employees may or may not join trade unions. Having considered one mechanism for articulating an employee 'voice', that of trade unions, the chapter moves on to consider a range of other mechanisms which seek to involve employees in the decision-making process in organizations through the processes of employee involvement and participation.

Employee or industrial relations?

In a recent analysis of the nature of employee relations in the UK economy CIPD (2005: 5) suggest that, 'the term "industrial relations" summons up today a set of employment relationships that no longer widely exist, except in specific sectors, and even there, in modified form'. In this view industrial relations can be thought of as denoting formal arrangements between employers and trade unions, in which collective bargaining would provide the mechanism for joint regulation that would give trade unions a say in key management decisions. This view of industrial relations held by CIPD is by no means universally held and amongst others Sisson (2005) responded with a wide-ranging rejoinder questioning whether the description of industrial relations as being anachronistic is indeed true. Whilst at one level this debate about the nature of 'industrial' or 'employee' relations might seem like a typical academic parlour game it is nevertheless important to recognize that at the heart of this debate are a number of crucial concerns which are likely to significantly influence arguments about the nature of employee involvement and participation. To appreciate such debates it is worthwhile briefly considering how industrial and employee relations may be considered different.

Industrial relations has its roots very much in the social sciences and draws on a number of academic disciplines such as economics, law, sociology, psychology, history and politics. The scope of industrial relations has traditionally encompassed the study of social institutions, legislative controls and social mechanisms and the way they provided the framework for interactions between the key actors in the employment relationship: government, employers and their organizations and employees and their organizations. At the heart of industrial relations lies the notion of how these partners manage the employment relationship, which denotes an economic, social and political relationship for which employees provide manual, mental, emotional and aesthetic labour in exchange for rewards allocated by employers. Often debates about the employment relationship would centre on the notion of the effort–reward bargain. As we saw in the previous chapter the effort–reward bargain refers to the manner in which employees are rewarded for the effort they expend on behalf of the organization. The potential conflict that would arise in the allocation of effort from employees and reward from employers would often be resolved through the use of, often adversarial, collective bargaining, where trade unions and employers would come together to attempt seek a resolution based on their relative strengths. Industrial relations, then, is often thought of as denoting the formal arrangements to manage the employment relationship that existed in large manufacturing plants where the world of work largely consisted of unionized male manual workers who worked full-time (Blyton and Turnbull, 2004).

By contrast, employee relations emerged as a term in the 1980s in an attempt to capture the changing nature of the employment landscape. In particular, as CIPD (2005: 3) argues, 'employee relations is now about managing in a more complex, fast-moving environment: the political, trade union and legislative climates are all shifting. In general, the agenda is no longer about trade unions'. Within this view of employee relations then a key aspect of what is considered distinctive about the term is a lack of trade union influence. In addition, employee relations has also tended to be considered as denoting the changing nature of employment in terms of the shift from manufacturing to service employment and the feminization of the labour market. These shifts have had a significant impact on employment and work, for example the increasing number of employees who work 'non-standard' hours or the much greater involvement of the customer as a third party in the employment relationship (Lucas, 2004).

As we acknowledged earlier there are many who would argue that these are rather simplistic interpretations of the terms (Sisson, 2005). To an extent though the above discussion does have an element of truth and at the least it is useful in denoting key shifts in the nature of employment in recent years. In particular, the shift from manufacturing to service employment and reliance on collective institutions to a more individualized view of the employment relationship are clearly apparent.

Frames of reference and the resolution of conflict

Notwithstanding the debate about the terms industrial and employee relations a key point that remains is the likelihood of conflict or competing interests existing in the employment relationship. Of course, these aspects may also exist alongside more co-operative relationships and this notion of how employers view both conflict and co-operation can be further appreciated by drawing upon the unitary and pluralist 'frames of reference' (Fox, 1966) through which the employment relationship can be viewed.

Within the unitary frame of reference the metaphor of a football team is often used to illustrate this perspective on the employment relationship (Marchington and Wilkinson, 2005). In this view organizations are conceptualized as a team in which all participants are aiming for the same goal, have similar objectives and are not in conflict with one another. The unitary perspective sees the organization as a cohesive and integrated team, where everybody shares common values, interests and objectives to achieve the goal of the efficient functioning of the enterprise. Within this approach a key element is the recognition of the managerial prerogative and the unrestrained 'right to manage'. Managers are the single source of authority and act in a benign and rational manner for the benefit of employees. Resultantly a unitary view of the employment relationship would be framed and constrained by the idea that conflict and dissidence are unnecessary, undesirable, irrational and pathologically deviant behaviour. Any conflict that does arise will be rationalized as being a reflection of frictional rather than structural problems within the organization. Consequently, trade unions are viewed as being an unimportant and unnecessary intrusion into the organization. One final point about the unitary perspective is the need to recognize there may be differing styles of management ranging from authoritarian to paternalistic, and the latter in particular may underpin a more sophisticated unitarism which finds organizational expression in talk of 'soft' HRM in particular. Although the unitary perspective may be easy to criticize for advocating an unrealistic view of the workplace, evidence suggests that many British managers still hold unitaristic views of the workplace. Indeed, Lucas (2004) suggests that unitaristic thinking is apparent in large parts of the tourism and hospitality industry; and often this unitaristic thinking is the less sophisticated version premised on cost-minimization and 'unbridled' individualism, which creates a 'poor' employment experience for many in the industry.

The 'them and us' attitude which unitarism eschews is something that is accepted as being integral to the pluralist perspective on the employment relationship. Conflict is accepted as being inevitable and rational because of the plurality of interests in the organizational setting, though the resolution of such conflict may be through differing approaches. In simple terms we can consider this in terms of both collective and individual approaches.

HRM in practice 10.1   Social partnership in Lufthansa

At a time when the airline industry has faced huge challenges in the 1990s and the post-9/11 era, Lufthansa has drawn on the institutionally-embedded social partnership approach common in Germany to stave of the worst effects of a downturn in the sector. At the heart of this social partnership is an understanding that the company will consult and negotiate with employees through works councils and trade unions. In particular, by considering the employee 'voice' the company has chosen to approach restructuring in a manner which has not led to redundancies and a short-term response to the challenges in the industry. This approach was in contrast to a number of other airline companies, such as British Airways (BA) and Aer Lingus who both made large-scale job cuts in the wake of September 11th. By a process of consultation and negotiation Lufthansa was able to agree wage concessions and enhanced labour flexibility, through things like changes in working time and voluntary unpaid leave to avoid redundancies. Though these changes were made, overall there was no major deterioration in the terms and conditions of employees. Consequently, the trust and co-operation between the social partners was able to survive the immediate post-9/11 era and allowed the company to consider a brighter future without the latent mistrust stemming from widespread redundancies, a problem which faced other airlines.

Source: Turnbull et al. (2004).

Collective approaches to conflict resolution will envisage a role for trade unions to represent the interests of employees, though there may be very different approaches adopted by trade unions depending on the institutional context in which bargaining with employers takes place. For example, in the UK the relationship has often been characterized as being reflective of a 'them and us' culture, where the relationship between employers and trade unions was antagonistic. In attempts to institutionalize conflict in such an environment the bargaining process would often be concerned with power bargaining or zero-sum 'winner takes all'-type bargaining. In such a process the relative economic strength of the employers and trade unions could determine the eventual resolution of any such dispute. By contrast, in a number of European countries the relationship between employers and trade unions has been rather more consensual and premised on notions such as 'social partnership' and 'social dialogue' (and see HRM in practice 10.1).

More recently, as we have already noted, many argue that British public policy has attempted to foster a climate which is more concerned with partnership along European lines, a process that has also been driven to an extent by a number of EU Directives encouraging greater consultation between employers and employees. As well as collective approaches to conflict, disagreement can also take place at a more individual approach. Again conflict is seen as inevitable but the resolution of such conflict does not take place within a collective framework or with the involvement of trade unions. Instead, the employment relationship is based on employment contracts determined by market forces and common law and 'freely' negotiated between employers and employees. Conflict may arise as employees seek the highest level of reward, best conditions and least exacting work, whilst employers seek the lowest level of payment, least costly conditions and most efficacious and flexible use of labour.

In addition a final perspective initially developed by Fox (1974) and then refined by others, adopts a more radical view of the employment relationship. In this radical/ Marxist approach the employment relationship is seen not so much in organizational terms, but in a much wider social, political and economic framework. In this broader analysis of capitalist society capital and labour are conceptualized as being engaged in an antagonistic 'power struggle' that is waged very much on capital's terms. Marxists or neo-Marxists argue that trade union power is illusory and only maintains the delusion of a balance of power. In its purest form the Marxist perspective suggests that only by the working class gaining workers' control will real equality be established. In contemporary market-driven economies moves to workers control are very unlikely. Nevertheless, it is important to recognize that the radical perspective provides the theoretical framework for more critical views of the employment relationship, such as labour process analysis.

Review and reflect

Think of your current workplace or where you have previously spent time on work placement and consider which frame of reference best describes how conflict is managed. Is this the best way to manage conflict?

In sum, then there have been a number of significant changes in the employment relations landscape in recent years. The shift from industrial to employee relations and the decline of trade union power and influence has led to increasing talk of a more unitaristic and individualistic view of the employment relationship. As a consequence there is often increasingly talk of the 'death' of trade unions, a view which is now considered in more detail.

Trade unions: in terminal decline?

A wide range of factors has contributed to a decline in trade union membership in the UK in recent years. In particular, the structural changes in the economy and the decline in so-called 'heavy' industries such as coalmining, shipbuilding and steel has particularly impacted on the unions. Equally, the legislative programme enacted by the Conservative Governments in the 1980s and 1990s can clearly be seen to be a significant influence. In addition to these aspects CIPD (2005) suggest that global competitive pressures and employee attitudes are equally important. In particular, younger people are unlikely to have ever belonged to a trade union and it is suggested that many of them see no point in trade unions (LRD, 2004a).

Review and reflect

Trade unions are increasingly looking to recruit younger employees and in sectors where they have previously had few members, such as tourism and hospitality. Think about your own view of trade unions and consider why you think trade unions have had little success in the past in recruiting members in the tourism and hospitality industry.

The decline in trade union membership is within a context in which for the first time in the UK there appears at first view to be much greater state support for trade unions. This situation is a change from the past where historically there has been little state support for trade union recognition in the UK and much of the twentieth century could be best characterized as being voluntaristic, with minimal intervention from the state in employment relations. More recently, though, there has been greater state intervention, including the area of union recognition. In this sense the Employment Relations Act (ERA) (1999) and (2004) means that trade unions may gain recognition even where employers are implacably opposed to the idea (LRD, 2006). Importantly though the legislation does not apply to small employers, defined as those with 20 or fewer workers, which of course is the majority of tourism and hospitality enterprises.

However, even within the changing employment relations landscape described above it is arguable the extent to which trade unions are likely to make a significant comeback. In part, this reflects a wider sense of managerial resistance to trade unions. In attempting to understand the reasons for such resistance, Gall (2004) notes how the period from 1979–1997 created what he terms a sense of 'managerial Thatcherism'. In essence, the legislative programme of primarily the Thatcher, but also the Major, Governments sought to change the employment landscape by severely restricting the ability of trade unions to organize and to take industrial action and thereby secure recognition and successfully pursue their members' interests in collective negotiations. For Gall one of the obvious outcomes that this period engendered is a present day situation of 'not insignificant employer opposition to granting recognition' (p. 36). Thus, despite the attempts by the Blair Governments to ostensibly create an employee relations public policy which foregrounds a stronger sense of partnership, it seems questionable, as Gennard (2002) argues, as to whether there really is a 'break with the past'. Indeed, some authors have gone so far as to suggest that New Labour's acceptance of the desirability of a largely deregulated labour market as a source of economic competitiveness denotes a marked convergence with the neo-liberal policies of the previous Conservative Governments and has led to what is termed 'Blatcherism' (Red Pepper, 2004).

Regardless of debates concerning what is the most compelling explanation for declining trade union membership and activity what is clear is the precipitous fall in trade union membership. In 1979 there were 13 289 million members, a density of over 50 per cent. By 2005 the figure had declined to approximately 6.4 million, a density of 29 per cent (DTI, 2006). Moreover, as Table 10.1 suggests low trade union membership is not confined to the UK, but is also be seen in the US, Australasia and large parts of Europe.

Whilst Table 10.1 outlines union density figures for the economy as a whole, often the figure will be lower again for the tourism and hospitality sector. For example, the International Labour Organization (ILO, 2001) has estimated that globally the average figure for the tourism and hospitality industry is 10 per cent. That said, we do have to exercise a degree of caution in recognizing this argument not least because there may be significant differences between sub-sectors like hotel and catering, compared to the airline industry, for example. Even then there may be national differences in the relative strength of trade unions in certain

Table 10.1 Union density in selected countries

Country	% Union density (2003)
US	12.4
Australia	22.9
Japan	19.7
Germany	22.6
France	8.3
Italy	33.7
Sweden	78
Netherlands	22
Ireland	35.3
New Zealand	22 (2002 figure)

Derived from Visser (2006).

sub-sectors. For example, within the hotel and catering industry in the UK the current trade union density is 4.2 per cent and trade unions have little real purchase or influence (DTI, 2006). Conventionally a number of reasons are forwarded for low levels of trade union density in the UK hotel and catering sub-sector (Macaulay and Wood, 1992; Aslan and Wood, 1993; Lucas, 2004 and see also HRM in practice 10.2).

- Ethos of hotel and catering – for example the suggested conservatism and individualism of the workforce and reliance on informal rewards tends to create a workplace culture which is antipathetic to trade unions. The self-reliance that this individualism tends to breed means that employees prefer to represent themselves in negotiating with management.
- The predominance of small workplaces and their wide geographical dispersion pose considerable challenges to trade union recruitment and organizing strategies. The existence of a 'family culture' in many small and medium-sized enterprises (SMEs) is also considered a significant barrier to organizing. For example, Lucas (2004) in her interrogation of the 1998 Workplace Employee Relations Survey (WERS) data found that hospitality employees in very small workplaces demonstrated a much higher level of positive endorsement for their manager's style of management.
- Structure of the workforce – the workforce has high numbers of young workers, students, part-timers, women, employees from ethnic minorities and migrant

HRM in practice 10.2   Failing to organize the Dorchester Hotel

Wills (2005) reports how the T&G targeted the world-famous Dorchester Hotel in 1999 in attempts to gain union recognition. The Dorchester was targeted as it was a stand-alone hotel which did not belong to a national or international chain, so for the purposes of 1999 ERA would be counted as a single bargaining unit. From 1999–2002 the T&G sought to gain union recognition. Although some employees did join the union, high levels of labour turnover and the ethnic diversity of the staff made it difficult to sustain a common union identity. When the T&G came to present its case to the Central Arbitration Committee in December 2002 the union was unable to present a sufficiently compelling case that a majority of workers constituting the bargaining unit would be likely to support recognition. In part, this was due to the Dorchester claiming more work-ers worked in the hotel than the T&G; although the union also found that a number of their claimed members were either duplicate members or were no longer employed. The failure to organize the Dorchester seems to point to the need for British unions to change their tactics in seeking recognition and to develop a broader geographical, occupational and sectoral focus, rather than concentrating on the level of the individual workplace.

workers, all groups who are not traditionally associated with trade union mem-bership. This situation is also exacerbated by high labour turnover.

- Employer and management attitudes – as we have already noted the industry is characterized by a unitary view of the employment relationship that sees no role for trade unions. Consequently employers and managers are hostile towards trade unions and will often pursue an active non-union policy.
- Role of trade unions – notwithstanding recent attempts by the Transport and General Workers Union (T&G) and the GMB to organize parts of the hospitality sector it is generally acknowledged that for too long trade unions failed to develop effective strategies to organize the sector.

Although trade unions have failed to establish any real foothold within the UK hotel and catering industry there is some evidence that they have had greater suc-cess elsewhere and in doing so improved the working lives of their members (and see HRM in practice 10.3 and 10.4).

As we noted earlier the relative lack of trade union presence is not universal in the tourism and hospitality industry in terms of the relative strength of trade

HRM in practice 10.3   Unions making a difference in the US

Research conducted by Bernhardt et al. (2003) in eight (half of which were unionized) high-end, full-service 'Class A' hotels in four US cities found that unions could make a difference to employees lives. The research focused on room attendants and food and beverage staff and amongst other things found that in the unionized hotels wages were higher, work intensity was lower, contract provisions on workload were more constraining and innovative bargaining was more prevalent. Such outcomes involve a partnership of unions and management. These union–management partnerships, it was suggested, can help to tackle industry-wide problems and demonstrate that 'win-win' or 'mutual gains' solutions are possible in the hotel industry.

HRM in practice 10.4   Enhanced labour flexibility in Australian hotels

Research by Knox and Nickson (2007) suggests that within Australia some hotel employers engage in successful firm-level bargaining with trade unions, with unionization rates across the industry far higher than in the UK. Case studies of two hotels found that management at hotels with enterprise bargaining had decided to pursue both service excellence and cost-minimization. This strategy focused on introducing employment practices that provided the dual benefits of quality enhancement and cost reduction in such a way that they were not in conflict with one another. This situation was achieved through partnerships and bargaining with the trade union. The employers believed that they could best achieve their aims by bargaining with the union rather than directly with employees because they were concerned with receiving the support and co-operation of the workforce. Sophisticated rostering systems were introduced in order to align the needs of employer and employee more effectively. The hotels also exhibited a strong commitment to enhanced functional flexibility, with initiatives directed towards improving multi-skilling, service quality, ongoing training and development and retention. In sum, the research highlighted Australia's unique institutional context and the potential benefits associated with regulation and union involvement.

unions in different sub-sectors. For example, Baum (2006) recognizes that the airline industry has always had a stronger trade union presence when compared to the hotel and catering sub-sector, even in the UK (and see HRM in practice 10.5).

HRM in practice 10.5   Conflict in BA

BA has had something of a chequered history in recent years in its dealings with trade unions. When in 2003 the company sought to introduce a new automated time recording system for check-in and ticketing staff it found itself involved in a costly industrial dispute. The row centred on the introduction of a new electronic clocking-on system at Heathrow airport, which staff feared would be used to push through other changes in pay and conditions, such as the introduction of split shifts and annualized hours. These concerns and the manner in which the system was being 'imposed' led to a two-day unofficial strike by members of the GMB, T&G and Amicus trade unions. The dispute led to the cancellation of over 500 flights affecting thousands of passengers. As well a PR disaster the dispute was estimated to have cost the company £50 million. More recently the company also found itself embroiled in an equally damaging dispute, albeit one not directly of its own making. In 1997 BA chose to outsource its in-house catering operation to a company called Gate Gourmet, who were the sole catering supplier for the company. Gate Gourmet was already paying relatively cheap wages to their workers when in an attempt to drive down wages even further the company employed 130 agency staff. This was despite the company's previous attempts at restructuring, which had led to redundancies. As a result the original staff held a meeting to wait for further news, which led to over 650 of them being sacked. In response BA found itself facing costly sympathy action by baggage handlers and ground staff, who were not only in the same trade union, T&G, as the Gate Gourmet workers, but in some cases were also the husbands and brothers of the sacked workers. Once again BA found itself having to cancel hundreds of flights, leading to over 100 000 passengers being stranded. As well as the immediate disruption caused by the action of the baggage handlers the dispute in Gate Gourmet dragged on for several months customer refreshments to some BA customer. The cost to BA of the strike action was estimated at between £35–45 million, though arguably the biggest cost was in terms of the company's damaged reputation and lost custom in the future.

Derived from BBC (2005), Clark (2003), Morgan (2003) Townsend (2005).

In sum, although there may be some pockets of trade union strength in the tourism and hospitality industry, generally trade unions remain a marginal presence. In a broader sense clearly any future for the trade union movement is contingent upon their ability to organize in the service sector. The evidence to date suggests that this may well be an uphill struggle for the trade union movement. As a consequence this lack of collective 'voice' provided by the trade unions means that most tourism and hospitality employees are likely to sustain an influence in managerial decision-making through the processes of employee involvement and participation.

Employee involvement and participation

As we have already noted there is a definitional and terminological debate on the meanings of terms such as 'employee involvement', 'employee participation' and 'industrial democracy' (Blyton and Turnbull, 2004). Hyman and Mason (1995) suggest that increasingly, talk of industrial democracy – which denotes a fundamental change in the balance of power in society generally and the workplace specifically, such as the establishment of employee self-management – has little currency in contemporary market-driven economies. Consequently we are left with the notions of 'employee involvement' and 'employee participation', which represent the 'two principal and in many respects contradictory approaches to defining and operationalizing employee influence' (Hyman and Mason, 1995: 1).

Employee involvement

Marchington and Wilkinson (2005) recognize that there are a number of mechanisms that have been introduced under the broad heading of employee involvement, for example teamworking and empowerment to name just two. Whilst there may be a number of differing initiatives there is nonetheless common agreement of the intent of employee involvement. In that sense most writers recognize that employee involvement is concerned with measures which are introduced by management to optimize the utilization of labour whilst at the same time securing the employee's identification with the aims and needs of the organization. Employee involvement is seen as being very much a phenomenon of the 1980s and closely linked with 'soft' HRM with its emphasis on unitarism and the creation of common interests between employer and employee. Employee involvement is managerially initiated and characterized as direct, 'descending participation', which is task-centred as it attempts to involve all individuals in the workplace (Salamon, 2000). In this way it seeks to provide employees with opportunities to influence and take part in organizational decision-making, specifically within the context of

Table 10.2 Direct communication and information sharing techniques

Technique	% of organizations using technique
Meetings with entire workforce or team briefings	91
Systematic use of management chain	64
Regular newsletter	45
Noticeboards	74
E-mail	38
Intranet	34
Suggestion schemes	30
Employee attitude surveys	42

Adapted from IRS (2005a).

their own workgroup or task. Therefore it is intended to motivate individual employees, increase job satisfaction and enhance the sense of identification with the aims, objectives and decisions of the organization. Organizations have a number of ways in which they can involve employees and Table 10.2 outlines the incidence of these aspects in British workplaces with 10 or more employees, as found in the 2004 WERS.

Marchington and Wilkinson (2005) note that these various techniques can be further broken down between those where the organization simply communicates downwards to employees, and those more concerned with upward problem solving. With regard to downward communication it can be seen from Table 10.2 that this form of employee involvement is especially prevalent amongst organizations. Direct communication to the individual can take a variety of forms and involve a variety of media both electronic and paper such as e-mail, intranet, company newsletters and noticeboards. IRS (2005b) recently surveyed over 70 organizations across the economy and found that the most important aim of their communication strategy was to keep employees informed about changes in the organization, closely followed by improving employee engagement and improving employee performance. Though downward communications can be useful in attempting to achieve these aims through informing and 'educating' employees about managerial actions and intentions they are also passive and are characterized by Marchington and Wilkinson (2005) as the most 'dilute' form of direct participation. Indeed, Hyman and Mason

(1995) suggest downward communications mechanisms are ultimately rather superficial and question the extent to which they denote meaningful involvement.

By contrast a number of upward problem-solving techniques are more likely to denote more meaningful involvement for employees, usually involving two-way communication. These techniques may be directed at either individuals or workgroups and are now considered. Suggestion schemes allow organizations to potentially tap into the creativity in their workforce to make significant improvements in just about every aspect of the business, for example improvements in customer service (IDS, 2003). As a result they can improve the motivation and commitment of workers, as they see their voluntary activity as being integral to company success. Equally, there may also be more instrumental and tangible benefits both to the individual, whereby employees are rewarded for ideas and for the organization, who may accrue significant cost savings from suggestions emanating from employees. A second technique which aims to encourage more active employee involvement is attitude surveys. More often than not employee attitude surveys will be a census of all staff usually yearly or bi-annually (IDS, 2004). Employees will usually be asked to give their views on a range of issues, including (IDS, 2004):

- The organization's strategic direction and leadership.
- Organizational culture.
- The organization as an employer.
- Pay and benefits.
- Working environment and conditions.
- Working relationships (i.e. with managers and colleagues).
- Company image.
- Overall satisfaction/commitment to the organization.
- Reaction to the survey and previous follow-up action.

The last point is important in delineating the need for organization's to be transparent in both disseminating results and being seen to act on them. As was alluded to in Chapter 8 there may also be opportunities for employees to appraise their manager's performance. The suggested benefits of employees commenting on managerial performance through employee attitude surveys are that it makes for better management, although again this is contingent upon management accepting and acting upon the results of surveys.

Review and reflect

Imagine you are a manager in a travel agency which is part of a large multinational company. As part of their involvement scheme the company runs an attitude survey which gives employees the opportunity to comment on your performance. In the last survey your employees have said that you are dictatorial and difficult to approach, how do you respond?

In a group sense, initiatives within tourism and hospitality which seek to encourage employees' involvement in upward communication are likely to be premised on the notion of improving quality within the organization and towards the customer, finding expression in techniques such as quality circles (QCs) and total quality management (TQM). Lashley (2001) notes how QCs are essentially concerned with consultation on the basis of management posing problems in the expectation of receiving suggestions from employees. Suggestions are likely to be directed towards improvements in service quality and productivity in particular. He also reports evidence from the Accor Group where QCs have been used successfully. Although employees were expected to act as volunteers and are not paid for taking part in the QCs there was still significant interest amongst employees. Amongst other things the QCs in Accor were able to speed-up customers breakfast service and guest check-out times on the basis of identifying problems, suggesting and testing solutions, measuring results and finally 'rolling out' the approved solution. A more all-embracing approach to quality is via the notion of TQM, which is more concerned to promulgate an integrated view of quality via company-wide improvements in quality both towards the internal customer (the employee) and the external customer. Baldachino (1995) reports a case study of a luxury hotel where the implementation of a TQM philosophy was beset by a number of problems including employee suspicion of the rhetoric of TQM, empowerment and involvement when faced with the realities of redundancy, industrial conflict and the more prosaic problem of a 'them and us' attitude emerging over the car parking situation for managers and employees at the hotel. More sanguine accounts of TQM claim several benefits from such a philosophy, including, improved organizational efficiency, greater employee involvement, consistently 'delighting the customer' by exceeding their expectations and reduced labour turnover (Hope and Muhlemann, 1998). An integral part of a TQM framework is the role of empowerment, which is often seen as being synonymous with greater employee involvement.

Empowerment may actually encompass a variety of employee involvement techniques (Wilkinson, 1998; Lashley, 2001), though for clarity we will talk here of empowerment as being predominately about encouraging front-line staff to solve customers problems on the spot, without constant recourse to managerial approval. As was discussed in Chapter 3 tourism and hospitality organizations are increasingly attempting to develop an organizational culture which places quality service at its centre. With customer expectations becoming ever more dynamic empowerment is increasingly sold as being the key to achieving not only high levels of service quality but also as a means to enhance the commitment and job satisfaction of employees. In principle, empowerment allows employees to exercise greater authority, discretion and autonomy in their dealings with guests. In reality, the latitude allowed to employees is often circumscribed. For example, Jones et al. (1997) in their study of the Americo hotel chain found that the use of a 'compensation matrix' would dictate employee responses and allowed management to monitor and measure such responses, creating tightly constrained discretion (see also Hales and Klidas, 1998). Thus, although the rhetoric of empowerment is about attempting to move decisively from a control-oriented organization to a commitment-oriented organization, Riley (1996: 171) pragmatically recognizes that whilst 'empowerment is giving the employees the right to "break the rules" to serve the customer' it is also nonetheless important to recognize that 'rules are always necessary for an organization. It is a balance between organizational rules and discretion which must be available quickly'.

Review and reflect

Can you really have empowerment which involves tightly constrained discretion?

As we recognized in Chapter 7 training and development of employees is also a crucial part in operationalizing empowerment strategies, with employees requiring training in areas like, social skills, communication skills, decision-making skills, problem-solving skills, planning skills and teamworking. Relatedly there will also be a need to re-orient managerial thinking towards a more facilitative and coaching style, which should also attempt to impart a greater sense of trust and confidence in the ability of the front-line staff to make suitable decisions. This does not mean that management's role is completely emasculated or abrogated but merely refined, although this may be particularly difficult for managers to accept (Wilkinson, 1998). Equally it is important to create a 'no blame' culture where 'well intentioned errors' are discussed in a supportive way in order that lessons can be learned from any mistakes in decision taking by employees.

This latter point can be seen as one of the obvious benefits of empowerment and a review of several writers suggests several other benefits to be derived from empowerment (Wilkinson, 1998; Lashley, 2001; Baum, 2006):

- Reduction in the so-called social distance between customers and employees, so service is not seen as servility.
- Improved quality and guest satisfaction, as the removal of close supervision creates a more responsive service delivery system.
- Enhanced motivation and job satisfaction for employees, leading to greater commitment and reduced labour turnover.
- More time for managers to engage in strategic planning and customer responsiveness.
- Cost savings and improvements from ideas generated by employees.
- Word of mouth advertising.

On the other hand there may also be a number of potential problems in empowering employees. We have already noted how reality may not match the rhetoric of companies in relation to the tightly constrained discretion which characterizes many empowerment schemes. In addition, employees may also see empowerment as about increasing risks and responsibilities without any commensurate extra reward for the additional skills and discretion they are expected to demonstrate. A further issue is that of job security, as empowerment may be used to justify delayering, which in turn leads to a drastic reduction in the number employed by the organization. There is also the vexed issue of the culturally-bound nature of empowerment, which is often seen as a very Americanized approach to service (Nickson, 1999). Consequently, and as we noted in Chapter 2, it may be especially difficult to create an empowered culture in countries such as China and the post-communist Eastern European states, though even within parts of Western Europe there is also evidence of significant resistance to the precepts underlying empowerment (Klidas, 2002).

Employee participation

Hyman and Mason (1995: 21) define participation as 'state [or supra-state] initiatives which promote the collective rights of employees to be represented in organizational decision-making, or to the consequence of the efforts of employees themselves to establish collective representation in corporate decisions, possibly in the face of employer resistance'. Salamon (2000) characterizes participation as being pluralist, power-centred, indirect, representative and 'ascending' in its focus on the managerial prerogative and attempts to extend employees collective interest into a variety of areas and decisions at higher levels of the organization. The expression of employee interests over company decisions may be via joint consultation, works councils and worker directors. With regard to joint consultative committees (JCCs), Lucas (2004) notes how data from WERS 1998 suggests that management committees for joint consultation, rather than negotiation, are rare in the tourism and hospitality industry. Moreover, where such committees do exist they tend to have quite a narrow focus in terms of what they will allow consultation on. As Lucas notes, 'Where committees function in the HI [hospitality industry], health and safety is most likely to be discussed, followed by training, working practices and welfare services and facilities. Pay and government regulations are the least frequently discussed issues' (p. 161). Consequently, in this section the focus is mainly on works councils, both European and national.

European and national works councils

Hyman and Mason (1995: 32) suggest works councils are, 'a representative body composed of employees (and possibly containing employer representatives as well) which enjoy certain rights from the employer'. Works councils have two principal rights; firstly, the right to receive information on key aspects of company activity, such as restructuring, HRM/personnel issues, health and safety, etc., and secondly, the right to consultation on such issues prior to their implementation by management. Works councils are common in Europe and often underpin approaches based on social partnership, but have been a relatively rare phenomenon in the UK with only a small number of companies setting up voluntary agreement (and see HRM in practice 10.6).

More recently though within the UK especially the situation has changed with European-inspired regulation, which has established European Works Councils

HRM in practice 10.6   PizzaExpress: Spreading the word

As was noted in Chapter 9 PizzaExpress' image was seriously damaged in 1999 following the revelation that they had been rather disingenuous in their interpretation of the minimum wage legislation in the UK. Clearly, the company had to start improving internal communication to pinpoint and address sensitive issues which arose from this dispute. To tackle this problem, the HR department gave the job of communications manager to Steve Perkins, who was then a member of the restaurant staff. Perkins decided to set up a company-wide works council system similar to those running in EU nations. The first step was to look at other companies' practices but Perkins was told to develop a system that best suited the company. The new communication system took more than 18 months to become fully effective. The work councils are now run at local, regional and national levels, from individual restaurants to headquarters. They involve managers and staff representatives alike. At the restaurant level, forum discussions are held every 2 months and involve managers, staff representatives and staff themselves who are encouraged to express their concerns. Problems can be settled at this stage, although unresolved issues can be taken to one of the seven regional councils held by regional managers and restaurant representatives. Again, issues can be brought to the national forum, which meets every 6 months and involves top-executives and board members. The new works council witnessed several breakthroughs. For instance, the system prevented massive complaints from employees about reduced wages, when the company was only trying to take out an amount of the wages to adjust it tax-wise and give it back at a lower tax rate. Thanks to the forum, representatives were able to identify and calm their colleagues' fears. From a company point of view the consultative process also has the advantage of avoiding negotiations with unions and resulting strike threats. Despite its successes, however, the communication system would not have worked without PizzaExpress' commitment, which was fundamental in gaining staff commitment to the process. As James Sydmonds, the national forum representative for Café Pasta, said, 'When I started on the forum, I was very suspicious … Every time I got to a different level and an issue was brought up, I'd think: "What is actually going to happen at the next level?" But the company involvement has surprised me, and I have been so impressed that I have wanted to get more involved and spread the gospel'.

Derived from Cooper (2001), Goymour (2000).

HRM in practice 10.7   Club Med

Club Med is a French company and one of the world leaders in holiday villages. The company operates in over 40 countries and has more than 20 000 employees. Club Med introduced its EWC in September 1996, though prior to this date the company had previously worked with unions to resolve issues such as re-employing seasonal staff and helping non-French nationals to settle into working in France. Initially the EWC agreement was signed for a period of 3 years, though in 1999 the agreement was renewed indefinitely. Employee representatives are provided by the trade unions, both at a European level and for several individual countries in which Club Med operates. The EWC allows for the provision of information, reflection and consultation between the partners. Information provided through the EWC encompasses economic and financial matters, strategic perspectives, the employment situation, organizational changes and their consequences. In difficult times, such as the post-9/11 period, the process of consultation allowed the EWC to engender consensus on issues such as restructuring in what were difficult circumstances. In sum, the Club Med EWC is suggested as having several benefits including: effective joint action during restructuring programmes with an impact on employment; production of ethics guidelines on sub-contracting to support local conflicts; and exchanges on strategic orientations or organizational changes within the group.

Source: EFILC (2005).

(EWCs) and national works councils. The Directive establishing EWCs was adopted in September 1994. It was not though till 2000 that the Directive was finally implemented in the UK. The Directive covers all companies with a presence in more than one EU Member State and with at least 1000 employees in total, of which at least 150 are located in each of two EU Member States (CIPD, 2006). Importantly, companies do not automatically have to establish a EWC, though both companies and employees (or their representatives) can trigger mechanisms to request a EWC (LRD, 2006). The voluntary nature of EWCs means that of the more than 2000 companies covered by the Directive only around a third have established EWC arrangements (CIPD, 2006). Within tourism and hospitality Lucas (2004) notes that a relatively small number of companies have introduced EWCs, a number of whom were headquartered in Europe (and see HRM in practice 10.7).

In addition to EWCs the EU parliament also adopted the information and consultation of Directive in March 2002, which was implemented in the UK as the Information and Consultation of Employees Regulations 2004 (ICE Regulations).

The Directive required Member States to ensure that employers are under an obligation to consult with their workforce on an ongoing basis in order that employees have a better idea of potential changes in their employment. As was noted earlier these types of arrangements are common in many parts of Europe, though much less so within the UK context. For example, if we take JCCs as a rough proxy for the sort of mechanisms required by the ICE Regulations then WERS 2004 found that JCCs were present in 14 per cent of all UK workplaces, though this varied markedly between size of the workplace, with the figures being 26 per cent in workplaces with 50–99 employees and 47 per cent in those with 100–199 employees (Kersley et al., 2006). From April 2005 the ICE Regulations applied to companies with more than 150 employees, though it will cover those with at least 100 from April 2007 and those with at least 50 from April 2008. Under the terms of the ICE Regulations employees will have the right to be (LRD, 2004b):

- Informed about the organization's economic situation.
- Informed and consulted about its current employment situation and employment prospects.
- Informed and consulted about decisions likely to lead to major changes in contractual decisions or work organization. This could cover a range of topics including working time and practices, training, equal opportunities and pensions.

Employers covered by the ICE Regulations will not automatically have to inform and consult with employees, and indeed some employers may have pre-existing arrangements that are considered acceptable. In workplaces without any existing arrangements employees can make a request for the establishment of information and consultation procedures. As long as 10 per cent of employees support such a request the employer then has to provide a mechanism for information and consultation (IDS, 2005). At the time of writing it is too early to say what effect the ICE Regulations are likely to have in the long term. However, it does seem set to continue the trend of Europeanization of employee relations activities in the UK, though whether this ultimately leads to real social partnership and dialogue remains to be seen.

Conclusion

In this chapter we recognized that whilst there may be broad agreement on the principle of ensuring that employees have a voice in managerial decision-making the form of influence will vary enormously. In some institutional contexts the voice may be provided by trade unions. This is especially true for a number of European countries where the principle of social partnership ensures that unions play an active part in organizational decision-making. In the UK though it is more likely that within the tourism and hospitality sector that employee influence will be sustained through a variety of involvement and participation mechanisms. There is much debate as to the efficacy – in relation to issues like improving employee morale and raising productivity – and democratic intent of employee involvement, and particularly the extent to which the various initiatives represent 'pseudo-participation' in their lack of a challenge to the managerial prerogative. On the other hand it remains to be seen whether the representative approaches which are now increasingly encouraged through a number of European Directives will provide the meaningful participation that is intended. Ultimately approaches to employee involvement and participation should aim to promote improved dialogue in the workplace. Workplaces that involve and engage their employees in matters that effect their employment experience are likely to benefit through increased commitment and motivation; something that social partnership seems to have achieved in a number of European contexts and from which lessons can seemingly be drawn by UK companies.

References and further reading

Aslan, A. and Wood, R. (1993) 'Trade unions in the hotel and catering industry: the views of hotel managers', *Employee Relations*, 15(2), 61–70.

Baldachino, G. (1995) 'Total quality management in a luxury hotel: a critique of practice', *International Journal of Hospitality Management*, 14(1), 67–78.

Baum, T. (2006) *Human Resource Management for Tourism, Hospitality and Leisure: An International Perspective*, Thomson Learning.

BBC (2005) 'Gate Gourmet settlement reached', at http://news.bbc.co.uk/1/hi/business/4284858.stm (accessed 6 July 2006).

Bernhardt, A., Dresser, L. and Hatton, E. (2003) 'The coffee pot wars: unions and firm restructuring in the hotel industry', in E. Appelbaum, A. Bernhardt and R. J. Murnane (eds.) *Low Wage America*, Russell Sage Foundation, 33–76.

Blyton, P. and Tunbull, P. (2004) *Dynamics of Employee Relations*, Palgrave MacMillan, 3rd edition.

Chartered Institute of Personnel and Development (2005) *What is Employee Relations?*, CIPD.

Chartered Institute of Personnel and Development (2006) *European Works Councils Factsheet*, CIPD.

Clark, A. (2003) 'Conflict and confrontation in the air', *Guardian*, 24 July, 5.

Cooper, C. (2001) 'Talking Italian', *People Management*, 14 June, 38–41.

Department of Trade and Industry (2006) *Trade Union Membership 2005*, DTI.

European Foundation for the Improvement of Living and Working Conditions (EFILC) (2005) 'EWC Case Studies: Club Med', at http://www.eurofound.eu.int/pubdocs/2005/7140/en/1/ef057140en.pdf (accessed 12 July 2006).

Fox, A. (1966) 'Industrial sociology and industrial relations', *Royal Commission Research Paper No. 3*, HMSO.

Fox, A. (1974) *Beyond Contract: Work, Power and Trust Relations*, Faber.

Gall, G. (2004) 'British employer resistance to trade union recognition', *Human Resource Management Journal*, 14(2), 36–53.

Gennard, J. (2002) 'Employee relations public policy developments, 1997–2001: a break from the past?', *Employee Relations*, 24(6), 581–594.

Goymour, D. (2000) 'Let's talk', *Hospitality*, May, 28.

Hales, C. and Klidas, A. (1998) 'Empowerment in five star hotels: choice, voice or rhetoric?', *International Journal of Contemporary Hospitality Management*, 10(3), 88–95.

Hope, C. and Muhlemann, A. (1998) 'Total quality, human resource management and tourism', *Tourism Economics*, 4(4), 367–386.

Hyman, J. and Mason, B. (1995) *Managing Employee Involvement and Participation*, Sage.

Income Data Services (2003) *Suggestion Schemes*, IDS Studies No. 752, June.

Income Data Services (2004) *Employee Attitude Surveys*, IDS Studies No. 777, July.

Income Data Services (2005) *Information and Consultation Arrangements*, IDS HR Studies No. 790, January.

Industrial Relations Services (2005a) 'Evolution, not revolution – the changing face of the workplace', *IRS Employment Review*, No. 832, 30 September, 8–15.

Industrial Relations Services (2005b) 'Dialogue or monologue: is the message getting through', *IRS Employment Review*, No. 834, 28 October, 8–16.

International Labour Organization (2001) *Human Resource Development, Employment and Globalization in the Hotel Catering and Tourism Sector*, ILO.

Jones, C., Nickson, D. and Taylor, G. (1997) 'Whatever it takes? Managing "empowered" employees and the service encounter in the international hotel industry', *Work, Employment and Society*, 11(3), 541–554.

Kersley, B., Alpin, C., Forth, J., Bryson, A., Bewley, H., Gix, G. and Oxenbridge, S. (2006) *Inside the Workplace: Findings from the 2004 Workplace Employment Relations Survey*, Routledge.

Klidas, A. (2002) 'Employee empowerment in the European cultural context: findings from the hotel industry', paper to the *CRANET 2nd International Conference on Human Resource Management in Europe: Trends and Challenges*, Athens.

Knox, A. and Nickson, D. (2007) 'Regulation in Australian hotels: is there a lesson for the UK?', *Employee Relations*, 29, 1.

Labour Research Department (2004a) 'What do young people know about unions', *Labour Research*, March, 17–19.

Labour Research Department (2004b) 'Be organized, be consulted', *Labour Research*, November, 17–19.

Labour Research Department (2006) *Law at Work*, LRD.

Lashley, C. (2001) *Empowerment HR Strategies for Service Excellence*, Butterworth and Heinemann.

Lucas, R. (2004) *Employment Relations in the Hospitality and Tourism Industries*, Routledge.

Macaulay, I. and Wood, R. (1992) 'Hotel and catering industry employees' attitudes towards trade unions', *Employee Relations*, 14(2), 20–28.

Marchington, M. and Wilkinson, A. (2005) 'Direct participation and involvement', in S. Bach (ed.) *Managing Human Resources: Personnel Management in Transition*, 4th edition, Blackwell, 398–423.

Morgan, O. (2003) 'Swipe strike costs BA £50m', *Observer Business Section*, 27 July, 1.

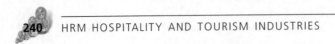

Nickson, D. (1999) *A Review of the Internationalization Strategies of Three Hotel Companies with a Particular Focus on Human Resource Management*, unpublished PhD Thesis, University of Strathclyde.

Red Pepper (2004) 'Red Pepper's 10th Anniversary', press release at http://www.redpepper.org.uk/Press/x-press-May2004.html (accessed 14 January 2006).

Riley, M. (1996) *Human Resource Management in the Hospitality and Tourism Industry*, 2nd edition, Butterworth-Heinemann.

Salamon, M. (2000) *Industrial Relations – Theory and Practice*, 4th edition, Prentice Hall.

Sisson, K. (2005) 'Responding to Mike Emmott: What "industrial relations" suggests should be at the heart of "employee relations"', at http://buira.org.uk/component/option,com_docman/Itemid,/task,doc_download/gid,2/ (accessed 5 July 2006).

Townsend, M. (2005) 'BA makes a meal of sari strike', *The Observer*, 14 August, 15.

Turnbull, P., Blyton, P. and Harvey, G. (2004) 'Cleared for take-off? Management–labour partnership in the European civil aviation industry', *European Journal of Industrial Relations*, 10(3), 287–307.

Visser, J. (2006) 'Union membership statistics in 24 countries', *Monthly Labor Review*, January, 38–49.

Wilkinson, A. (1998) 'Empowerment: theory and practice', *Personnel Review*, 27(1), 40–56.

Wills, J. (2005) 'The geography of union organizing in the low-paid service industries in the UK: lessons from the T&G's campaign to unionize the Dorchester in London', *Antipode*, 37(1), 139–159.

Websites

The Trades Union Congress website gives a sense of their views on a range of employment and political issues http://www.tuc.org.uk

There are a number of case studies concerning employee participation in European companies at http://www.eurofound.eu.int/areas/participationatwork/index.htm

The hospitality, leisure, sport and tourism support network has a useful guide to empowerment, involvement and participation at http://www.hlst.heacademy. ac.uk/resources/guides/empowerment.html

http://www.ilisimatusarfik.gl/eng/index_eng-filer/index_eng.htm is an international site with links to many organizations involved with employee participation and involvement.

Chapter **11**
Welfare, health and safety

Chapter objectives

This chapter considers the range of issues concerned with the development of welfare policies in tourism and hospitality. Recognizing the ethical, legal and business aspects of welfare this chapter aims to:

- Appreciate the differing rationales for developing welfare policy.
- Consider the balance between the public and private life of organizational members.
- Recognize the increasing business emphasis in the development of welfare policies.
- Assess the extent to which welfare issues are particularly resonant within the tourism and hospitality industry.

Introduction

Every year thousands of people suffer serious injury or even death in the workplace. Many more suffer from work-related illnesses or are absent from work due to work-related stress. In order to alleviate dangers in the workplace and ensure that employees are working in a healthy or happy environment it is essential that tourism and hospitality organizations consider the development of appropriate welfare policies. Goss (1994: 122) recognizes how, 'Welfare provision generally refers to those policies which are directed at some aspect of employee well being, both in a physical and emotional sense.' Torrington et al. (2005) suggest that the physical aspects of a broader welfare policy stem from measures to improve health and safety in the workplace, as well as issues such as the provision of paid holidays and reduced working hours. From an emotional/psychological perspective organizations are likely to be concerned with the mental well being of their employees, or more broadly anything involving the 'human relations' needs of people at work. Of course, in reality there is a degree of interconnectedness between physical and mental aspects of welfare, though it is also important to consider the potential distinctions that may be made between them.

From the above discussion we might ask ourselves why should organizations have a welfare policy and indeed whether the subject of the more sensitive aspects of welfare-related issues should remain personal and private. To answer these questions we should recognize various reasons for the existence of welfare policies. Goss (1994) suggests that organizations have usually developed welfare provision within the paradigm of three common 'welfare rationales', these being: legal-reactive, corporate conscience and company paternalism and these are now briefly discussed.

- *Legalistic-reactive*: In this approach an organization's approach to welfare policy is primarily driven by legislative requirements, for example responding to health and safety legislation. With such an approach the organization does not see developing welfare policy as an important part of its core objectives but rather something that has to be complied with.
- *Corporate conscience*: Here, Goss notes how historically the role of personnel had a strong welfare orientation and, arguably, how over time this welfarist approach became increasingly seen as 'soft' and 'indulgent', especially within a more competitive business environment.

- *Company paternalism*: This approach is concerned with the 'fatherly' manner in which organizations would seek to look after all aspects of their employees lives. By taking an 'encompassing' approach, company's that practiced company paternalism would be concerned not only with the immediate work environment, but the manner in which employees lived their lives outside of work. Underpinning company paternalism is a strong sense of religious and moral commitment and employees would be expected to lead a live which fitted with this ethos (see also Nickson (1997) for a description of company paternalism in the Marriott, Hilton, Holiday Inn and Forte organizations).

In many respects the above description of differing welfare rationales has a clear overlap with some of the discussion in Chapter 6 on equal opportunities. In the earlier chapter on equal opportunities the question was considered as to whether organizations should develop policies due to legal, ethical or business aspects and the same arguments can be made with regard to the welfare of employees. Clearly within this discussion the legal dimension is one that cannot be ignored and this aspect will be a concern throughout the chapter. To an extent the notion of corporate conscience and company paternalism would seem to rest more on an ethical view of welfare. Increasingly though it is argued that the main argument for developing welfare policies is from the point of view of the HRM business case/efficiency argument. Much of this discussion about adopting a more efficient approach to welfare is generally seen through the lenses of savings costs by reducing absence and improving the performance of employees in the workplace by addressing any problems or concerns that they might have. Clearly then welfare is an important topic, which may conceivably cover a variety of different issues. In this sense we can think of a welfare 'alphabet', encompassing a range of issues, such as: absence management, AIDS/HIV, alcohol/drug misuse, smoking, stress, working time and workplace violence. These aspects are now considered.

Absence management

Increasingly organizations are attempting to take a more proactive approach to the management of absence, recognizing both its direct and indirect costs. With regard to direct costs IDS (2005a) note how absence can be a significant drain for organizations in terms of the cost of occupational sick pay, lost production or the need to

HRM in practice 11.1   The UK: The sick man of Europe?

IRS (2004a) reports recent research by the European Union (EU) which suggests that the UK has a particularly poor health record with more than one in four working age adults having a long-term health problem. This figure was second only to Finland (32.2 per cent) and higher than direct competitors such as Germany (11.2 per cent), France (24.6 per cent) and Holland (25.4 per cent). The lowest figures in the survey were Romania (5.8 per cent) and Italy (6.6 per cent). For those actually in employment, the UK again has one of the highest rates of employees suffering long-term health problems at 20.4 per cent (surpassing only Finland and France), compared to the EU average of 12.7 per cent.

bring in replacement staff. CIPD (2005a) note that 9 out of 10 organizations report that absence is a 'significant' or 'very significant' cost to the business. Overall, the cost of absence to the UK economy is £11 billion (Simms, 2005), and more specifically CIPD (2005a) notes how the cost per employee is £601 (see HRM in practice 11.1).

More indirectly, and less easy to quantify, absences may place burdens on other organizational members, leading to poor morale, lower productivity, reduced customer retention and profitability (IRS, 2001; IDS, 2005a). In the CIPD (2005a) annual survey of rates of sickness absence hotels, restaurants and leisure had an absence rate of 3.2 per cent and on average employees took 7.3 days off sick. In comparing these figures to other sectors, hospitality and tourism has higher absence rates than private services generally (3.0 per cent and 6.8 days), yet compares favourably with the economy as a whole (3.7 per cent and 8.4 days). There is also the vexed issue of whether sickness absence is 'genuine'. The absence survey by the CIPD (2005a) suggested that 14 per cent of absence across the economy as a whole is not genuine. Indeed, a previous survey conducted in 2004 by the Confederation of British Industry found a similar figure (15 per cent), whilst also noting that retail and distribution, hotels and restaurants were amongst the sectors with the highest levels of non-genuine absence (respectively, 21 per cent and 19 per cent) which arguably points to underlying employment and HRM-related problems (IRS, 2004b).

CIPD (2006a) notes that in broad terms there are two types of absence, short term and long term – defined as 10 days or more (Simms, 2005). Short-term sickness absence will usually be uncertificated, self-certificated or covered by a doctor's note. For longer-term absence there may be a need to involve occupational health professionals or utilize rehabilitation programmes in order to get the employee back to work (CIPD, 2006a), though this may be more likely in larger organizations (IRS, 2004b). There are a number of causes of absence, though the most prevalent is usually minor illness, such as colds or flu. Other reasons for absence include aspects such as back pain, musculo-skeletal injuries, stress, mental ill health and recurring medical conditions (CIPD, 2005a).

Regardless though of the nature of the absence and whether it is short or long term increasingly it is suggested that there is a need for organizations to adopt a more proactive approach, especially if the costs described previously and so-called non-genuine illness are taken into account. For example, it is suggested that organizations are making progress in measuring absence and taking specific steps to address the most obvious causes. Though it is also important that such an approach is seen as part of a broader integrated approach to create a healthy, high-quality workplace, where the link between employer performance and employee satisfaction is clearly understood. At the least though the organization should have a basic sickness absence policy, which should aim to (CIPD, 2006a: 3):

- Provide details of contractual sick pay terms and its relationship with statutory sick pay.
- Outline the process employees must follow if taking time off sick – covering when and whom employees should notify if they are not able to attend work.
- Include when (after how many days) employees need a self-certificate form.
- Contain when they require a medical certificate (sick-note) from their doctor to certify their absence.
- Mention that the organization reserves the right to require employees to attend an examination by a company doctor and (with the employee's consent) to request a report from the employee's doctor.
- Include the provision for return-to-work interviews as these have been identified as the most effective intervention to manage short-term absence.

HRM in practice 11.2 notes an attempt by British Airways to take a more proactive approach to managing absence, which amongst other things demonstrates the importance of training line managers to become involved in the process of managing absence.

In an even more proactive vein some companies are also moving towards using a new trend imported from the US, that of 'wellness' or health management at work, which may be particularly apposite in those leisure-oriented sub-sectors of the tourism and hospitality and is considered in HRM in practice 11.3.

HRM in practice 11.2   Tackling absence at British Airways

British Airways had previously had real problems with levels of absence in the company. In 2002, the company acknowledged the scale of the problem by choosing to go 'loud, proud and wide' on the issue. By October 2004, the average absence per employee was 16.7 days per year, well above the sectoral average. Around 90 per cent of this absence was short term and the overall cost to the company was put at £70 million. It was at this time that British Airways introduced a new absence management policy, which developed a single set of clear absence policies and procedures for all staff. The aim of the new approach was to reduce absence by March 2006 to an average of ten days per employee, thus saving the company an estimated £30 million annually. As Peter Holloway, British Airways head of people and organizational development, recognizes, 'absence management is not fun, sexy or exciting; it is about day to day following through of simple management practices'. Recognizing this point, amongst other things the new policy sought to encourage regular attendance at work, promote early intervention from line managers and HR managers and provide support for those with legitimate reasons for absence with the intent of assisting their return to work at the earliest opportunity. Resultant policy interventions included employees having to have a conversation with their line manager as soon as possible regarding the nature of their absence and a standard informal return-to-work discussion after every occasion of absence. There was also a tightening of absence recording mechanisms, which are now done electronically. Line managers were also tasked with taking a more active role in absence management and 'triggering' an 'absence review interview', a more formal version of the return-to-work interview. The absence review interviews are triggered if an employee is absent more than twice in 3 months or takes more than 10 consecutive days off. When conducting the absence review interviews managers have a degree of discretion in considering the personal circumstances of the employee and aspects such as the Disability Discrimination Act. Although there were some teething problems with the new policy, especially in terms of the manner in which line managers applied discretion and some inconsistency in interpretation of the new rules, the policy appears to have been very successful with the company suggesting that employee absences are now around 8 days per employee.

Derived from IDS (2005a); Simms (2005).

HRM in practice 11.3   Prevention is better than cure

Manocha (2004) recognises how wellness management seeks to adopt a proactive approach in creating a healthy organization. It aims to help employees to look and feel better and to be physically healthy or fit. The emphasis is less on managing employees when they get sick, but instead seeks to manage healthy employees so they do not get sick. Such initiatives are likely to be part of a broader package of HRM policies which aim to create a great place to work. Wellness is likely to be facilitated by aspects such as a gym on site in the workplace and the provision of expert advice in areas such as nutrition. Employers adopting a wellness programme are also likely to measure the results of such an approach by monitoring aspects such as employees' heart rate, blood pressure, cholesterol and body weight.

In sum, organizations are increasingly seeking to adopt more proactive approaches to absenteeism. In part, this approach can be achieved by integrated absence management approaches which look to address short- and long-term absences and importantly also recognizes the potential for underlying causes for absence that may be explicable by broader HRM failings.

AIDS/HIV

AIDS, which stands for Acquired Immune Deficiency Syndrome, was first diagnosed in 1981. It is caused by the human immunodeficiency virus (HIV) which attacks the body's natural defence system and leaves it open to various infections and cancers. Worldwide there are now nearly 40 million people with HIV, many of them in sub-Saharan Africa (MacAskill, 2006). Within North America, Western and Central Europe the figure stands at 3.5 million (MacAskill, 2006). Currently, approximately 10 per cent of known HIV-positive individuals have developed AIDS (ACAS, 2006). Importantly, many people who are HIV positive are well most of the time, but develop some minor symptoms such as swollen lymph glands. In this sense HIV infection alone does not affect people's ability to do their job, at least until employees develop illnesses that may make them unfit for work. Till that point there is no reason why someone who is HIV positive cannot continue to work normally as long as they are fit to do so. Moreover a person who is HIV positive is no real danger to others at work in that transmission during normal working activities is virtually impossible.

It is difficult to be definitive in terms of identifying the number of people who may be HIV positive or have AIDS within the workplace. Ladki (1994) notes that 96 per cent of those diagnosed with AIDS in the United States were in their prime employment years (20–64 years). Similarly, Breuer (1995), again writing in the US context, suggests that 1 in 300 employees may be HIV positive or have AIDS; and that 90 per cent of HIV infected Americans are in the workplace. Clearly then AIDS/HIV is something that organizations have to respond to as a major environmental feature, for example with regard to aspects such as employee education and understanding the legal implications of how best to respond to employees who are HIV positive. AIDS then presents a major managerial challenge encompassing moral, social and medical issues resulting from health, safety, legal and humanitarian problems (Arkin, 2005). Consequently, as Bratton and Gold (2003: 172) note, 'a textbook on human resource management for the next millennium would be incomplete if no reference were made to society's most recent menace.'

Indeed, it may well be that these sentiments have a particular resonance within the tourism and hospitality industry for a number of reasons including (Adam-Smith and Goss, 1993):

- *Age composition and accommodation arrangements*: Many organizations within the sector rely to a great extent on young workers. This is the group in society perceived to be at the most risk of infection through high-risk behaviour, whether that be drug abuse or unprotected sex. For example, most of those infected with HIV are in the age groups that have the highest level of economic activity, thus half of all know infections are in those between the ages of 15–24 years (Goss, 1997). It is also possible that there is a greater concentration of high-risk behaviour when many young workers are living together in shared accommodation, or working in a potentially sexually charged environment (see HRM in practice 11.4).
- *Perceived high concentration of homosexual males working in the industry*: Despite research suggesting that this group has now changed their sexual practices there may be a number who were affected before the risks became apparent.
- *The nature of the work in certain sub-sectors, such as working in kitchens and restaurants*: Here, there may be a very slightly greater risk of infection than in other workplaces. For example, blood being transmitted through accidents in the

HRM in practice 11.4   Sexual activity in the tourism industry

Guerrier and Adib (2004) in their study of tour reps in Mallorca found that male reps in particular where much more likely to instigate sexual relations with customers. Often these approaches and liaisons would take place after organized night outs where male reps were also more than likely than female reps to drink with customers. Guerrier and Adib recognize that for the male tour reps engaging in this type of behaviour was an attempt to reinforce their masculine identity, which they suggest is especially important in feminized environments when it may be in doubt.

HRM in practice 11.5   Responding to sensitive issues

Read the following scenarios:

A member of staff in your travel agency comes to you and informs you that they are HIV positive. How do you react?

A male cook who works in your restaurant kitchen is quite open about the fact that he lives in a homosexual relationship. Most of the other people in the kitchen are aware of this. One day a rumour is started that he is HIV positive. Despite this rumour being *untrue* very quickly a number of his colleagues have been to see you to ask for him to be dismissed. How do you handle this situation?

Review and reflect: How, as a manager, would you respond to these scenarios?

kitchen or hypodermic needles being found in hotel bedrooms or clubs/discos and the risk of blood contact through violent encounters.

● *Sensitivity to public fears*: Despite medical advice to the contrary the public may feel that there is a significant risk of HIV being transmitted through food and in the 1990s employers in the American restaurant industry saw AIDS as the number one long-term issue facing the industry (Ladki, 1994).

Much of the above discussion points to the need for a considered managerial response. Before we move on to discuss this point further first of all consider the issues outlined in HRM in practice 11.5.

HRM in practice 11.6   Public misperceptions about AIDS

Barrows et al. (1996) report how a well-known Californian restaurant, Bon Appetit, found that its business was seriously affected when news emerged that a former employee had died of AIDS. Customer counts declined significantly when the media released a story that an executive chef who had previously worked in the restaurant had died of AIDS. The owner of the restaurant, Ralph Granthem, chose to take a proactive response to the situation by holding a press conference, where he recognized the overwhelming medical evidence that suggests that AIDS is not transmitted by food handling. Greater clarity was also offered by a well-publicised visit from the Director of the California Department of Health Services. Along with his wife the Director ate in the restaurant and also produced a statement recognizing that people do not get AIDS from restaurants. By taking a proactive approach the restaurant was able to reverse the decline in business, but the case illustrates the possibility for uninformed public responses to AIDS.

Having considered your response to these scenarios now consider HRM in practice 11.6 which outlines how one organization dealt with a very similar problem.

HRM in practice 11.6 illustrate the need for a clear and sensible approach to managing AIDS/HIV, though some of the difficulties in developing such an approach are nicely encapsulated by the view of one manager quoted in Bratton and Gold (2003: 172) who recognizes that, 'I was not trained to manage fear, discrimination, and dying in the workplace.' Much of the discussion above stems from potential misinformation about the nature of AIDS/HIV and in particular the notion of perceived risk of infection. Adam-Smith and Goss (1993) identify three potential responses to the perceived risk of infection in the workplace.

- *Rational response*: In this response individuals fully understand the probability of risk and on this basis make an informed choice about the acceptability of working with somebody who is HIV positive. As we have already noted the risk of transmission in a normal workplace situation is minimal and as long as employees are aware of this point then their rational response is such that they would have little or no fear of contracting the disease or working with somebody who is HIV positive.
- *Bounded rationality response*: In this response individuals are likely to view the issue on the basis of factually incomplete or incorrect information, often leading

to a misunderstanding of the degree of risk. Consequently, employees may overemphasize the perceived hazard of AIDS/HIV and for example refuse to work with a fellow employee who is HIV positive because of an inflated sense of risk.

- *Subjective response*: This response is largely driven by moral or subjective beliefs that determine the level of acceptability of working with somebody who is HIV positive. For example, somebody who is homophobic may see AIDS/HIV as being a disease that is 'self-inflicted' and refuse to work with a homosexual colleague who is HIV positive.

Adam-Smith and Goss recognize that in reality, 'individuals are likely to use a complex mix of these decision-making processes in their assessment of risk' (p. 28). Furthermore the organizational context will also be important in determining employees' assessment of risk, a point we touched on earlier.

Policy responses to AIDS/HIV

To a large extent the discussion above also points to the manner in which organizations can develop a response to the issue of AIDS/HIV, which can take one of several forms:

- Total denial that AIDS/HIV is a workplace issue.
- Wait and see approach.
- Deliberate no-policy decision and reliance on existing arrangements.
- AIDS/HIV to be treated as any other life-threatening disease.
- Introduce specific policy.

Given much of the discussion above a more proactive response seems appropriate. In this way the reasons for having a policy include things like countering misunderstanding, lack of knowledge, fear and prejudice. Although ostensibly there is no statutory obligation for such a policy, the designation of HIV under the Disability Discrimination Act, wherein someone with HIV is deemed to have a disability, means that organizations should be proactive, particularly with regard to the notion of making 'reasonable adjustments' to address progressively disabling conditions. In developing a policy there are a number of aspects organizations can consider as being integral to a successful policy, including (e.g. see IRS, 1997; ACAS, 2006):

- A general statement of the company's commitment to non-discrimination.
- Affirmation of usual hiring procedures so there is no discrimination in recruitment against applicants on the grounds that they are HIV positive or have AIDS.
- Assurance of continued employment.
- Employees who are HIV positive will be redeployed to alternative employment at their own request and will not be prevented from continuing work, except where they are deemed 'medically unfit' through the standard procedures.
- Equitable benefits.
- Guarantee of medical confidentiality.
- Access to employee assistance programmes (EAPs), for example counselling services.
- A statement that individuals who refuse to work normally with people with AIDS or who are HIV positive will be interviewed to find out the circumstances of their refusal and if appropriate dealt with under the organization's disciplinary procedure.
- Arrangements for staff who travel overseas.

A policy such as that suggested above may also be developed in conjunction with an education programme to ensure that all employees are fully aware of AIDS/HIV and particularly the lack of any real risk in normal workplace situations.

Alcohol/drug misuse

Drink- and drug-related problems are one of the commonest causes of sickness absence in the workplace. Figures suggest that in the UK one in three men and one in five women drink over the recommended limits (IDS, 2005b) with 1 in 13 Britons said to be dependent on alcohol (BBC, 2003). The result is that for those drinking over the recommended number of units (21–28 for men; 14–21 for women) are twice as likely to take sick leave (IDS, 2005b). It is estimated that alcohol-related sickness or illness costs UK employers around £6.4 billion, with up to 17.4 million working days lost in 2003 (Roberts, 2003). Moreover research from Alcohol Concern suggests that one in four accidents at work are due to alcohol misuse (TUC, 2003). Across the EU it is estimated that the cost of lost productivity through absenteeism, unemployment and lost working years through premature deaths resulting from alcohol abuse is €59 billion a year (Institute of Alcohol Studies, 2006). Similarly, research in the US has suggested that workplace alcohol use and impairment affects approximately 15 per cent of the workforce (Alcohol Concern, 2006). Problem drinkers are also absent from work in the US, on average, 22 days per year and are twice as likely as non-alcohol drinkers to have accidents at work (Corsun and Young, 1998). Whilst problem drinking is a significant workplace concern the same is also true for drug misuse. In 2004, a third of British workers under the age of 25 years took illegal drugs in the previous year, with the figure being 1 in 10 for all workers (IDS, 2005b). Drug abuse costs British industry around £800 million a year (Hilpern, 2001). In the US one in four workers either has used or knows someone who uses illegal drugs and it is suggested that drug abuse costs US business $60 billion annually (Eade, 1993).

Therefore the direct and indirect of alcohol and drug abuse can be seen in a number of ways, such as costs of accidents, lower productivity, poor quality work, bad decisions, damage to the organization's reputation, absenteeism and unreliability, managers losing time in dealing with problems and increased labour turnover. Many argue that alcohol and drug misuse has a particular resonance in the tourism and hospitality. For example, the industry is often suggested as being fast paced and having a 'work hard, play hard' culture where employees may unwind with alcohol or drugs. In addition, other factors that create an environment which arguably encourages alcohol and drug abuse include:

- Long working hours.
- Sociability of the workplace.
- Availability of alcohol in the workplace, and often the expectation that employees will drink as part of their employment.
- Stress, for example employees having to sustain emotional labour so that even during stress-inducing encounters with customers, employees are expected to be positive, friendly, cheerful and helpful.

Reflecting the above discussion it is unsurprising to find that hospitality and tourism workers have been identified as particularly at risk with regard to alcohol and drug abuse. For example, a recent survey of 1000 hospitality professionals found that 40 per cent of respondents had seen colleagues take illegal drugs while at work, with 59 per cent noting how they had seen colleagues drinking to excess on duty (Bignold, 2003). Similarly, publicans top the list of liver cirrhosis mortality with other hospitality occupations, such as cooks and kitchen porter and caterers not far behind (Mullen, 2001).

Developing policy on alcohol and drugs

On the question of a policy it is worthwhile initially considering the extent to which employers can seek to intervene in something that may be taking place outside the workplace. As we noted earlier, in developing welfare policies there may be times when employers are intervening in an employee's private life outside the organization. Proponents of the business case for welfare would argue that if an employee attends work whilst still impaired through the use of alcohol or drugs then it is likely to significantly affect their performance. Consequently they would dismiss concerns as to the appropriateness of an employer taking an active interest in an employee's life outside of work.

Of course, within the workplace the issue is less ambiguous and employers have a legitimate right to develop policies for alcohol and drug misuse. A further issue which impacts on the development of such a policy is the difference between alcohol and drugs in that rules on drugs at work are inevitably more stringent because many drugs are illegal (IDS, 2004a). In terms of developing policy it is useful to acknowledge the view of IDS (2004a: 10) who recognize that, 'there is an increasing trend towards treating long-term alcoholism and, to a lesser extent, dependence on illegal drugs as serious illnesses'. When viewing alcohol and drug misuse in this light the organization is likely to be supportive rather than punitive and will encourage an employee who has a drink or drug problem to seek voluntary help, although this may be facilitated by establishing links with outside organizations, such as those providing EAPs, who can provide expert advice and support. That said, even supportive policies will also usually contain provision for a more punitive approach if there is no improvement in the employee, for example an employee may face disciplinary action and ultimately dismissal on the grounds of capability. Furthermore, IDS (2004a) also note that there may be circumstances where an employee recklessly or even deliberately disregards company rules or acceptable standards of conduct on alcohol and drugs where dismissal on the grounds of misconduct may be acceptable. Within this context then an organization's alcohol and drug policy may contain the following (IDS, 2004a):

- A general statement covering the background to the policy, including any legal obligations.
- A clear outline of the aims and purposes of the policy, including the balance between the discipline and support for employees.
- Details of the responsibilities of different staff and the training and guidance available.
- Who is covered by the policy and if there are tighter restrictions for any particular groups.
- Rules and procedures around drug use, including definitions of what constitutes alcohol and drug misuse and rules regarding prescription medicine.
- The disciplinary action that will be invoked following a policy breach, and what the company's stance is regards to misconduct relating to alcohol or drugs, but not dependency.
- Information for employees on safe drinking limits, classes of drugs, the effects of alcohol and drugs, and where to receive help.
- Details of how an employee can refer themselves for treatment, the support the company will offer and what action the company will take if treatment is declined, not completed or the employee relapses.
- Overview of any testing process, including an explanation of why tests are carried out and when, who administers the tests and what happens if a test proves positive or an employee admits to a dependency during the testing process (see HRM in practice 11.7).

Review and reflect

To what extent do you agree that 'peer pressure' is likely to have more impact on changing behaviour with regards to alcohol or drugs than organizationally directed interventions?

HRM in practice 11.7　Drug and alcohol testing: An ethical or legal issue?

There are debates about the usefulness of drug and alcohol testing in the workplace, with concerns being expressed about the moral, ethical and legal aspects of testing; and particularly whether testing is the best way to address the problem of misuse. For example, within the European context some argue that under the Human Rights Act 1998 random testing impinges on an individual's right to privacy. Where testing does take place there are significant differences on who is likely to be tested, depending on aspects such as the country and sectoral context. In the US it is suggested that around 70 per cent of companies across all industries screen employees for illegal substances. More specifically, research conducted in the 1990s in the hotel sector found that nearly 50 per cent of a sample of 110 hotels conducted drug testing both for applicants for jobs and existing employees. In the UK, the figure is much lower with some estimates suggesting it is as low as 4 per cent. As well as the national differences there may also be differences in terms of occupations. For example, jobs in industries which are considered 'safety critical' are much more likely to have testing on the job, this would include some parts of the tourism industry, such as the airline industry. The British Airline Pilots Association (BALPA), a trade union representing around 8000 pilots and cabin crew, have voiced concerns about random testing of pilots, suggesting that this approach merely drives the problem underground. Instead, their solution to alcohol and drug misuse is support via 'peer pressure'. In this approach flight crew are encouraged to confront a colleague with a problem and urge them to seek help. Evidence seems to suggest that this approach is more successful in detecting the problem and helping individuals deal with it and has recently been endorsed by the International Federation of Airline Pilots Association, which represents pilots worldwide. The ferry and cruise ship industries also tends to operate a strict 'no-alcohol at work' policy for both sea- and shore-based employees, and will often randomly test on-board employees for alcohol or drugs.

Derived from Casado (1997); IRS (2002); Shanahan (2005).

Sexual harassment

Whilst definitions of sexual harassment are generally similar there may still be different perceptions as to what constitutes sexual harassment (see, for example, ILO (1999) for a review of practices across a number of companies and countries).

HRM in practice 11.8   What constitutes sexual harassment?

Consider the following list/scenarios and place a tick by what you would consider sexual harassment:

Patting, hugging or touching a co-worker.
Comments about the way a women looks.
Lewd remarks or glances directed towards a male employee from a female employee.
Questions about an employees sex life.
Requests for sexual favours.
Allowing suggestive posters of either sex in the workplace.
Intimate physical contact within the workplace.
A manager begins a sexual relationship with one of his/her subordinates.

Before we move on to consider the substance of this statement first of all consider HRM in practice 11.8.

In 2002, the Council of Ministers and European Parliament agreed the text on a new directive on the equal treatment of women and men, which included a new definition of sexual harassment. As of 1st October 2005 this new European wide definition was introduced into law and suggests that sexual harassment is 'any form of unwanted verbal, non-verbal or physical conduct of a sexual nature (which) occurs with the purpose of violating the dignity of a person, in particular when creating an intimidating, hostile, degrading, humiliating or offensive environment' (cited in LRD, 2005a: 21). Sexual harassment therefore is unwanted behaviour which a person finds intimidating, upsetting, embarrassing, humiliating or offensive and in that sense is unique to the individual. The individual nature of sexual harassment means that, at certain times, it may be rather subjective and behaviour that one person may consider as acceptable could be seen as harassment by another. For example, you may have indicated all of the aspects in HRM in practice 11.8 as denoting sexual harassment, yet the next person might have indicated something different. There is also the added complication that increasingly many of us now meet our partners in the workplace, which means that romantic conduct or romantic liaisons are increasingly evident in the workplace. For example, according to IRS (2000), whilst the majority of UK employees disapproved of overt sexual activity in the workplace, the majority of survey respondents were comfortable with flirting and almost 40 per cent were or had been involved in workplace romantic or sexual relationships. This estimate is cautious given that such relationships are often deliberately covert but is also confirmed by Kakabadse and Kakabadse's (2004) recent international study of romance in the workplace. With the workplace 'becoming a common meeting ground for romantic liaisons' (Kakabadse and Kakabadse, 2004: 42) there is a need to recognize the line between legitimate and accepted behaviour and that considered sexually harassing.

Where behaviour does err on the side of unacceptable it is usually women who are worst affected by sexual harassment, although men can suffer as well. Equally, there may be occasional cases of same sex harassment (Sherwyn et al., 2000). Generally, though it is women who experience sexual harassment. For example, the Industrial Society (now Work Foundation) produced a report in the mid-1990s which suggested that 93 per cent of sufferers of sexual harassment were women (Coupe and Johnson, 1999). Often it is a male superior who is the harasser. Gilbert et al. (1998) note how two-thirds of sexual harassment complaints in the largest companies in the US were made against immediate supervisors and upper management. Moreover the extent to which sexual harassment is experienced is widespread. IRS (1996), for example, reporting their own and other survey data suggests that well over 50 per cent of women had suffered harassment at work. More specifically, Worsfold and McCann (2000) reporting on the experience of 274 students on supervised work experience in the hospitality industry found that 156 (57 per cent) had experienced instances of sexual harassment.

Despite the fact that it is often viewed as a 'joke', 'just a bit of fun' or 'a bit of harmless flirting', sexual harassment is, in reality, usually about the misuse of power as well as being humiliating and degrading for the recipient and therefore likely to effect confidence and job performance. It can also have a serious impact on physical and mental health and lead to absenteeism. Clearly, then there are several reasons why employers should take action to prevent sexual harassment. Some of these may be pragmatic, such as protecting the company image and avoiding litigation as the courts increasingly view the prevention of harassment as the responsibility of the employer; some may be concerned with business aspects such as reducing absenteeism. Arguably though the strongest argument lies in our earlier identification of the ethical dimension of broader welfare policies. No employee should have to suffer sexual harassment and the workplace should be

HRM in practice 11.9   If you can't stand the heat...

The kitchen is often felt to be a very masculine environment with a very macho culture, which may lead to sexist attitudes being prevalent. It is suggested that to fit in employees may have to swear, ogle pornography and generally act like men. Such an environment can create attitudes where sexually harassing behaviour could be construed as just a 'bit of a laugh'. One female chef reporting on her experiences working in a kitchen notes several incidences of sexual harassment, including a colleague having her trousers pulled down in front of an all-male kitchen. She also notes the experiences of female chefs in the US where sexism seems equally prevalent, for example one noting how she was routinely groped.

Derived from Packer (1998); Roche (2004).

a place where every employee has the right to be treated with dignity and not suffer from harassing behaviour (ILO, 1999).

Tourism and hospitality: a breeding ground for sexual harassment?

It is important to realize that sexual harassment may be particularly prevalent in the tourism and hospitality industry. For example, Coupe and Johnson (1999: 37) note that, 'Female employees within traditional service spheres of employment, such as operative employees in the hospitality industry, will be extremely vulnerable to sexual harassment'. Why is this the case? First, within the hospitality sub-sector in particular there is the notion of many departments often being dominated by a single gender, for example men in the kitchen (see HRM in practice 11.9).

A further issue is the extent to which tourism and hospitality organizations may either tacitly or even deliberately exploit women's sexuality. As Gilbert et al. (1998: 49) note 'the inherent characteristics of service organizations create a prime breeding ground for sexual harassment'. Within tourism and hospitality many accounts (e.g. Hall, 1993; Adkins, 1995; Tyler and Abbott, 1998) recognize the manner in which some organizations may sanction sexuality as part of the performative aspects of their front-line employees. In this way tourism and hospitality workplaces may be in Mano and Gabriel's (2006) view 'hot' climates. Workplaces which are considered 'hot' climates often have a high degree of aestheticization of the workplace which emphasizes the importance of appearance, style and sensuousness, which in turn creates what Mano and Gabriel term a 'sexual simmer'. Workplaces which have this sexual simmer are also likely to encourage flirtation, sexualized language, innuendo and an emphasis on appearance and image. This notion of certain service workplaces being inherently sexualized is supported by Guerrier and Adib (2000). In their study of sexual harassment of hotel workers they suggest a contributing factor is that hotels often suggest the promise of sexual activity:

> The space of the hotel is laden with sexuality. In particular, the hotel's function is sexualized. Hotel bedrooms provide a space for guests to engage in sexual activity. The sexualization of the hotel space is reflected in the sexualization of hotel workers. In many of the incidents of harassment in this study, assumptions were made about the hotel workers and their roles as service providers within a sexualized setting (p. 720).

Beyond the hotel sub-sector, Guerrier and Adib (2000, 2004) also note how other tourism- and hospitality-related setting such as restaurants, airlines and working in a resort as a tour rep are also inherently sexualized environments (see HRM in practice 11.10).

As can be seen from the above discussion it is women who are more likely to face sexualization and potentially sexual harassment. Adkins (1995) is one of several authors who recognize how female employees have greater pressure from tourism and hospitality organizations to sustain an 'attractive' or alluring appearance. She reports how managers in the leisure organization she studied would enforce uniform requirements which required that women would have their dresses pulled down off the shoulder. Indeed, she even notes how male managers would often physically pull down employees' dresses into that position. In this way potentially neutral dress and appearance standards are sexualized by managerial action. Organizations may also encourage a degree of flirting in the interaction with customers and crucially alcohol consumption, indeed often excessive consumption, is an integral part of many tourism and hospitality workplaces, frequently loosening the tongues and morals of customers in particular. For example, Hall (1993) notes the importance of 'job flirt' to the waiting staff she studied. Taking part in such activities could potentially be gender neutral in that both men and women might conceivably engage in this type of behaviour in the work setting. Guerrier and Adib (2000) note how the restaurant chain TGI Fridays encourages both

HRM in practice 11.10   Skilled professional or 'trolley dolly'?

Historically the process of sexualization of airline cabin crew has been one which has changed over time. At the outset of the airline industry flying was an all-male preserve, including the job of air steward. Though there was a limited experimentation with the recruitment of female air stewards in the 1930s it was not until the mid-1940s that the job was really feminized. In the 1950s and 1960s airlines began to sexualize their stewardesses, mainly through their advertising and marketing by portraying the 'sexy' image of female cabin crew. Sexually suggestive advertising slogans used in the past have included Delta's 'Ready when you are', National's 'I'm Anne, fly me' and Continental's 'We really move our tail for you'. This portrayal of what have often been described as 'trolley dollies' was one which seemingly became increasingly anachronistic as airlines were accused of sex discrimination and sexism, especially by the trade unions representing stewardesses. By the mid-to-late 1970s the selling of overt sexuality seemed to wane. However, a recent review of aesthetic labour in the airline industry offers evidence as to how some airlines still seem to mobilize their employees' physical disposition to move beyond an aesthetic appeal to one where the appeal seems to be to the sexual desires of customers. The examples cited are Virgin Blue and Air Asia, two new airlines operating in the low-cost carrier market. An examination of the advertizing and marketing of these two airlines points to the manner in which female employees are sexualized, particularly in Virgin Blue, which was described in one newspaper as the world's sexiest airline. For example, one advert produced by the company featured smiling, attractive and youthful flight attendants and was captioned 'Plane Fares, Beautiful Service'.

Derived from Mills (1996); Spiess and Waring (2005).

male and female waiters to flirt with customers to increase customer spend and their own tips. Nevertheless, Hall (1993: 465) notes how, 'although playing the flirting game is an accepted part of interacting with customers, waitresses are more likely than waiters to be the subject of sexual approaches' (see HRM in practice 11.11).

What the above discussion points to is that within tourism and hospitality there is not only the potential for sexual harassment in terms of the superior/subordinate relationship, but also via potentially pernicious customer interactions. The latter aspect in particular is one where some tourism and hospitality organizations may allow for a certain amount of ambiguity to creep in. For example, in Loe's (1996)

HRM in practice 11.11   Hooters: An acceptable form of sexualization?

Although selling itself as 'a family restaurant' (though 70 per cent of customers are men aged 25–54 years) the Hooters company uniform of short shorts, and a choice of either a tight tank top, crop or tight T-shirt suggests that the intent of the company is to project an image of sexy, eager waitresses. Golding (1998: 7) notes how the company 'unashamedly uses nubile young waitresses dressed in skimpy tops to attract customers' – the so-called 'Hooters Girls'. The success of the company is such that they now have over 400 restaurants in the US as well as a presence in 19 other countries. Additionally, until recently the company also had an airline, Hooters Air, which in addition to the airline crew also featured two Hooters Girls on each flight. A recent case study of Hooters in *Fortune* recognizes the extent to which Hooters is considered a mainstream business success (Helyar, 2003). Indeed, the company's marketing and branding strategy has survived a challenge in the American courts on the basis that the company brand is 'female sex appeal' (Prewitt, 2003). It is also interesting to note the reaction of the then editor of *Caterer and Hotelkeeper* to the arrival of the first Hooters restaurant in the UK. In an opinion piece the editor saw little to worry about in the emergence of Hooters. In answer to his own question of whether 'the moralists and protectors of womens' rights [are] being distracted by a bit of harmless fun?', he goes on to suggest that: 'Blatant titillation has become widely accepted in the selling of countless commodities, from fast cars to chocolate bars, from drinks to holidays … If we are not offended by this, then we shouldn't get upset about Hooters, because the principle is much the same' (Mutch, 1998: 23).

Review and reflect: To what extent do you agree with the sentiment of Mutch?

thinly disguised ethnographic study of 'Bazooms', she notes how new employees had to sign the official Bazooms sexual harassment policy, which states that 'In a work atmosphere based upon sex appeal, joking and innuendo are commonplace' (p. 400). Of course, there is potentially a thin line between innuendo and what may be thought of as harassing behaviour. Such an issue seemed less of a concern for the company and the Bazooms employee handbook described sexual harassment in the following manner:

Sexual harassment does not refer to occasional compliments of a socially acceptable nature. It does not refer to mutually acceptable joking or teasing. It refers to behaviour which is unwelcome, that is personally offensive, that debilitates morale, and that, therefore, interferes with work effectiveness (quoted in Loe, 1996: 412).

Whilst ultimately the manner in which some tourism and hospitality organizations portray a certain 'style' may be one which is debated in terms of the extent to which it encourages customers to engage in unacceptable behaviour, the key point remains that sexually harassing behaviour can have a significantly harmful impact on employees. Consequently, it is important that the organization develops a suitable policy response.

Developing policy for sexual harassment

Therefore as a way of preventing sexual harassment organizations should implement an effective policy, which should aim to (CIPD, 2006b):

- Set out what is considered to be inappropriate behaviour, as well as defining positive and supporting behaviours.
- Explain the damaging effects and why it will not be tolerated.
- Affirm that sexual harassment will be treated as a disciplinary offence with appropriate penalties attached.
- Explain complaints procedure, including how to get help and make a complaint, formally and informally.
- Affirm that the complaint will be treated seriously, speedily and confidentially and that there will be no victimization for making a complaint.
- Make it a duty for supervisors/managers to implement policy and ensure it is understood.

By offering a clear policy employees who are being sexually harassed can feel confident that the issue will be taken seriously. This point is important as in bringing forward a complaint of sexual harassment the employee should not have to fear reprisals or continued harassment or equally be worried about things like risking future promotion opportunities. Once a complaint is made the investigation should begin as soon as possible and provide (CIPD, 2006b):

- A prompt, thorough and impartial response.
- Independent, skilled and objective investigators.
- Representation for both parties.

- Complaint details, the right to respond and adequate time to respond.
- A time scale for resolving the problem.
- Confidentiality for all parties.

Investigations of sexual harassment may either be by formal or informal means, though often the preference will be for an informal resolution (IDS, 2003). If though there is a more formal investigation, depending on the outcome of any investigation there may be a range of potential decisions. For example, if the harassment is sufficiently serious it could lead to the dismissal of the perpetrator. Alternatively, there may be disciplinary action short of dismissal, counselling for the person whose behaviour is unacceptable and often the perpetrator may be transferred. There may be occasions where individuals are unclear how their behaviour may be seen as harassing and ensuring that they are aware of acceptable and unacceptable behaviour at work will prevent ambiguity and stop harassment reoccurring.

Smoking

In a recent review of smoking in the restaurant industry, Nickson (2000) noted that much of the work in this area could be distilled into two broad themes:

- The responsibility of the employer to maintain a safe environment for employees and customers.
- The necessity of satisfying the needs of all consumers (i.e. smokers and non-smokers) to remain profitable.

From a health and welfare perspective most of the concerns about smoking in the workplace are linked to the phenomenon of environmental tobacco smoke, or as it is rather more popularly known, passive smoking. In the past many tourism and hospitality workplaces, such as restaurants and pubs, would be considered as being a relatively smoky atmosphere, and consequently possibly more damaging to employee health. The issue of passive smoking has been at the centre of an intense debate between pro- and anti-smoking groups, with each side contesting the validity of each other's statistics. Increasingly though it appears that those against passive smoking are winning the argument as a number of countries have now moved to banning smoking in public places, including pubs, hotels and restaurants (see HRM in practice 11.12).

HRM in practice 11.12   A global curb on smoking

Australia: Smoking is banned in all airports, government offices, health clinics and workplaces in Australia. Restaurants in most states and territories are also smoke free zones.

France: Attempted to cut smoking levels by raising the price of cigarettes by 20 per cent in October 2003. Despite this price hike it was reported that there was no noticeable difference in Paris' traditionally smoke-filled cafes and bars.

Italy: Imposed a ban on smoking in all enclosed public places including bars and restaurants in 2005. The ban has not been welcomed by all, with some bar owners and smokers saying they will ignore the ban on the grounds that cigarettes and smoking are an integral part of Italian bar and cafe culture. The new rules allow smoking in special sealed-off areas fitted with smoke extractors; however many bar owners say fitting the automatic doors and forced ventilation systems required by law is too expensive.

The Netherlands: A tough crackdown on smoking from 1 January 2004 saw cigarettes banned from many public places including railway stations, trains, toilets and offices. Hotels, bars and restaurants are likely to face a ban from 2009. Some 30 per cent of the Netherlands' 16 million population are smokers – a higher rate than all other EU countries except Spain, Greece and Germany.

Norway: A national ban was imposed on smoking in restaurants, bars and cafes from June 2004. The government says the ban is to protect staff working in these establishments from passive smoking and to 'de-normalize' smoking as a social pastime.

Spain: Smoking was banned in offices, shops, schools, hospitals, cultural centres and on public transport from 1 January 2006. The government says the ban is necessary because smoking is the biggest killer in Spain, with 50 000 smoking-related deaths annually.

Sweden: Smoking was prohibited in all bars and restaurants from May 2005. Establishments wanting to allow smoking are required to have a closed-off section with specially designed ventilation, where no food or drink can be served. Most venues were not expected to be able to afford such renovations. The ban followed lobbying by the country's licensing sector which said bar and restaurant staff were more likely to suffer lung cancer than in any other profession.

United States: Many cities and states enforce bans on smoking. California has some of the toughest and most extensive anti-smoking legislation anywhere in the world. Smoking is also banned in restaurants, bars and enclosed workplaces – and on beaches – throughout the state. In New York, smoking has been banned in bars, clubs and restaurants since March 2003.

Derived from BBC (2005).

At the time of writing within the UK the picture is currently mixed. Within Scotland the introduction of the Smoking, Health and Social Care (Scotland) Act 2005 led in 2006 to the banning of smoking in public places, including restaurants, bars and pubs. In a similar vein legislation will lead to a smoking ban in England from summer 2007. It is suggested that creating healthier workplaces lies at the heart of the legislation and ultimately the development of smoking bans marks a significant intervention by government to improve occupational health.

Stress

Stress has increasingly become a major issue in the workplace with a seemingly ever larger part of the workforce suffering from work-related stress. Indeed, CIPD (2005b) note how the Health and Safety Executive (HSE) have indicated that stress is likely become the most dangerous risk to businesses in the twenty-first century. In simple terms stress is the adverse reaction people have to excessive demands or pressure when trying to cope with tasks and responsibilities in the workplace (LRD, 2006a). At one level, stress is a normal part of everyday life and within the workplace many writers talk about so-called 'good' stress, or 'eustress'. This optimum level of stress is felt to be important to sustain high performance and will of course vary with individuals. Once an employee feels unable to cope or control the pressure then they will experience stress as 'distress', which will lead to declining performance. The most recent research conducted by the HSE indicates that over half a million workers in the UK were suffering from work-related stress, depression or anxiety caused or made worse by their current or past work. As a consequence it is estimated that there were 12.8 million lost working days due to work-related stress in 2004–2005 (LRD, 2006a). European-wide research has suggested that over 40 million EU workers are affected with work-related stress, with the European Commission suggesting that the 'conservative' estimate of the cost of this stress being €20 billion (£16 billion) (LRD, 2002).

Review and reflect

Think about what makes you stressed at work and how you can address this. To what extent is your stress at work alleviated by the organization and its work processes and to what extent by your own initiative? Where should the responsibility lie, with the organization or the individual?

Individual	Organizational
Anxiety	Impaired job performance
Alcohol abuse	Increased absenteeism
Drug abuse	Decreased commitment and motivation
Job dissatisfaction	Higher turnover rates
Depression	Higher accident rates
Panic attacks	Lower productivity
Irritability	Lower morale
Low self-esteem	Damaged reputation
Disturbed sleeping patterns	Recruitment problems
Poor concentration	
Frequent headaches	
Gastric and intestinal problems	
High blood pressure	
Heart disease	

Adapted from IDS (2004a)

Figure 11.1 Some negative effects of stress for the individual and organization.

As with a number of other aspects discussed in this chapter organizational responses to stress are likely to reflect both legal and business arguments. From a legal point of view employers have a general duty of care under section 2 of the Health and Safety at Work Act (HASWA) 1974 to ensure the health, safety and welfare at work of all of their employees and this includes their mental health. In addition, there is also European-inspired regulation and Regulation 3 of the Management of Health and Safety at Work Regulations 1999 requires employers to undertake risk assessment in order to minimize the hazards facing staff, including ensuring that employees health is not placed at risk by excessive and sustained levels of stress. Failure to comply with the duties contained in the HASWA and the Management of Health and Safety at Work Regulations may result in significant compensation being paid by employers. For example, a number of recent court and out of court settlements in the UK have seen figures of up to £300 000 paid by employers (LRD, 2002). From a business point of view Figure 11.1 outlines a number of possible negative effects of stress, which will have a deleterious impact physiologically and psychologically on individuals, which in turn is likely to significantly hamper organizational performance.

As we noted above there is a need for organizations to be proactive in recognizing and responding to potential stressors in the workplace. The HSE has sought to develop a management standard which classifies some of the key areas which, if mismanaged, can become workplace stressors, these are (HSE, 2005):

Demands – including issues like workload, work patterns and the work environment. The standard expects that employees are able to cope with the demands of their jobs. To achieve the standard the organization should provide employees with adequate and achievable demands in relation to the agreed hours of work; ensure that people's skills and abilities are matched to the job demands; that jobs are designed to be within the capabilities of employees; and that any employee concerns about their work environment are addressed.

Control – is primarily concerned with how much say the person has in the way they do their work. The standard suggests that employees are able to have a say about the way they do their work. To achieve the standard the organization should aim where possible to ensure that employees have control over their pace of work; that employees are encouraged to use their skills and initiative to do their work; that employees are encouraged to develop new skills to help them undertake new and challenging pieces of work; the organization encourages employees to develop their skills; employees have a say over when breaks can be taken and employees are consulted over their work patterns.

Support – includes the encouragement, sponsorship and resources provided by the organization, line management and colleagues. The standard suggests that employees should receive adequate information and support from their colleagues and superiors. To achieve the standard, the organization should have policies and procedures to adequately support employees; that systems are in place to enable and encourage managers to support their staff; that systems are in place to enable and encourage employees to support their colleagues; that employees know what support is available and how and when to access it; employees know how to access the required resources to do their job and employees receive regular and constructive feedback.

Relationships – includes promoting positive working to avoid conflict and dealing with unacceptable behaviour. The standard expects that employees should not be subjected to unacceptable behaviours (e.g. bullying and harassment) at work. To achieve the standard, the organization should promote positive behaviours at work to avoid conflict and ensure fairness; employees share information relevant to their work; the organization has agreed policies and procedures to prevent or resolve unacceptable behaviour; that systems are in place to enable and encourage managers to deal with unacceptable behaviour and that systems are in place to enable and encourage employees to report unacceptable behaviour.

Role – includes whether people understand their role within the organization and whether the organization ensures that the person does not have conflicting roles. The standard expects that employees understand their role and responsibilities. To achieve the standard, the organization should ensure that, as far as possible, the different requirements it places upon employees are compatible; the organization provides information to enable employees to understand their role and responsibilities; the organization ensures that, as far as possible, the requirements it places upon employees are clear and systems are in place to enable employees to raise concerns about any uncertainties or conflicts they have in their role and responsibilities.

Change – includes how organizational change (large or small) is managed and communicated in the organization. The standard expects that the organization will frequently engage with employees when undergoing an organizational change. To achieve the standard the organization should provide employees with timely information to enable them to understand the reasons for proposed changes; the organization ensures adequate employee consultation on changes and provides opportunities for employees to influence proposals; employees are aware of the probable impact of any changes to their jobs. If necessary, employees are given training to support any changes in their jobs; employees are aware of timetables for changes; employees have access to relevant support during changes.

A number of the above aspects can be seen in research examining stress in the tourism sector. Ineson et al. (2001) conducted in-depth interviews with 10 UK tour managers and identified 117 critical incidents that induced stress. These aspects were grouped into four categories relating to colleagues, clients, nature of the job and poor management. For example, with regard to the nature of the job the particular work environment of tour managers means that they may face situations such as medical emergencies or logistical problems such as breakdowns and getting stuck in traffic jams. Similarly, a number of the tour managers recalled instances where clients had questioned and contradicted their commentaries, which had undermined their professional authority as they appeared to be incompetent. Interestingly though the most common source of stress was employer/management-induced stress. Examples of such stress included lack of training from the employer and a lack of management communication and support. Similar results were also apparent in Law et al.'s (1995) study of 102 front line staff from 14 Australian tourist attractions. Again, poor management was the reason mentioned most often by respondents as a source of stress. A number of the other stressors tended to revolve around the interactions with customers, such as difficulties in controlling crowds. While it might seem self-evident that difficult customers are an occupational hazard for tourism and hospitality employees there is a need to ensure that they are properly trained to deal with such situations. This and other aspects are clearly reliant on proactive management and in considering workplace stressors it is clear that there is significant responsibility on employers and managers to address these issues in a proactive manner, including developing a stress policy.

Developing policy

IDS (2004b) recognize the importance of having a stress policy in bringing the subject out into the open, ensuring that stress is not seen as a taboo subject and employees do not feel stigmatized for feeling 'stressed'. They also recognize that a standard stress policy is likely to have the following aspects:

- A definition of stress.
- A description of the symptoms of stress and stress-related illnesses.
- An outline of the organization's responsibilities for managing stress.
- An outline of managers' and employees' responsibilities for managing stress.
- A list of both internal and external sources of help for stress-related issues (see HRM in practice 11.13).

Working time

Excessive working time has often been linked to stress (LRD, 2006a) and clearly is deleterious to a healthy work-life balance. Estimates suggest that around 11 per cent of UK employees currently work more than 48 hours a week, this figure is the highest in the EU, creating concerns about 'burn out' (LRD, 2006b). Additionally, the UK tops the European hours league with a usual working week of 42.7 hours, compared to an EU average of 41 hours (LRD, 2006b). Interestingly

HRM in practice 11.13 EAPs: Helping employees in the workplace

EAPs are external help services provided by employers which aim to assist in the identification and resolution of employee concerns that affect performance. EAPs originated in the US and remain popular there, with over 85 per cent of the largest *Fortune* 500 companies using their services. Outside the US the uptake is rather patchier. In Europe EAPs are rarely used, though there is evidence that more UK employers are using their services, which now cover around 15 per cent of employees. EAPs typically provide a 24-hour, 365 days-a-year telephone counselling service for employees on issues such as stress, bullying, violence, and drug and alcohol misuse. A recent decision in the Court of Appeal on work-related stress has given EAPs a significant boost. The ruling from the Court of Appeal suggested that the provision of EAP provision to address stress pointed to a proactive employer response and consequently employers who use such services are less likely to be found to be in breach of the duty of care expected in health and safety legislation.

Source: LRD (2003a).

though compared to non-EU countries, the UK has shorter working hours than Australia, Japan and the US (CIPD, 2006c). Many would argue that debates about long working hours are particularly pertinent to tourism and hospitality. The long hours culture in the industry means that many employees work excessive hours, which is likely to have a harmful impact on their health. A recent survey of nearly 700 hotel, restaurant and bar employees reported in *Caterer and Hotelkeeper* (9th June 2005, 'Long working hours the norm') found that 93 per cent worked more than 40 hours, with nearly a fifth (17 per cent) working more than 60 hours a week. The same is also very much true for managers and operators of small business, with a survey of 1400 small hospitality businesses finding that 46 per cent of publicans, 43 per cent of hoteliers and 13 per cent of restaurateurs worked more than 70 hours a week (Cushing, 2004).

The continuing prevalence of excessive working time for many tourism and hospitality employees may seem surprising given the introduction of the Working Time Regulations (WTR) in 1998. The introduction of the WTR in the UK was not without controversy. The WTR were initially introduced as a health and safety measure. Despite this, the government of John Major sought to challenge the legality of the measure via the European Court of Justice (ECJ), but eventually lost the case in November 1996, as the ECJ ruled that working hours were a health and safety issues as opposed to a more general social issue. As a result the UK government eventually introduced the WTR into law in October 1998 and the main provisions are (CIPD, 2006c):

- A maximum working week of not more than 48 hours a week, including overtime, normally calculated over a rolling 17-week period.
- Employees are entitled to a daily rest period of 11 hours.
- Night workers are limited to an average of 8 hours work in 24 hours.
- Employees are entitled to 4 weeks paid holiday.
- Where the working day is longer than 6 hours, workers will be entitled to a rest break of 20 minutes.
- In each 7-day period, workers will be entitled to 1 day's rest, in addition to the above 11-hour period set out above.
- Free health assessments must be made available to night workers.

When they were first introduced it was felt that the WTR would have a significant impact on UK organizations. In particular, the extension of paid annual leave to the UK, the only EU country not to previously have a legal right to paid holidays, affected around 2.5 million workers, mostly part-timers and women. Moreover just over four million workers had less than 3 weeks leave and six million less than 4 weeks leave (Milne, 1998). In reality though the impact of the WTR has proved to be less than thought, in part because of a series of derogations which the UK government negotiated (Hurrell, 2005). Chief among these is the ability of companies to offer an 'opt-out' where employees sign away their right to a 48-hour limit on their working week. This measure is one which has been adopted by a large number of tourism and hospitality employers. Although the European Commission has recently sought to restrict the UK's right to offer an opt-out clause, at the time of writing the UK government seems determined to retain the opt-out (LRD, 2006b). Finally, even the provision of paid leave is far from straightforward. Due to the WTR never specifying whether public and bank holidays would be included in the 20-day calculation some employers have taken advantage of this loophole and have used bank holidays in calculating their employees' holiday entitlement. Resultantly, around 3.4 million employees have not been getting 20 days minimum paid leave a year, with around one million of these employees being in the leisure and retail industries (LRD, 2005b). More recently it appears that this loophole is now likely to be closed with the Government announcing plans to rectify this anomaly (LRD, 2006c).

Workplace violence

Tourism and hospitality establishments rank high on the list of workplaces with high incidences of violence. LRD (2003b) reports evidence from the British Crime Survey on the number of workers reporting assaults or threats which occurred while the victim was working and were perpetrated by a member of the public. Across all occupations the percentage of workers who faced violence was just 1.2 per cent. However, for leisure service providers the figure rises to 3.7 per cent and for publicans and bar staff it rises significantly to 11.5 per cent. Boyd (2002) in a survey of nearly 1200 employees in the airline and railway industries also found that 70 per cent of her respondents reported an increase in the number of abusive passengers over the previous year. Such abuse was both verbal with 74 per cent of respondents experiencing verbal abuse from passengers at least once a month. More worryingly still, nearly 40 per cent of her respondents had experienced at least two types of physical abuse and 26 per cent had experienced at least three types of physical abuse. Instances of such abuse included being pushed, punched, kicked, slapped, struck with an object and spat at.

These relatively high figures reflect the fact that many employees in the tourism and hospitality sector have to deal with members of the public, exchange or collect money, work at night and work alone, or in small numbers. Added to these aspects many workplaces in tourism and hospitality involve the consumption of alcohol, often to excess. Certainly, alcohol seems to have a catalytic effect in many instances of workplace violence in tourism and hospitality. Morgan and Nickson (2001) in a review of 'air rage' in the airline industry found that excessive alcohol consumption was by far the most commonly cited contributory factor to passenger violence or aggression. Other reasons included being deprived of nicotine and the inherently stressful nature of flying.

Workplace violence is undoubtedly a complex issue, though again there is a need for organizations to be proactive. Certainly an argument could be made that the Management of Health and Safety at Work Regulations would encourage organizations to assess and act upon any potential risks of violence. Amongst other things organizations could consider issues such as the underlying cause of

HRM in practice 11.14   A proactive response to 'air rage'

IDS (2000) report on how Virgin Atlantic have sought to address violence at work, and specifically air rage, by improving their HR approaches. Within the recruitment and selection process for instance Virgin look for key skills in relation to communication skills, assertiveness and customer service orientation, and although not a primary consideration in the selection process there is an assessment of how potential employees may respond to difficult scenarios involving aggressive customers. Employees also receive training in observation skills to help them identify potentially disruptive passengers at an early stage. Staff are taught how to recognize potential precursors of an air rage incident, such as the tapping of fingers or the reddening of a passengers face, and in response to these use calming techniques, such as using friendly gentle tones and body language, to defuse the situation. As a result of these approaches the need to have recourse to actual physical restraint has significantly decreased in Virgin Atlantic. If a major incident does occur though the company also looks to provide a supportive response. There is an automatic debriefing to the whole flight crew, even those employees not directly affected by the incident. Attendance at such debriefings is mandatory and this recognizes that they may be a delayed response from employees to what is a potentially very stressful experience Further to that Virgin also provide follow-up counselling, if necessary, through their occupation health department. Finally, the company also offers legal and financial support to employees who wish to pursue legal action against assailants.

the violence, working practices, and the provision of suitable training and support needs (see HRM in practice 11.14).

Conclusion

Welfare, health and safety issues have become increasingly important to tourism and hospitality organizations as the business case for proactive responses has become recognized. In considering the 'alphabet' of welfare issues a number of these issues seems to have a particular resonance within the tourism and hospitality sector. The presence of demanding customers, the blurring of work and leisure and often catalytic effect of alcohol create particular circumstances where the duty of care of employers seems particularly pronounced. That said, it was also recognized that in seeking to intervene in often sensitive issues that the balance between an organizational members public and private life is far from clear cut. Undoubtedly managers in modern organizations require an awareness of these issues and how best to intervene for the benefit of both the organization and individual; a task that is far from easy in dealing with potentially sensitive issues.

References and further reading

Adam-Smith, D. and Goss, D. (1993) 'HIV/AIDS and hotel and catering employment: some implications of perceived risk', *Employee Relations*, 15(2), 25–32.

Adkins, L. (1995) *Gendered Work – Sexuality, Family and the Labour Market*, Open University Press.

Advisory, Conciliation and Arbitration Service (2006) *Health and Employment*, ACAS.

Alcohol Concern (2006) *Acquire: Alcohol Concerns Quarterly Information and Research Bulletin*, Alcohol Concern.

Arkin, A. (2005) 'Out of the shadows', *People Management*, 24 November, 24–28.

Barrows, C., Gallo, M. and Mulleady, T. (1996) 'AIDS in the hospitality industry: recommendations for education and policy formulations', *International Journal of Contemporary Hospitality Management*, 8(1), 5–9.

BBC (2003) 'Millions hooked on alcohol', at http://newsvote.bbc.co.uk/mpapps/pagetools/print/news.bbc.co.uk/1/hi/health/281781.stm (accessed 1 June 2006).

BBC (2005) 'Smoking curbs: the global picture', at http://news.bbc.co.uk/1/hi/world/3758707.stm (accessed 10 June 2006).

Bignold, D. (2003) 'Hospitality sector reaches drink and drugs crisis point', *Caterer and Hotelkeeper*, 9 October, 21–23.

Boyd, C. (2002) 'Customer violence and employee health and safety', *Work, Employment and Society*, 16(1), 151–169.

Bratton, J. and Gold, J. (2003) *Human Resource Management – Theory and Practice*, Palgrave, 3rd edition.

Breuer, N. (1995) 'Emerging trends for managing AIDS in the workplace', *Personnel Journal*, June, 125–134.

Casado, M. (1997) 'Drug-testing practices in US hotels', *International Journal of Hospitality Management*, 16(4), 393–401.

Chartered Institute of Personnel and Development (2005a) *Absence Management: A Survey of Policy and Practice*, CIPD.

Chartered Institute of Personnel and Development (2005b) *Stress at Work Factsheet*, CIPD.

Chartered Institute of Personnel and Development (2006a) *Absence Management Factsheet*, CIPD.

Chartered Institute of Personnel and Development (2006b) *Harassment at Work Factsheet*, CIPD.

Chartered Institute of Personnel and Development (2006c) *Working Hours in the UK Factsheet*, CIPD.

Corsun, D. and Young, C. (1998) 'An occupational hazard: alcohol consumption among hospitality managers', in P. Cummings, F. Kwansa and M. Sussman (eds.) *The Role of the Hospitality Industry in the Lives of Individuals and Families*, 187–211.

Coupe, V. and Johnson, K. (1999) 'Sexual harassment: "That'll do nicely sir"', *Hospitality Review*, April, 36–41.

Cushing, K. (2004) 'Concerns raided over UK long-hours culture', *Caterer and Hotelkeeper*, 11 June, 9.

Eade, V. (1993) 'Drug abuse in the hospitality industry', *Florida International University Hospitality Review*, 11(2), 81–86.

Gilbert, D., Guerrier, Y. and Guy, J. (1998) 'Sexual harassment issues in the hospitality industry', *International Journal of Contemporary Hospitality Management*, 10(2), 48–53.

Golding, C. (1998) 'Britain gets first look at Hooters', *Caterer and Hotelkeeper*, 30 April, 7.

Goss, D. (1994) *Principles of Human Resource Management*, Routledge.

Goss, D. (1997) *Human Resource Management: The Basics*, International Thomson Business Press.

Guerrier, Y. and Adib, A. (2000) '"No we don't provide that service": the harassment of hotel employees by customers', *Work, Employment and Society*, 14(4), 689–705.

Guerrier, Y. and Adib, A. (2004) 'Gendered identities in the work of overseas tour reps', *Gender, Work and Organizations*, 11(3), 334–350.

Hall, E. (1993) 'Smiling, deferring and flirting: doing gender and giving "good service"', *Work and Occupations*, 20(4), 452–471.

Health and Safety Executive (2005) *Tackling Stress: The Management Standards Approach*, at http://www.hse.gov.uk/pubns/indg406.pdf (accessed 6 June 2006).

Helyar, J. (2003) 'Hooters: a case study', *Fortune*, 1 September, 140–146.

Hilpern, K. (2001) 'What's your poison', *Guardian Office Hours*, 19 November, 2–3.

Hurrell, S. (2005) 'Dilute to taste? The impact of the working time regulations in the hospitality industry', *Employee Relations*, 27, 5, 523–546.

Income Data Services (2000) *Violence at Work*. IDS Studies No. 683, February.

Income Data Services (2003) *Harassment Policies*, IDS Studies No. 743, February.

Income Data Services (2004a) *Alcohol and Drug Policies*, IDS HR Studies No. 771, April.

Income Data Services (2004b) *Stress Management*, HR Studies No. 775, June.

Income Data Services (2005a) *Absence Management*, IDS HR Studies No. 810, November.

Income Data Services (2005b) 'Alcohol, drugs and employment law', *IDS Brief*, No. 779, April, 10–17.

Industrial Relations Services (1996) 'Sexual harassment at work (1): incidence and outcomes', *IRS Employment Trends*, No. 615, September, 4–10.

Industrial Relations Services (1997) 'HIV and AIDS: a workplace issue', *IRS Employment Trends*, No. 633, June, 8–16.

Industrial Relations Services (2000) 'Sex at work: everything that you wanted to know but were afraid to ask', *IRS Employment Trends*, No. 713, October, 5–10.

Industrial Relations Services (2001) 'Counting the cost of absence', *IRS Employment Review*, No. 739, 1 November, 46–47.

Industrial Relations Services (2002) 'Alcohol and drug testing', *IRS Employment Review*, No. 757, 5 August, 43–46.

Industrial Relations Services (2004a) 'UK has the second-worst health rate', *IRS Employment Review*, No. 792, 23 January, 17.

Industrial Relations Services (2004b) 'Measuring the performance gap: CBI absence statistics', *IRS Employment Review*, No. 802, 18 June, 19–20.

Ineson, L., Batty, L. and Wynne, J. (2001) 'Tour management and occupational stress', paper to *2001 EuroChrie Conference*, Switzerland.

Institute of Alcohol Studies (2006) *Alcohol in Europe: A Public Health Perspective*, at http://ec.europa.eu/health-eu/news_alcoholineurope_en.htm (accessed 1 June 2006).

International Labour Organization (1999) *Sexual Harassment: An ILO Survey of Company Practice*, ILO.

Kakabadse, A. and Kakabadse, N. (2004) *Intimacy*, Palgrave.

Labour Research Department (2002) 'Europe "must address stress"', *Labour Research*, October, 20–22.

Labour Research Department (2003a) 'Can "help firms" really stop staff stress?' *Labour Research*, August, 9–11.

Labour Research Department (2003b) 'Can "zero tolerance" deliver?' *Labour Research*, May, 12–15.

Labour Research Department (2005a) 'Legal changes define sexual harassment', *Labour Research*, November, 21.

Labour Research Department (2005b) 'Millions wait for holiday rights', *Labour Research*, July, 9–10.

Labour Research Department (2006a) *Stress at Work*, LRD.

Labour Research Department (2006b) 'Labour clings to long-hours opt-out rule', *Labour Research*, February, 12–14.

Labour Research Department (2006c) 'Two million workers to get paid extra eight days' paid leave', *Labour Research*, July, 5.

Ladki, S. (1994) 'Strategies for combating fear of AIDS in the hospitality industry', *Hospitality and Tourism Educator*, 6(1), 75–77.

Law, J., Pearce, P. and Woods, B. (1995) 'Stress and coping in tourist attraction employees', *Tourism Management*, 16(4), 277–284.

Loe, M. (1996) 'Working for men at the intersection of power, gender and sexuality', *Sociological Enquiry*, 66(4), 399–421.

MacAskill, E. (2006) 'US blocking international deal on fighting aids', *Guardian*, 2 June, 18.

Mano, R. and Gabriel, Y. (2006) 'Workplace romances in cold and hot organizational climates: the experiences of Israel and Taiwan', *Human Relations*, 59(1), 7–35.

Manocha, R. (2004) 'Well adjusted', *People Management*, 8 April, 26–30.

Mills, A. (1996) 'Strategy, sexuality and the stratosphere: airlines and the gendering of organizations', in L. Morris and E. Stina Lyon (eds.) *Gender Relations in Public and Private: New Research Perspectives*, MacMillan, 77–94.

Milne, S. (1998) 'Holiday rules will aid 4m', *Guardian*, 6 April, 9.

Morgan, M. and Nickson, D. (2001) 'Uncivil aviation: a review of the air rage phenomenon', *International Journal of Tourism Research*, 3(6), 443–457.

Mullen, R. (2001) 'Drink the destroyer', *Caterer and Hotelkeeper*, 28 June, 28–31.

Mutch, F. (1998) 'Sex sells – so why not in restaurants?' *Caterer and Hotelkeeper*, 30 April, 23.

Nickson, D. (1997) 'Colorful stories' or historical insight? A review of the auto/biographies of Charles Forte, Conrad Hilton, J.W. Marriott and Kemmons Wilson, *Journal of Hospitality and Tourism Research*, 21(1), 179–192.

Nickson, D. (2000) 'Should smoking be banned in restaurants? The debate so far', R. C. Wood (ed.) *Strategic Directions in Food and Beverage*, Butterworth Heinemann, 208–224.

Packer, N. (1998) 'Women driven away by kitchen culture', *Caterer and Hotelkeeper*, 21 May, 5.

Prewitt, M. (2003) 'Critics say "good looks" win job advantages while others shut out', *Nation's Restaurant News*, 37, 19, 1 & 6.

Roberts, Z. (2003) 'Glass ceiling required', *People Management*, 9 October, 14–15.

Roche, E. (2004) 'If you can't stand the heat … get some balls', *Guardian: G2*, 28 January, at http://www.guardian.co.uk/g2/story/0,03604,1132605,00.html (accessed 12 June 2006).

Shanahan, A. (2005) 'You've got the job. Now please take the drug test', *Guardian Office Hours*, 4 July, 5.

Sherwyn, D., Kaufman, E. and Klausner, A. (2000) 'Same-sex sexual harassment: how the "equal opportunity harasser" became a legitimate defence', *Cornell Hotel and Restaurant Administration Quarterly*, 41(6), 75–80.

Simms, S. (2005) 'Better by design', *People Management*, 29 September, 24–29.

Spiess, L. and Waring, P. (2005) 'Emotional and aesthetic labour: cost minimization and the labour process in the Asia Pacific airline industry', *Employee Relations*, 27(2), 193–207.

Torrington, D., Hall, L. and Taylor, S. (2005) *Human Resource Management*, Prentice Hall, 6th edition.

Trade Union Congress (2003) *Alcohol and Work: A Potent Cocktail*, TUC.

Tyler, M. and Abbott, P. (1998) 'Chocs away: weighting watching in the contemporary airline industry', *Sociology*, 32(3), 433–450.

Worsfold, P. and McCann, C. (2000) 'Supervized work experience and sexual harassment', *International Journal of Contemporary Hospitality Management*, 12(4), 249–255.

Websites

http://www.managingabsence.org.uk/ provides employers with comprehensive information on cost-effective approaches to managing short-term sickness absenteeism.

Two charitable organizations that campaign on issues related to AIDS/HIV are the Terence Higgins Trust and the National Aids Trust, http://www.tht.org.uk/ and http://www.nat.org.uk/

The Ark Foundation is a service offered by Hospitality Action, set up for the purpose of educating hospitality industry students, employees and management as to the dangers of alcohol dependency and other drug misuse, http://www.thearkfoundation.co.uk/

DrugScope offers some interesting views on policy issues surrounding drugs and can be found at http://www.drugscope.org.uk/

Women Against Sexual Harassment is a global organization that campaigns against sexual harassment, http://www.washrag.org/

The Health and Safety Executive's stress at work page can be found at http:// www.hse.gov.uk/stress/index.htm

The Health and Safety Executive's violence at work page can be found at http:// www.hse.gov.uk/violence/index.htm

The Department of Trade and Industry has details of the Working Time Regulations and other case studies on how reduce long hours http://www.dti.gov.uk/employment/employment-legislation/working-time-regs/index.html

Chapter **12**

Grievance and disciplinary procedures

Chapter objectives

This chapter examines the importance of rules and regulations in the employment relationship, focusing on grievance and disciplinary procedures. Specifically, the chapter aims to:

- Consider the complementary nature of grievance and disciplinary procedures.
- Identify sources of employee grievances.
- Assess the differing severity of organizational responses to breaches of discipline.
- Recognize the need for fairness in dismissing employees.

Introduction

It is generally accepted that there is a need for procedures in the employment relationship to ensure that both managers and employees are aware of the expectations of the organization (Marchington and Wilkinson, 2005). In this sense managers need a framework in which to direct and guide behaviour of employees in the workplace. Similarly employees need to understand their place in the organization and its expectations. Thus, there is a need for some articulated order which is likely to be important to sustain organizational effectiveness. Consequently rules are needed which cover the whole range of human resourcing, such as what work is done, how jobs are constituted, training and promotion, hours of work, health and safety and standards of behaviour and performance. Equally, there is a need for procedures to provide a framework which allows for notions of organizational justice and reciprocity. This point is particularly true when we think of grievance and disciplinary procedures. We can conceptualize grievance and disciplinary procedures as being complementary, but also distinct. In this way the former is a mechanism whereby employees can challenge management's power, either collectively or individually, and the latter is a way of establishing and maintaining standards which are acceptable to management. Whilst much of this discussion may seem rather prosaic it is important to recognize that all managers should have at least a working knowledge of grievance and disciplinary procedures, particularly with regard to the ultimate sanction of dismissal. Edwards (2005) notes how dismissal represents the 'dark' or 'murky' side of HRM and is often omitted in many discussions of the subject. It is though a fact of organizational life, in much the same way as employees choosing voluntarily to leave the organization. Ultimately, then, as Torrington et al. (2005: 554) rather neatly express it, 'The two complementary processes are intended to find ways of avoiding the ultimate sanction of the employee quitting or being dismissed, but at the same time preparing the ground for those sanctions if all else fails'.

Setting the scene on grievance and disciplinary procedures

Salamon (1992: 568) defines grievance as, 'a formal expression of individual or collective employee dissatisfaction primarily, but not exclusively, in respect of the application or non-application of collective agreements, managerial policies and actions or customs and practice'. In recognizing the distinction between individual and collective aspects of dissatisfaction many writers suggest that grievances are usually about individual concerns, whilst collective dissatisfaction is likely to become a dispute, especially if a trade union is involved. On the other hand, discipline is defined by the same author as, 'formal action taken by management against an individual or group who have failed to conform to the rules established by management within the organization' (Salamon, 2000: 565). Often grievance and disciplinary procedures will be conceptualized in quasi-judicial terms wherein a body of recognized rules is administered under a judicial-type procedure.

Although the argument in support for the establishment of clear rules and regulations in an organizational setting seems compelling research undertaken in the tourism and hospitality industry suggests that in the past some organizations have been slow to develop policy. For example, Price (1994) found that only 24 per cent of 241 organizations she surveyed had a well-developed disciplinary procedure. More recently though there is greater prescription emanating from legislation and since 1st October 2004 all employers, regardless of size, have to have a disciplinary and grievance procedure and to notify their employees of it, in order to comply with the Employment Act 2002 (LRD, 2006). In developing a policy an obvious starting point is the influential Advisory Conciliation and Arbitration Service (ACAS) Code of Practice on disciplinary and grievance procedures. Originally produced in 1977 and most recently revised in 2004 the code of practice provides a series of recommendations on how best to approach grievance and disciplinary procedures. Indeed, an awareness of procedure may be particularly apposite for tourism and hospitality managers as evidence suggests that they may be more likely to find themselves enmeshed in either a grievance or disciplinary situation. For example, the Chartered Institute of Personnel and Development (CIPD, 2004) in a recent survey of nearly 1200 UK and Irish companies (including 142 tourism and retail employers) found that private sector service employers had twice as many grievance and disciplinary cases compared to the manufacturing, public and voluntary sectors.

Grievance procedures

What is a grievance? Generally, as we have noted a grievance is the right of employees to express and attempt to resolve dissatisfaction that they might have in the work situation. Pigors and Myers (1977: 152, cited in Torrington et al., 2005) outline degrees of discontent which employees may have in the workplace:

- *Dissatisfaction*: anything that disturbs an employee, whether or not the unrest is expressed in words.
- *Complaint*: a spoken or written dissatisfaction brought to the attention of the supervisor and/or trade union representative.
- *Grievance*: a complaint that has been formally presented to a management representative or to a union official.

Review and reflect

What makes you unhappy at work? Would you be willing to articulate this dissatisfaction as a grievance? If not, why not?

Grievances can take a number of forms and Salipante and Bouwen (1990) have provided a widely used schema to categorize sources of conflict and grievance. They suggest that conflict can be distinguished in three ways:

- *Environmental conflict* is primarily concerned with working conditions and nature of work. These problems will encompass the economic terms and conditions of the job, the physical job conditions and job demands either being too great or too little for the individual's skills and abilities.
- *Social substantive* these grievances stem from perceived inequalities in treatment or disagreements over goals or means. Conflict of this nature may be precipitated by organizational policy or management action, which creates a perception of inequity arising from how decisions are taken.
- *Social relational* grievances arise from the relationships between individuals and groups within the organization, for example, personality conflicts, racism and sexism.

The findings of the 2004 Workplace Employment Relations Survey echo the above categorization, whilst also suggesting that the bulk of grievances raised are more likely to be in relation to Salipante and Bouwen's environmental and social substantive aspects. In that sense pay and conditions, relations with supervisors/ line managers and work practices, work allocation and the pace of work were the most common grievances raised by employees (Kersley et al., 2006).

As suggested by our earlier recognition of Pigors and Myers work all of us at some point in our organizational lives will have a degree of dissatisfaction with our work situation, though the extent to which we will be willing to formally articulate this will vary. Ordinarily, it is unlikely that we will choose to formally register our dissatisfaction as a grievance. Instead, employees may express their dissatisfaction in a number of ways short of formally registering a grievance. For example, employees may simply impose their own unilateral solution through things like increased absenteeism, withdrawing their goodwill or in a reduction in morale/motivation. Ultimately the dissatisfaction may be such that the employee chooses to leave and the high rate of labour turnover in hospitality and tourism suggests that many employees take such a course of action. If however an individual chooses to stay in the organization and decides to formally present a grievance it is important that it is properly considered and addressed. The ACAS code of practice offers a clear procedure for addressing grievances, based on a three-stage approach (ACAS, 2004):

- The employee informs the employer of their grievance in writing.
- The employee should be invited by the employer to a meeting to discuss the grievance where the right to be accompanied will apply and be notified in writing of the decision. The employee must take all reasonable steps to attend this meeting.
- The employee is given the right to an appeal meeting if they feel the grievance has not been satisfactorily resolved and be notified of the final decision.

Ordinarily, employees would initially raise the grievance with their line manager, unless somebody else is specified in the organization's procedure. Once received a grievance will then lead to a meeting between the employee and manager where the grievance will be discussed (and see Torrington et al., 2005 for details of how to approach grievance and disciplinary interviewing). Finally, the decision will be communicated in writing to the employee, who if they are still unhappy will then have the right to appeal, which ordinarily would be dealt with by a more senior manager, who again will write to the employee with the final decision. Importantly, if an employee is to subsequently seek to take a grievance further through the employment tribunal (ET) system, then they automatically have to have first gone through the organization's grievance procedure.

Disciplinary procedures

Having examined grievance procedures we can now consider discipline in the organization. In discussing discipline in the organization it is interesting to note the extent to which we are likely to be predisposed to obey rules and authority.

Review and reflect

What might explain our pre-disposition to respect rules and authority?

Torrington et al. (2005: 555–556) draw on the work of the famous social psychologist Stanley Milgram to suggest a number of features which explain our propensity to be obedient towards authority and how this is likely to shape workplace behaviour:

- *Family*: the inculcation of respect for adult and parental authority encourages us to generally respect authority.
- *Institutional setting*: in school, university and work we learn how to function in an organization, often accepting our subordinate position.
- *Rewards*: compliance brings rewards, disobedience brings punishment.
- *Perception of authority*: authority is normatively supported, so we are generally predisposed to follow organizational and managerial rules, but where this does not happen the organization may have to take disciplinary action.

Again in developing a disciplinary procedure the ACAS code of practice provides a template suggesting that good disciplinary procedures should (ACAS, 2004):

- Be in writing.
- Specify to whom they apply.
- Be non-discriminatory.
- Ensure matters are dealt with without unnecessary delay.

- Allow for information about proceedings, witness statements and records to be kept confidential.
- State the disciplinary actions which may be taken.
- Specify the levels of management which have the authority to take the various forms of disciplinary action.
- Provide for employees to be informed of complaints against them and where possible all relevant evidence before any hearing.
- Give employees the opportunity to state their case before a decision is reached.
- Provide employees with the right to be accompanied by a trade union representative or fellow employee at any hearing.
- Ensure that except for gross misconduct, no employee is dismissed for a first breach of discipline.
- Ensure that disciplinary action is not taken until the case has been carefully investigated by management.
- Ensure that employees are given an explanation for any penalty imposed.
- Provide employees with rights to appeal, normally to a more senior manager.

Implicit in the guidelines is recognition of the differing severity of organizational responses in terms of misconduct and ordinarily the distinction is made between minor misconduct, serious misconduct and gross misconduct. For many instances of minor misconduct or unsatisfactory performance a quiet word from a manager may be all that is needed to improve an employee's performance and resolve the issue. However, if this informal action does not bring the desired improvement then an employer may take a more formal approach. As with grievance procedures the ACAS code of practice outlines a three-stage approach to discipline. First, the employer signals to the employee in writing what they have done wrong. There will then be a meeting to discuss the problem, where the employee will be allowed to ask questions, present evidence, call witnesses and be given an opportunity to raise questions about information provided by witnesses. Lastly, the employer must then decide on the basis of the meeting whether the disciplinary action was justified and if that is the case the nature of any sanction against the employee. The decision on disciplinary action will clearly be influenced by the nature of misconduct and in that sense Figure 12.1 outlines a typical disciplinary procedure with commensurate organizational responses.

Examples of minor/serious misconduct could include things such as persistent absenteeism, poor timekeeping, failure to adhere to dress codes or appearance

Nature of the disciplinary matter	Management response and action
Minor misconduct	Recorded oral warning
Serious misconduct or repeated minor misconduct for which a written or oral warning has been received	Written warning followed by final written warning
Gross misconduct or further misconduct for which a final written warning has been received	Action short of dismissal: • Transfer • Demotion • Reward deferment • Suspension Dismissal

Figure 12.1 Typical disciplinary procedure

standards or unacceptable performance and if employees do receive a oral or written warnings they are likely to have a specified 'life', after which they are disregarded. For example, for an oral warning the period is likely to be for 6 months, whilst for a written warning it will be 1 year and a final written warning, 2 years (CIPD, 2005). For gross misconduct ACAS (2004) notes how instances of such misconduct are likely to be decided by the organization given their own particular circumstances, whilst still noting some typical examples, including:

- theft or fraud;
- physical violence or bullying;
- deliberate and serious damage to property;
- serious misuse of an organization's property or name;
- deliberately accessing internet sites containing pornographic, offensive or obscene material;
- serious insubordination;
- unlawful discrimination or harassment;
- bringing the organization into serious disrepute;

- serious incapability at work brought on by alcohol or illegal drugs;
- causing loss, damage or injury through serious negligence;
- a serious breach of health and safety rules; and
- a serious breach of confidence.

Recent research undertaken by Industrial Relations Services (IRS, 2005) is useful in pointing to the reasons for disciplinary action. In a survey of over 100 employers in all sector of the economy they found that the most likely issues for disciplinary action were attendance, performance and capability, timekeeping and general behaviour and conduct. Clearly, most of these aspects are likely to fall into the minor/serious misconduct category so it is likely to be rare for employees to be dismissed for gross misconduct. Regardless though of whether an employee is dismissed for gross misconduct or repeated minor or serious misconduct a key point is that any dismissal should follow due procedure, something that we now consider.

Employers need to ensure that disciplinary procedures are fully utilized to ensure that any dismissal is considered 'fair', both in a legal and moral sense. For example, an organization might consider it has acted ethically in dismissing an employee, but even if an organization or individual acting on behalf of the organization has acted in good faith, an ET may decide the dismissal was unfair if the correct procedure is not followed. Clearly, then, a key point in any dismissal is the notion of whether the organization has acted in an reasonable, equitable and procedurally fair manner, if not then the organization could be faced with a claim for unfair dismissal. In considering whether a dismissal is fair or unfair we should firstly consider acceptable reasons for dismissal. Taylor and Emir (2006) note how the number of potentially fair reasons was originally five as outlined in the Employment Rights Act 1999, with a sixth being added under the Employment Relations Act 1999 and further reasons relating to Transfer of Undertaking Regulations (TUPE) and mandatory retirement being added in 2006. The most likely reasons for dismissal though are likely to be (and see HRM in practice 12.1):

- *Lack of capability*: this may refer to when employees may encounter difficulties in their performance and struggle to fulfil their responsibilities; alternatively there may also be situations where an employee is unable to do their job due to ill-health.
- *Misconduct*: as we noted above this can range from minor to gross misconduct with differing sanctions.

HRM in practice 12.1   Prime candidates for dismissal?

Rayner (1998) reports on the controversy created in the late 1990s when it emerged that some local authorities were sending managers on a course to learn how to sack troublesome employees. The course was run by an American company, Padgett-Thompson. Amongst other things the course offered participants advice on how to 'deal with employees who drive you crazy' or good performers who had 'know it all attitudes'. The course also offered 'a tried and tested technique for silencing employees who want to argue about being dismissed'. In addition the course identified four employee types who managers are likely to want to dismiss. These types were the chatterbox (who keeps everyone away from work by constantly talking with colleagues), the plotician (who collects the dirt on colleagues and enjoys manipulating those around them), the shark (who enjoys making people squirm and chews up anyone who gets in their way) and the snoop (who delves into other people's personal things and private lives).

- *Redundancy*: the law in redundancy is quite complex, though in simple terms a redundancy will arise when a business is closing, a workplace is closing or there is a diminishing need for employees to do particular kinds of work in an organization.
- *Statutory bar.*
- *Some other substantial reason*: this category is deliberately vague as it is intended to give employers scope to dismiss employees in circumstances that were not envisaged when the legislation was drawn up.

Review and reflect

To what extent is a course of the nature described in Box 12.1 ethical?

In further considering the notion of whether a dismissal is fair it is important to recognize that there are a number of things which would be considered automatically unfair regardless of the qualifying period, these being (LRD, 2006):

- Dismissal on grounds of pregnancy or assertion of paternal paternity or adoption leave rights.

- Dismissal on grounds of trade union membership or stating an intention to join a trade union.
- Refusing to work on a Sunday (in the case of retail workers).
- Dismissal on grounds of actual or proposed trade union activity undertaken at an appropriate time.
- Dismissal resulting from individual's refusal to join a trade union.
- The dismissal of an employee without going through the required disciplinary procedure.
- Dismissal connected with the transfer in the organization's ownership – TUPE (2006).
- Where no reason for dismissal is given.
- Where the employee has been unfairly selected for redundancy.
- Dismissal on basis of past criminal offence which is spent.
- Unfair dismissal on the basis of sex, race, disability, sexual orientation or religion/beliefs.
- During the first 12 weeks of official industrial action (i.e. action sanctioned by a trade union executive body).
- Asserting a statutory right, for example the national minimum wage (NMW).
- 'Blowing the whistle' on malpractice in the workplace.
- Refusal to do something on health and safety grounds.

In 2004–05 there were nearly 40 000 claims for unfair dismissal submitted to the Employment Tribunal Service (ETS, 2005). Of these, the vast majority were withdrawn or settled with the intervention of ACAS. Ultimately, just over 7500 cases reached a formal ET hearing. Of those cases that were heard by the tribunal service over 50 per cent were dismissed, with 46.3 per cent being upheld (ETS, 2005). Clearly in assessing the fairness or otherwise of the dismissal the ET will assess whether dismissal was carried out in line with procedures (reiterating the need for organizations to have well-established and transparent procedures related to disciplinary issues). To judge whether a dismissal is fair the ET is likely to consider the following issues:

- Was dismissal for admissible reason?
- Was dismissal fair in sense of equity of treatment between employees?
- Was dismissal fair in the sense of the offence or the employee record justifying the dismissal?
- Did the employer follow proper procedures?

As noted above the success rate for employees in ETs is not very high, but if they win their case then there are several options open to the ET. The first is the basic award, which depends on length of service and age and is based on the same rate as statutory redundancy pay (LRD, 2006):

- *aged under 22*: half a week's pay for each complete year worked under this age;
- *aged 22–40*: one week's pay for each complete year worked between these ages; and
- *aged 41–65*: one and a half week's pay for each complete year worked between these ages.

In addition, there is also a compensatory award, which considers aspects such as loss of earnings, loss of pension rights and the cost to an employee of time and effort in seeking new work. In awarding a compensatory award the ET can also award an amount that it considers 'just and equitable' given the circumstances (LRD, 2006). Recent changes in the law now mean that there is no upper limit for cases where dismissal was based on discrimination, for health and safety or whistle blowing reasons. For other cases the maximum compensatory aware is £58 400 (LRD, 2006). In 2004–05 the highest award was £75 250, though the median award was £3476 and average award £7303 (ETS, 2005). The final option is either reinstatement (where the employee gets their old job back) or re-engagement (where they are given a different but comparable job). In reality, very few people take this option and in 2004–05 just 14 successful claimants chose this course of action (ETS, 2005).

Conclusion

The chapter has considered the need for a clearly articulated order in the organization, particularly with regard to grievance and disciplinary procedures. Evidence suggests that these issues may have a particular resonance within tourism and hospitality; yet at the same time tourism and hospitality organizations often seem to lack the formal policies which sustain a sound approach to towards these issues. Although the predominance of small and medium-sized enterprises (SMEs) may go some way to explain this lack of formal policies and procedures, legislation means that all organizations should now have well-established grievance and disciplinary procedures. Establishment of such procedures mean that employees have a channel in which to express their dissatisfaction and employers a means by which to articulate concerns about employee performance or behaviour. Though characterized as the 'murky' or 'dark' side of HRM, dismissal is an organizational reality and all managers should be aware of what constitutes a fair or unfair dismissal. Although a relatively small numbers of cases end up at the ET those that do may lead to an organization facing significant costs for a badly handled dismissal. In this way it is clear that rules and procedures in the employment relationship are integral to ensure that decisions taken by organizations are both ethically and procedurally fair and a sense of natural justice prevails in the organizational setting.

References and further reading

Advisory Conciliation and Arbitration Service (2004) *Disciplinary and Grievance Procedures Code of Practice*, ACAS.

Chartered Institute of Personnel and Development (2004) *Managing Conflict at Work: A Survey of the UK and Ireland*, CIPD.

Chartered Institute of Personnel and Development (2005) *Disciplinary and Grievance Procedures Factsheet*, CIPD.

Edwards, P. (2005) 'Discipline and attendance', in S. Bach (ed.) *Managing Human Resources: Personnel Management in Transition*, Blackwell, 4th edition, 375–397.

Employment Tribunal Service (2005) *Annual Report and Accounts 2004–05*, The Stationary Office.

Industrial Relations Services (2005) 'Disciplinary and grievance policies at work', *IRS Employment Review*, No. 825, 10 June, 9–18.

Kersley, B., Alpin, C., Forth, J. et al. (2006) *Inside the Workplace: Findings from the 2004 Workplace Employment Relations Survey*, Routledge.

Labour Research Department (2006) *Law at Work*, LRD.

Marchington, M. and Wilkinson, A. (2005) *Human Resource Management at Work: People Management and Development*, 3rd edition, CIPD.

Pigors, P. and Myers, C. S. (1977) *Personnel Administration*, McGraw Hill, 8th edition.

Price, L. (1994) 'Poor personnel practice in the hotel and catering industry – does it matter?', *Human Resource Management Journal*, 4(4), 44–62.

Rayner, J. (1998) 'Bolshie staff? We have ways of purging them', *Observer*, 13 December, 6.

Salamon, M. (1992) *Industrial Relations – Theory and Practice*, Prentice Hall.

Salamon, M. (2000) *Industrial Relations – Theory and Practice*, 4th edition, Prentice Hall.

Salipante, P. and Bouwen, R. (1990) 'Behavioural analysis of grievances: conflict, sources, complexity and transformation', *Employee Relations*, 12(3), 17–22.

Taylor, S. and Emir, A. (2006) *Employment Law: An Introduction*, Oxford University Press.

Torrington, D., Hall, L. and Taylor, S. (2005) *Human Resource Management*, 6th edition, Prentice Hall.

Websites

ACAS has a number of useful resources at http://www.acas.org.uk/index.aspx?articleid=360&detailid=548

The Department of Trade and Industry's page on dispute resolution can be found at http://www.dti.gov.uk/employment/Resolving_disputes/index.html

Chapter 13
Concluding comments

This book has sought to offer a comprehensive review of competitive strategies, and concomitant HRM practices in the international tourism and hospitality sector. It has painted a complex picture of the sector, and particularly the differing routes to competitive advantage which organizations may adopt. Clearly, the book has demonstrated that it is virtually impossible to entirely generalize the employment experience in tourism and hospitality. In particular, the extent to which organizations may be aspiring to best practice HRM remains a point worthy of further debate and research.

Clearly recognition of this point has a major impact on the nature of work, employment and people management in tourism and hospitality industry. In that sense from a HRM point of view, in crude terms, there is much evidence to support an approach in the tourism and hospitality sector to HRM which is more 'best fit' than 'best practice'. Marchington and Grugulis' (2000: 1121) view that 'best practice, it seems, is problematic' is certainly borne out by the tourism and hospitality sector. Much as policy-makers would like the sector to be characteristic of a high wage, high skill, high quality, high value-added approach, clearly the low and mixed skill context of the tourism and hospitality sector a more nuanced approach is called for. Large numbers of tourism and hospitality employers do not necessarily need to look to develop high value added approaches. As a consequence, high value added approaches have to be seen in relation to 'a broader package of environmental, cultural and structural features that can nurture and support high performance, high value added industries and sectors' (Keep and Mayhew, 1999: 4). These conditions do not exist universally across the tourism and hospitality sector and resultantly the 'best fit' approach of designing HRM practices which are contingent upon the particular customer definition of 'good service' would seem apposite. Notions of 'good service' will differ markedly across market segments and between tangible and intangible aspects of the tourism and hospitality product. Given this reality, practices which may be desirable to employees such as levels of high pay, extensive training and job security, are not necessarily cost effective for many tourism and hospitality organizations, a point which Riley et al. (2000) strongly advocate in their arguments about economic determinism. In this sense then the 'poor' personnel practices of tourism and hospitality organizations that are noted by a number of authors may reflect any number of reasons. However it is important to stress that there is still an element of choice for employers and claims to the immutability of 'poor' personnel practice should be treated with some caution. As the DfEE (2000: 13) notes in describing employment practices in the sector:

> Some of these deficiencies reflect labour market circumstances, commercial constraints and lack of awareness of options, but some reflect poor human resource management, unwillingness to take risks or invest in innovation and short termism: most vividly exemplified by the low pay, crisis management culture of the less impressive establishments.

Equally, though, there is clearly some evidence for good practice HRM in the tourism and hospitality industry and the book has sought to highlight such practices throughout. An obvious question stemming from this recognition of good practice, which we have sought to answer is: if best practice does exist, what does it look like? More often than not it is likely to be large, often multinational organizations who exemplify a number of the practices, as described by the likes of Hoque (2000) and illustrated by a number of examples in this book. Indeed, recognizing the nature of the small and medium enterprise (SME) sector it may well be that notions of best practice need to reconfigured within this particular sector. As Worsfold (1999: 346) notes, 'In the case of small hotels we may need to abandon the search for formal HRM approaches and attempt to establish whether "caring management" can provide the "concern for employee well being" which appears to be linked to service quality.'

Generally, whilst this book concludes that the HRM strategies of firms are heavily shaped by contextual contingencies, including national, sectoral, organizational and occupational factors, and therefore are more redolent of best fit, such a conclusion does not necessarily invalidate best practice thinking. For example, Haynes (1999: 200) argues that in relation to best practice HRM in the hospitality sector:

> Sometimes the critical verges on the hysterical … In an industry characterized by relatively low levels of pay and high levels of arbitrary management practice, the adoption of many of the HRM practices in question would undoubtedly improve the work experience of hospitality workers. For that reason alone the model should not be rejected out of hand by hospitality researchers.

As Boxall and Purcell (2000: 1930) suggest '… there are certain broadly applicable principles and processes of good labour management.' The diffusion of these practices as best practice does remain problematic and difficult to achieve throughout the tourism and hospitality sector. However, the fact that diffusion of these sorts of practices is potentially limited does not invalidate their utility. Thus, although the 'deluxe' version of best practice may remain out of reach of large numbers of tourism and hospitality organizations, at the very least there should be aspirations to at least go for the 'economy' version to offer a more rewarding and meaningful employment experience for the many who work in the sector.

References

Boxall, P. and Purcell, J. (2000) 'Strategic human resource management: Where have we come from and where should we be going?', *International Journal of Management Reviews*, 2(2), 183–203.

Department for Education and Employment (2000) *Employers Skill Survey: Case Study Hospitality Sector*, DfEE.

Haynes, P. (1999) 'A new agenda for researching hospitality HRM: comment on Lashley and Watson', *Tourism and Hospitality Research*, 1(3), 199–204.

Hoque, K. (2000) *Human Resource Management in the Hotel Industry*, Routledge.

Keep, E. and Mayhew, K. (1999) 'The assessment: knowledge, skills and competitiveness', *Oxford Review of Economic Policy*, 15, 1–15.

Marchington, M. and Grugulis, I. (2000) '"Best practice" human resource management: perfect opportunity or dangerous illusion?' *International Journal of Human Resource Management*, 11(6), 1104–1124.

Riley, M., Gore, J. and Kelliher, C. (2000) 'Economic determinism and human resource management practice in the hospitality and tourism industry', *Tourism and Hospitality Research*, 2(2), 118–128.

Worsfold, P. (1999) 'HRM, performance, commitment and service quality in the hotel industry', *International Journal of Contemporary Hospitality Management*, 11(7), 340–348.

Index